Beverly Cleary

 Twayne's United States Authors Series
Children's Literature

Ruth K. MacDonald, Editor
Purdue University Calumet

TUSAS 572

BEVERLY CLEARY
Photograph by Margaret Miller

Beverly Cleary

Pat Pflieger
West Chester University

Twayne Publishers • Boston
A Division of G. K. Hall & Co.

PS 3553.
L 3914
Z 88
1991

Beverly Cleary
Pat Pflieger

Copyright 1991 by G. K. Hall & Co.
All rights reserved.
Published by Twayne Publishers
A Division of G. K. Hall & Co.
70 Lincoln Street
Boston, Massachusetts 02111

Copyediting supervised by Barbara Sutton.
Book production by Gabrielle B. McDonald.
Book design by Janet Z. Reynolds.
Typeset in 10/13 Century Schoolbook
by Compset, Inc. of Beverly, Massachusetts.

10 9 8 7 6 5 4 3 2 1

Library of Congress Cataloging-in-Publication Data

Pflieger, Pat.
    Beverly Cleary / Pat Pflieger.
        p.   cm.—(Twayne's United States authors series ; TUSAS
    572. Children's literature)
    Includes bibliographical references and index.
    ISBN 0-8057-7613-3
    1. Clearly, Beverly—Criticism and interpretation.   2. Children's
stories, American—History and criticism.   I. Title.   II. Series:
Twayne's United States authors series ; TUSAS 572.   III. Series:
Twayne's United States authors series.   Children's literature.
PS3553.L3914Z88   1991
813′.54—dc20   90-23346
                                                          CIP

For the multitude of Cleary's readers, and especially for Cindy Kaye, who had a fine set of curls for boinging.

Contents

Preface

It seems impossible to grow up in the United States in the last half of the twentieth century without having been touched by the works of Beverly Cleary. While researching this work, I met few Americans under the age of forty who did not betray a nostalgic delight in Cleary's books. The college professor with a secret yen for a dress like Ellen Tebbits's; the bored bookstore clerk suddenly eager to talk over the life of Henry Huggins; the world-weary college freshman instantly alive at the mention of Ramona Quimby—all have made their own special connections with Cleary's books. For the ten-year-old so deep in the adventures of Ralph S. Mouse as to ignore the Pennsylvania landscape unrolling 10,000 feet below outside the plane window, the connection still is being made, as strong as ever.

As Margaret Novinger has noted, however, "Beverly Cleary has been more read than written about."[1] Apart from biographical pieces and articles emphasizing the breadth of Cleary's work, few critical studies have been published. James Zarrillo's "Beverly Cleary, Ramona Quimby, and the Teaching of Reading" discusses the way that the Ramona books provide a wealth of information for reading teachers about the mind of the child who is learning to read.[2] Novinger's article itself—while focusing on biography and on description of Cleary's works—contains some analysis. For the most part, however, Cleary's works have struggled for equal time in articles on the works of two or more authors: Suzanne Rahn's "Cat-Child: Rediscovering Socks and Island MacKenzie" discusses the often-ignored *Socks* with Ursula Williams's *Island Mackenzie*[3]; David Rees compares Cleary's works with those of British author Rodie Sudbery in "Middle of the Way: Rodie Sudbery and Beverly Cleary," a chapter in *The Marble in the Water*[4]; Susan Thompson includes a few paragraphs on *Fifteen* in part 1 of her discussion of works for adolescents, "Images of Adolescence."[5] In-depth critical discussions, however, are almost nonexistent. Cleary's popularity may be one reason for the lack of critical attention; almost all her works have remained in print since first publication, and Cleary has received almost every award American children can give their favorite authors. Most readers seem to content themselves with exploring the range of and reasons for this popularity. So lucid are the works themselves that they do not at first glance seem to repay serious study. But such lucidity is itself an art, and, taken together, Cleary's body of work is wonderfully rich and rewarding. Focusing on the everyday—so different now from what it was when Cleary first began to write, yet essentially unchanged—Cleary's works give the reader a view of the extraordinary qualities of ordinary life that can reward not only the young reader but the adult scholar as well.

Because so many of Cleary's works seem to be series based around a particular character, I have chosen to examine most of them in groups rather than singly. Each work is discussed individually, but analysis centers on the group around which each chapter is built as a whole. This approach proves especially rewarding, as it allows for comparison of the individual works in each series. One can thus get a sense of Henry Huggins's growing maturity and the changes Ramona Quimby has gone through while noting how Cleary's vision of her characters may have changed. Chapter 1 discusses Cleary herself, with a biography and a discussion of her work methods and the philosophy behind what she produces. Chapter 2 discusses the books about Henry Huggins; chapter 3 focuses on those about Ramona Quimby. Chapter 4 discusses the nonseries works about children: Cleary's picture books, her adaptations of episodes from "Leave It to Beaver," and *Ellen Tebbits, Otis Spofford, Mitch and Amy,* and *Emily's Runaway Imagination.* Chapter 5 is built around the works about animals: the Ralph S. Mouse trilogy and *Socks. Dear Mr. Henshaw,* Cleary's most complex work to date and the winner of the most prestigious prize, the Newbery, deserves deep analysis on its own and receives it in chapter 6. The four works for adolescents serve as the nucleus for chapter 7, while the afterword provides a brief overview.

Preface

It is impossible to do a project of this size totally unaided, and
I would like to acknowledge the help of the following: Dr. Brai-
dotti, Foreign Languages, West Chester University, West Chester,
Pennsylvania; the Delaware County Library System, Delaware
County, Pennsylvania; the Chester County Library and District
Center, Exton, Pennsylvania; the Kerlan Collection, University
of Minnesota–Twin Cities; the staff of Interlibrary Loan, Illinois
State University, Normal; the staff of Harvey Green Library, West
Chester University; the staff of the Graduate Department of Li-
brary Science, Library Science Library, Villanova University,
Villanova, Pennsylvania; David Reuther and Melanie S. Dono-
van, William Morrow & Company, Inc.; Charlene K. Coates;
Deidre Johnson; Beverly Cleary; and my students at Illinois State
University, Normal, and West Chester University, whose bound-
less enthusiasm for Cleary's works is always cheering.

Chronology

1916 Beverly Bunn Cleary born 12 April in McMinnville, Oregon.

1922 Bunn family moves to Portland, Oregon.

1934 Beverly leaves home for college in California.

1938 Earns a B. A. in English, University of California at Berkeley.

1939 Earns a B. A. in librarianship, University of Washington, Seattle. Takes job as children's librarian, Yakima Public Library, Yakima, Washington, until 1940.

1940 Marries Clarence Cleary; they move to California.

1942–1945 Post Librarian, U. S. Army Hospital, Oakland, California.

1948 Clearys move to Berkeley, California.

1950 *Henry Huggins.*

1951 *Ellen Tebbits.*

1952 *Henry and Beezus.*

1953 *Otis Spofford.*

1954 *Henry and Ribsy,* winner of the Pacific Northwest Library Association Young Readers' Choice Award (1957).

1955 *Beezus and Ramona.*

1956 *Fifteen,* winner of Dorothy Canfield Fisher Children's Book Award (1958).

1957 *Henry and the Paper Route,* winner of Pacific Northwest Library Association Young Readers' Choice Award (1960).

1958 *The Luckiest Girl.*

1959 *Jean and Johnny.*

1960 *Leave It to Beaver. The Hullabaloo ABC. The Real Hole* (reissued 1986).

1961 *Emily's Runaway Imagination. Beaver and Wally. Here's Beaver. Two Dog Biscuits* (reissued 1986).

1962 *Henry and the Clubhouse.*

1963 *Sister of the Bride.*

1964 *Ribsy,* winner of Dorothy Canfield Fisher Award (1966); Nene Award (1968).

1965 *The Mouse and the Motorcycle,* winner of William Allen White Children's Book Award (1968); Pacific Northwest Library Associations Young Reader's Choice Award (1968); Nene Award (1969); Sue Hefley Award (1973); Surrey School Book of Year Award (1974); Great Stone Face Award (1983).

1967 *Mitch and Amy.*

1968 *Ramona the Pest,* winner of Georgia Children's Book Award (1970); Nene Award (1971); Sequoyah Children's Book Award (1972); Pacific Northwest Library Association Young Readers' Choice Award (1972).

1970 *Runaway Ralph,* winner of Nene Award (1972); Charlie May Simon Award (1972–73).

1973 *Socks,* winner of William Allen White Award (1976); Golden Archer Award (1977).

1975 *Ramona the Brave,* winner of Golden Archer Award (1977); Mark Twain Award (1978). "Ramona and the Three Wise Persons" appears in December issue of

Family Circle. Cleary receives Laura Ingalls Wilder Award.

1977 *Ramona and Her Father,* Newbery Honor book (1978); Boston Globe Horn Book Honor book (1978); winner of Nene Award (1979); Garden State Children's Book Award (1980); Northwest Library Association Young Reader's Choice Award (1980); Tennessee Children's Choice Award (1980); Utah Children's Choice Award (1980); listed on International Board on Books for Young People Honor list (1980); winner of Land of Enchantment Children's Book Award (1981); Texas Bluebonnet Award (1981); a Sue Hefly Award honor book (1982).

1979 *Ramona and Her Mother,* winner of American Book Award for children's fiction in paperback (1981); Garden State Children's Award (1982); Surrey School Book of the Year Award (1982).

1980 Cleary wins Regina Medal.

1981 *Ramona Quimby, Age 8,* Newbery Honor Book (1982); winner of Charlie May Simon Children's book Award (1983–1984); Garden State Award (1984); Michigan Young Readers Award (1984); runner-up for Sunshine State Young Readers Award (1984); Buckeye Children's Book Award (1985).

1982 *Ralph S. Mouse,* winner of Golden Kite Award (1982); Parents' Choice Award (1982); Garden State Children's Book Award (1985): Iowa Children's Choice award (1985); is runner-up for Sunshine State Young Readers Award (1985); West Virginia Children's Book Award (1986–87). Cleary receives University of Southern Mississippi Silver Medallion.

1983 *Dear Mr. Henshaw,* winner of Commonwealth Club of California Award (1983); Parents' Choice Award (1983); one of the New York Times Outstanding Books (1983); Newbery Medal (1984); Christopher

Award (1984); Dorothy Canfield Fisher Award (1985); Massachusetts Children's Book Award and Sequoyah Award (1986); Nene Award (1989). Cleary receives George G. Stone Award.

1984 *Lucky Chuck. Ramona Forever,* a New York Times Notable book (1984); winner of Parents' Choice Award for literature (1984); Iowa Children's Choice Award (1987).

1985 "Josie Lays Her Down to Sleep" appears in February issue of *Woman's Day.* Cleary saluted by the Children's Book Council.

1987 *Janet's Thingamajigs. The Growing-Up Feet.* Cleary receives Jeremiah Ludington Award.

1988 *A Girl from Yamhill.*

1990 *Muggie Maggie.*

1

An Ordinary Life

An Ordinary Childhood

"If my books are popular with children," Cleary wrote in 1957, "it is because my childhood was bounded by the experiences of an average American child."[1] Cleary's childhood, spent first on a small family farm and then in Portland, Oregon, has provided a wealth of material for her books, from experiences to emotions. The reader of Cleary's 1988 autobiography, *A Girl from Yamhill*, cannot help but realize the richness of her childhood memories, in a 279-page work that explores only the first eighteen years of her life. Memories of the specific events—fears, joys, and confusions—of her childhood fill Cleary's works with authentic emotions and with "the little everyday experiences that do not seem important to adults, but which are so terribly important to children." Cleary remembers that children's "lives do not seem eventful, but they are eventful in the little ways that loom large to a child" ("Writing," 11).

Yamhill
Cleary's life began on 12 April 1916, in McMinnville, Oregon. Born to Chester Lloyd and Mable Atlee Bunn, Beverly was descended from Oregon pioneers, whose fortitude and courage Bev-

erly came to resent being reminded of each time she found something difficult.[2] But Beverly loved the house her grandfather had enlarged from a wheelwright's house into the "first fine house in Yamhill, with the second bathtub in Yamhill County" (*Yamhill*, 8); she loved the eighty-acre farm her father worked; and, especially, she loved life in Yamhill, Oregon.

Writing of those first six years of her life, Cleary has called them "exceptionally happy."[3] The only child on the farm, she learned quickly to amuse herself and was given the run of the place because her father had taught her the rules she was to follow for her own safety—rules which Beverly obeyed, but which did not preclude such activities as picking flowers, feeding baby birds the worms out of Bing cherries, throwing rotten eggs, or tripping chickens with a long pole (*Yamhill*, 24). The rules Beverly's mother taught her seemed more arbitrary, dealing as they did with etiquette and social graces. But it was her mother who told Beverly, "Never be afraid" (*Yamhill*, 39), and it was her mother who instilled an early love of a good story. Though Yamhill did not yet have a library, Mrs. Bunn sparked Beverly's imagination with remembered recitation pieces and fairy tales as well as with stories of her own Michigan childhood. The lack of a library did not mean that young Beverly did not know of the magic of books. In fact, she had loved her first book at age four:

My first experience with a book was fraught with peril. When I was four years old and lived on a farm outside Yamhill, Oregon, a neighbor showed me a picture book which so delighted me that she invited me to look at it any time I pleased. Unfortunately her bachelor son had made a deal to sell me for a nickel to another neighbor, Quong Hop, who was planning to return to China to die. To reach the book I had to pass Quong Hop's house, and since I did not want to go to China, but I did want to see that book, I snaked on my stomach through tall grass and arrived damp with spitbug spit. Alert for the son's footsteps so I could hide in the pantry, I perched on a kitchen chair and studied the pictures of red-coated men on horseback chasing a fox with a pack of hounds. At the end of the book they held the fox's tail triumphantly aloft. Fascinating! Nothing like this went on in Yamhill. The crawl home left me even damper with spitbug spit and longing for more books.[4]

Beverly's own books were a Mother Goose and a copy of *The Three Bears* printed on linen (*Yamhill*, 60).

More books came when Beverly was five; her mother launched a campaign for a town library "when other homesteaders would come for miles around just to borrow her one book" (Ernest Thompson Seton's *The Biography of a Grizzly*)—sent from Michigan (*Yamhill*, 20).[5] The library, housed in the Commercial Clubrooms over the Yamhill Bank, was a "dingy room filled with shabby leather-covered chairs and smelling of stale cigar smoke" ("Writing," 7), but it was the means of a revelation to Beverly: that there were other books for children, exciting books such as Jacobs's *More English Fairy Tales* and Beatrix Potter's *The Tailor of Gloucester, Johnny Crow's Garden,* and *The Curly-Haired Hen.* That charming and gruesome story of the Hobyahs—who "run, run, run," "creep, creep, creep," and "trip, trip, trip" up on the peasant's house—was a favorite, with Beverly insisting on taking Jacobs's work to bed with her "instead of my teddy bear" ("Writing," 7); the mouse embroidery in Potter's work intrigued Beverly, who was learning needlework ("Books").

In Yamhill, Beverly felt a part of everything since her uncle was mayor, her father was on the town council, and her mother was the librarian. Children were expected to be a part of everything in Yamhill, so Beverly acted in pageants and went to church picnics, dances, and the Fourth of July parade (*Yamhill*, 43–44). All of this changed when Beverly turned six: the good harvest brought little money, and Mr. Bunn decided to quit farming. He was probably the only one in his family distressed at the prospect of moving: Mrs. Bunn, unprepared to be a farmer's wife, disliked the hard work of farming, and Beverly looked forward to moving to the big city of Portland, Oregon. Although she could amuse herself on the farm, Beverly longed to play with other children, making do with her stolid cousin, Winston; her mother's pregnancy when Beverly was four had ended in miscarriage, so Beverly had remained an only child. Now she would "have children close by to play with, school, a real teacher who would teach me to read. Even though adults had troubles, I was secure. Yamhill had taught me that the world was a safe and beautiful place, where children were treated with kindness, patience, and tolerance" (*Yamhill*, 64–65).

Portland

Portland taught her different. Excited by the wonders of the city, by the enormous children's room of the Portland Library Association, and by the joy of playing with the many neighborhood children, Beverly was eager to plunge into her new life. School was interesting but sometimes puzzling and arbitrary: Beverly did not understand why she was wrong to pick up a pencil in the closest hand (her left) and why she suddenly had "a right or wrong hand" (*Yamhill*, 75–76); Beverly already knew how to add and subtract but was taught again. Reading was "dull but easy" (*Yamhill*, 77) until a bout of chicken pox put Beverly behind the other students. Now "the boundaries of childhood closed like a trap" ("Wilder," 363). Used to the freedom of the farm, Beverly hated the classroom, which was crowded by forty students, hated the primer which bore "the symbol of a beacon light, presumably to guide us and to warn us of the dangers that lay within,"[6] and was confused by Miss Falb, her teacher, who punished without explaining. Smallpox seemed wonderful, for it meant Beverly did not have to go to school. However, it put her even farther behind in reading, and when Beverly returned to school the class had been divided into reading groups: Bluebirds, the best readers; Redbirds, the next best; and Blackbirds, the worst readers. Beverly was a Blackbird, which meant sitting closest to the blackboard and farthest from the windows, reading from flashcards, and learning monotonous word lists; Beverly also learned that, despite her mother's assurances, reading was *not* fun ("Low," 288). Afraid at school, Beverly also became afraid at home. Beverly was afraid that the earthquake that had ravaged Japan would be repeated in Portland, that something would happen to her father as he worked nights, that (as her nightly prayer hinted) she might die before she woke, and afraid to tell her mother, who had taught her to be brave (*Yamhill*, 81). When Mrs. Bunn visited the classroom to find out why her daughter begged to stay home from school, Miss Falb "was so kind to me that my mother was reassured, and I learned a bitter lesson of childhood—an adult can be a hypocrite" ("Wilder," 363).

During the summer between first and second grades, Beverly regained her self-confidence; in second grade, Beverly loved her teacher and learned to read. But she refused to read outside of school, though while ill with tonsillitis Beverly was languidly surprised to learn that a book could tell her something she did not already know (*Yamhill*, 87). It was on a boring afternoon when she was eight that Beverly picked up Lucy Fitch Perkins's *The Dutch Twins* "to look at the pictures" and realized that, not only was she reading, but she was enjoying it (*Yamhill*, 93). In Perkins's work about two ordinary children and their often-humorous adventures, Beverly found a "great feeling of release"[7]; suddenly she "felt young, and it is a marvelous thing to feel young at the age of eight" ("Wilder," 363). Soon Beverly was devouring Perkins's entire series, then all the fairy tales in her branch of the library, and, finally, *all* the works for children in her library, working her way from Alcott to Zwilgmeyer ("Books"). She also turned her newfound love to practical use: a review written for the *Oregon Journal* earned Beverly a copy of *The Story of Dr. Dolittle* (*Yamhill*, 93).

School life improved as Beverly moved through the grades, despite multiplication tables and an incident in which a beloved teacher called her a "nuisance" (*Yamhill*, 100). Having moved once, the Bunns moved again, to a lively neighborhood in which Beverly felt comfortable. However, now Mrs. Bunn decided to "mold Beverly's character," a process seemingly designed to make her independent; now she was exhorted to "Try" (*Yamhill*, 105). Trying earned Beverly $2 when hers was the only entry in a contest "for the best essay about an animal"; trying earned her $1 from the *Shopping News* when it published a letter from her

(*Yamhill*, 105). However, Beverly's contribution was rejected by the St. Nicholas League ("Writing," 9).

Now there was tension at home because Mr. Bunn, educated to work a farm and not to work in the city, was unhappy in his indoor job. Mrs. Bunn prayed that the family would not go back to the farm. Tensions began, too, between Beverly and her mother, with battles over woolen underwear and high brown shoes (*Yamhill*, 116). These tensions escalated when the inflation of 1927 brought new money worries to the family. Mrs. Bunn took the only job she could find, telephoning for subscribers to *McCall's* magazine: "When I came home from school that dark and dreary winter, I felt as if Mother, bundled up in an old sweater, had shut me out by endlessly repeating the merits of *McCall's* to strangers over the telephone" (*Yamhill*, 124). Beverly's relationship with her mother was not openly affectionate. Surprised once to find that her best friend's mother kissed her daughters, Beverly confronted her mother and received a hug and a kiss in "a sweet, isolated moment" that "was never repeated" (*Yamhill*, 113–14). Feeling shut out, Beverly took refuge in books, reading Carroll Watson Rankin's *Dandelion Cottage* over and over and finding comfort in a story of a mother devotedly searching for her daughter, the story of Demeter and Persephone: "In my imagination I became Persephone. . . . At home, the wet Oregon winter with its sodden leaves became the dark underworld, and somehow Mother's telephone soliciting kept the world from blooming" (*Yamhill*, 124–25). Demeter found Persephone only as Beverly was "emerging from the dark underworld of anesthesia" after a tonsillectomy, with Mrs. Bunn calling her by endearing names for the first, and only, time (*Yamhill*, 126–27).

The possibility of going back to the farm vanished when Mr. Bunn sold it, and for a time the Bunns enjoyed a certain amount of prosperity, buying a car, getting Beverly's teeth straightened, and buying a house near Klickitat Street. Now, Beverly began to find pleasure in writing, especially after she was encouraged by a seventh-grade teacher whose assignments required imagination. "Journey through Bookland," in which Beverly wrote about her favorite characters, brought the comment that Beverly should write for children when she grew up, a comment Beverly took seriously, vowing to write "the kind of books I wanted to read" ("Writing," 9). Encouraged by her mother to think about a steady job as well, Beverly blithely decided to become a librarian (*Yamhill*, 147).

An incident in the summer before Beverly entered eighth grade left her more bewildered than anything, when an uncle made sickeningly clear to Beverly that his feelings toward her were more than avuncular. On the other hand, eighth-grade boys were not confusing; they were "horrible" (*Yamhill*, 161). Graduation from the eighth grade marked the beginning of adulthood, when each graduate was given an adult library card as she or he crossed the stage.

In the summer of 1930, another tense time began in Beverly's life, when her father lost his job. Suddenly, the depression was upon them (*Yamhill*, 173). Feeling claustrophobic from the effort to live as cheaply as possible and from the pain of seeing her father so defeated, Beverly revelled in a week spent with a friend away from home. Mindful of her possible career in librarianship, Beverly took college preparatory classes in high school, though there was no possibility that the family's dwindling resources would cover the costs. Domestic tensions had deepened after Mr. Bunn decided, and failed, to sell the house. This was balanced by Beverly's success in writing, when, taking her mother's advice to be funny and to keep things simple, she wrote stories that her teachers praised. One—"A Green Christmas," about a boy accidentally dyed green—was published, though under another's name (*Yamhill*, 186–87).

As the depression deepened, Beverly's father found a job, though the family's skills in making do still were tested. Once Mr. Bunn was working, Beverly and her mother began to disagree openly, as Beverly began to resent her mother's attempts to dominate her life and compared Mrs. Bunn with her best friend's mother, who did not pressure or "interfere" (*Yamhill*, 205). High school was fun for Beverly, though she disagreed with the emphasis some students put on being popular. Her view of boys, too, had improved, though Beverly had no thoughts of dating. One evening, however, while delivering Christmas decorations to the local lodge during a dance, Beverly—most unsuitably dressed and painfully aware of her lack of skill—was astonished to be asked to dance, and Mrs. Bunn had her take a class in ballroom dancing as a result.

Dancing class resulted in something more, when Beverly met a young man of whom her mother approved. Though the man, whom Beverly calls "Gerhart" in her autobiography, had nothing in common with Beverly and though Beverly found that her dates with him—and his kisses—were not that enjoyable, they continued to go out together, for Gerhart gave Beverly an escape from her mother (*Yamhill*, 225). As their relationship continued, Beverly began to find school more interesting than did Gerhart, who poked fun at her articles and who grew more and more possessive. Beverly's dates with another boy made her realize that there were boys more interesting than Gerhart, and a fumbled kiss at the end of the junior play—co-authored by Beverly—proved to her that there were kisses better than his as well (*Yamhill*, 232, 236).

That summer brought several realizations: Beverly learned how much she disliked Gerhart and also saw that her mother would always make her feel guilty and would always feel the need to be right (*Yamhill*, 250). She resisted both realizations during her senior year, breaking up with Gerhart but having to endure his visits, which were engineered by her mother. Beverly wanted to go to college but knew that her family could not afford it. The answer to everything seemed to lie in an invitation from Beverly's great-aunt to come to California for the winter and attend junior college tuition-free—an invitation that was at first dismissed as impractical. Mr. Bunn, however, seeing a chance to have his worries about Beverly's future allayed and to help her break off completely with Gerhart—whom he had never liked—decided to let her go.

Beverly was sent to college "not to catch a husband, as was the custom for young women of that time and place, but to become independent."[8] Studying at the University of California–Berkeley, she earned a B.A. in English in 1938; in 1939 she earned a B.A. in librarianship from the University of Washington–Seattle. Her first job as a librarian was as children's librarian in Yakima, Washington, which was important to Cleary's development as a writer. Here she met the children who wanted to read humorous books about children like themselves, and here she learned to tell stories to children.[9]

At college she had met Clarence T. Cleary ("Newbery," 431), whom she married in 1940. Then she gave up her job and moved with her new husband to Oakland, California. The Cleary family, which doubled in the 1950s with the birth of twins Marianne Elisabeth and Malcolm James, has lived in California ever since. Cleary used her librarian's skills again during World War II when she worked as post librarian at the Oakland Army Hospital.[10] Still interested in writing for children, Cleary bided her time. A job in the children's book department of a Berkeley bookstore seems to have provided the final incentive for her writing: "Surrounded by books, she was sure she could write a better book than some she saw there, and after the Christmas rush was over, she says, 'I decided if I was ever going to write, I'd better get started'" (Reuther, 441).

The Author at Work

Cleary's working methods seem to have changed little since she wrote that first book in pencil on typing paper that previous owners had left in the linen closet of her home. *Henry Huggins* was begun on 2 January; she has begun most of her works on the anniversary of that date.[11] Writing longhand on a legal pad, Cleary begins the story wherever it starts: "I often begin books in the middle or at the end and play about with my characters in my poor handwriting until I am satisfied with their behavior, which is often a surprise to me."[12] There are no outlines, for Cleary learned as a sophomore in high school that outlining was no help to her (*Yamhill,* 213). Working on weekday mornings, Cleary may take six months to a year to complete a book (Reuther, 442). Then it is typed by a professional, for she "finds typing the most difficult part of writing" ("Why," 42). Cleary does

not try out her manuscripts on children, for she is distrustful of
the response—"I wonder how valid those reactions would be. . . .
Children are conditioned to please adults"[13]—and distrustful of
the method: "Authors who solicit a number of opinions so often
try to follow everyone's advice, only to find their story dissipating
to the point of losing impact on the reader" (Roggenbuck, 59). Advice has come from her children when she has used their experiences in a book, but otherwise Cleary has shown only finished
manuscripts to her "interested, supportive, and uncritical" family
(Roggenbuck, 59).

Cleary's first book was accepted immediately by William Morrow and Company, which has published almost all her books since
then. Editor Elisabeth Hamilton was replaced by Connie Epstein
and then by David Reuther; Cleary appears to have enjoyed her
relationships with all three editors. She has been equally fortunate in the illustrators who have interpreted her words. Louis
Darling's Henry Huggins, Otis Spofford, and Ellen Tebbits are
solid, freckle-faced, and all-American; his Ribsy is the essence of
"muttiness," and—especially in *Ribsy*—Darling has emphasized
the mental processes going on between those ragged ears. His
illustrations have a humor all their own: in *Ramona the Pest,* he
takes literally the teacher's calling the classes' two Erics Eric J.
and Eric R. "because we don't want to get our Erics mixed up"
and presents us with a picture of two Erics exactly alike and sure
to be mixed up in life as well as on paper;[14] at the beginning of
chapter 8 he "Xs out" Ramona, the kindergarten dropout. Having
read idly of Miss Binney's sixty-eight students, which she is
trying to get into parade formation, the reader is astonished and
amused to count exactly sixty-eight little stick figures standing
in line, pushing, and chasing each other in Darling's tiny illustration of the scene ("Pest," 145).

After Darling's death, other illustrators stepped in with their
own visions. Darling's dainty Ralph S. Mouse became more solid
and expressive in Paul O. Zelinsky's hands. Zelinsky's somewhat
grittier illustrations ground *Dear Mr. Henshaw* firmly in reality.
Alan Tiegreen's Ramona became the one most people remember:

a nose, a smile, two dot-eyes, and a mop of hair on skinny little neck attached to a skinny little body. Tiegreen's pictures of Ramona emphasize not what she really looks like but how she feels: awkward, innocent, and misunderstood, a child surrounded by more perfectly formed adults. Beatrice Darwin's illustrations for *Socks* have the sketchy grace of Oriental art oddly appropriate for her subject; with only a few heavy strokes on page 129 she shows us an Old Taylor truly too frightening to challenge. The delicacy of Joe and Beth Krush's illustrations for *Emily's Runaway Imagination* are appropriate for the nostalgic tone of that book; their even more delicate works for *Fifteen, Jean and Johnny,* and *Sister of the Bride* emphasize the fragility of young romance.

The Author and the Child

Material for Cleary's books has come from her own life, from the nostalgic glow of Yamhill preserved in *Emily's Runaway Imagination* and the dark fears of her early years in Portland, which crop up in her works about Ramona, to her troubles with Gerhart, which inform the difficult relationships in some of her works for adolescents. "Why did adults think children had no feelings at all?" young Beverly had wondered, and Cleary clarifies in her works just how deep these feelings lie (*Yamhill,* 117). Just as important, her early struggles with reading and her subsequent longing for books about ordinary American children have influenced her work: stories about everyday life and ordinary children solving everyday problems, filled with appropriate humor and with a sense that even ordinary life—while not perfect—still has something extraordinary about it. Focusing on the trivialities of daily life, Cleary shows us how important and even interesting they are, for, Cleary constantly reminds her adult readers, the things adults consider trivial loom large in a child's life.

Cleary's philosophy of what makes a good children's book came to her early. Having overcome her difficulties with reading, she became "an opinionated young lady" who knew exactly what she wanted to read.[15] What she did *not* want to read included

> any book in which a child accepted the wisdom of an adult and reformed, any book in which a child reformed at all, any book in which problems were solved by a long-lost rich relative turning up in the last chapter, any book in which a family was grateful for the gift of a basket of groceries, usually on Christmas Eve, or any book in which a child turned out to be lord of the manor or heir to a fortune. These things did not happen in my neighborhood. Neither did I want to read about a noble dog who died in the last chapter after a long journey home on bleeding paws nor any book in which a pioneer girl ran through the forest to warn settlers of Indians. ("Regina," 23)

It also included any book or story in which education was disguised like a pill in a spoonful of jelly; approaching a revision of *The History of Little Goody Two Shoes* "with a brave heart and high hopes" as she struggled out of her reading difficulties, Beverly was at first irritated, then disillusioned, by what had appeared to be a "real" story turned into a treatise on reading, complete with phonics, as Goody taught the village children to read "ba, be, bi, bo, bu." The author had "cheated me. He had used a story to try to teach me. I bitterly resented this intrusion into my life."[16] Young Beverly especially knew that authors should stay out of their books—something the author of *Goody Two Shoes* had been unable to do. Or at least they should

> have the courtesy to hide themselves so the reader did not know they were there. My copy of "Pinocchio" began:
> "There was once upon a time . . .
> "'A king!' my little reader instantly exclaim.
> "No, children, you are wrong. There was a piece of wood."

Any child capable of reading a "chapters" book consid-ers himself a big reader. And what was the author doing in the book in the first place? He should keep still in-stead of interrupting one of my favorite stories with paragraphs beginning, "I leave it to my readers to imag-ine" when I was imagining very nicely without any in-terference from him. First person books, in which the protagonist was presumably the author, presented a dif-ferent problem. Most children in the 1920's and 1930's refused to read them, for "finding ourselves" was un-heard of. Maybe we had not found ourselves, but we knew where we stood. Anyone who talked about himself for an entire book had to be conceited. And "conceited" was an epithet, as in, "You're so conceited you think you're the whole cheese!" The central character of an "I" book was only pretending modesty.

The most disliked author, if he could be called an au-thor, wrote our arithmetic books. He stated a problem and then ordered us to *Think*. We knew we were sup-posed to think. We didn't need any author sneaking into the book to remind us. The first day of school, I went through my arithmetic book and angrily blacked out every *Think*. There. Take that, you old author. ("Why," 42)

Out of school, young Beverly tolerated little description, cultivat-ing the art of creative skipping and imagining:

Too much description bogging down the story? Skip it! A blue-eyed, fair-haired heroine when the reader was a brunette who wanted to be the heroine in the story? . . . Make her a brown-eyed, brown-haired girl in my imagi-nation. An author trying to use his story to teach his readers to be better boys and girls? Ha-ha, you old au-thor! You aren't my mother or father. This isn't school. You can't tell me what to do! I won't be a better girl.

Maybe I won't even finish your old book. So there! An
author who paused to say, "And now dear reader—" Skip
that, too. What makes him think I am his dear reader?
He's got to tell me a good story before I will be his dear
reader. ("Talking," 6)

What young Beverly did want to read were books about "plain,
ordinary" children like the ones she knew, "as they were, not as
they should be in the opinion of adults," who lived in neighbor-
hoods like hers, books in which the authors skipped "all that tiresome description" and allowed something to happen on every
page ("Low," 290; "Regina," 23). Above all, these children should
have problems they could solve themselves ("Regina," 23). The
kind of books she had in mind were books such as Carolina Snedeker's *Downright Dencey,* published in 1927, and Carroll Watson
Rankin's *Dandelion Cottage,* published in 1904. *Downright Dencey,* with its nineteenth-century Nantucket setting, is nevertheless the story of a young girl intent on solving her own problems,
though these problems include teaching a stubborn young boy
to read; young Beverly sympathized with Jetsam's struggles
("Books"). It was the book's compelling depiction of a warm family
life and of the stubborn little heroine staunchly trying to do what
she thinks is right and occasionally making mistakes of enthusiasm, however, which seems to have caught Beverly's imagination.
Dandelion Cottage was a work Beverly read over and over again.
An often-humorous book about four girls keeping house in an
abandoned parsonage, Rankin's story is very much a product of
its time. But its protagonists are ordinary, lively girls playing
games of keeping house, with their adventures arising naturally
out of the situation and their problems being solved by themselves with energy and creativity. These are not the patient, long-
suffering heroines of the books Beverly disliked; for, while they
are not terribly bad, these girls bicker with each other and with
the girl next door. The author, having plenty of opportunity to
moralize, refuses to do so, and there is no sense of sugarcoating
in the book: the girls' parents are loving but pragmatic and even-

tually insist the girls earn what they need for their playhouse; the girls get the cottage at the end of the book only because the adults have realized that it is too dilapidated to turn a profit.

The books Cleary did and did not enjoy as a child have influenced her writing: "In my own books I write for the only child I really know and that is the child within myself. I simply write the books I wanted to read as a child" ("Writing," 11). Though *Downright Dencey* and *Dandelion Cottage* reflect their times—as Cleary's do hers—there are parallels in their themes of ordinary children looking to themselves to solve their problems, children who are neither very good nor very bad, living lives that are not perfect but that are filled with family love. In her works, ordinary children lead ordinary lives, though these lives have changed since publication of *Henry Huggins* in 1950. Cleary's characters solve their problems by themselves, though they are clever enough to accept adult help if offered.

One of the chief delights of Cleary's work is her writing style: clear, direct, and disarmingly simple, it is the essence not only of good humorous writing, but of good writing in general. Though the words and sentence structure Cleary uses are simple and straightforward, there is no sense that Cleary is stripping her writing to accommodate her audience; instead, there is a sense that these are simply the right words for what Cleary wants to say. In part, this simplicity is a legacy from Cleary's mother, who advised her in high school to "[a]lways remember, the best writing is simple writing" (*Yamhill,* 186). Remembering the child who loved *Dandelion Cottage,* in writing her own books, Cleary also has remembered the child who disliked books in which the main character conceitedly told the story, books with too much description, books with a message, books with an author who kept popping in to harangue the reader. *Dear Mr. Henshaw,* the only work in which a child essentially tells his own story, is basically epistolary: Leigh's letters and diary are reproduced as if edited by Cleary herself. Description is sparse in Cleary's works, especially since Beverly's eighth-grade teacher handed back a paragraph of description "inflamed with red pencil corrections," having "changed almost every word": "For years I avoided writing description, and children told me they liked my books because there isn't any description in them" (*Yamhill*, 169).

There isn't any author, either, or any explicit message in Cleary's books. She does not lead her readers to the right reading of the work. Wryly pointing out that adults who insist to children that reading is fun also seem to insist to authors of children's books that a message is essential, she has answered their claims again and again in her fiction for children, with its implicit messages, and, more bluntly, in her speeches and articles aimed at adults:

> The writer of fiction for children must be, first of all, a story-teller, and if he cannot tell a story his books will not last with children. A story, according to my dictionary, is "a narrative, either true or fictitious, designed to interest or amuse the hearer or reader." The definition does not include the word "teach." Any message conveyed by the story must be implicit in the story, and this implicit message stems from the personality of the author, from his experience, his emotions and his convictions and not from any desire to teach or to get into a market. . . .
>
> No child wants to read for pleasure a book written in a controlled vocabulary, tested on other children the way detergents are tested on housewives, and designed to teach. I certainly would not want to write such a book. It sounds like a tiresome task. Books for children should be written out of the desire to tell a story. If the reading is to be satisfying to the child, the writing should be satisfying to the author who is collaborating with his child self. ("Talking," 7–8)

Besides, Cleary maintains, "[c]hildren would learn so much more if they were allowed to relax, enjoy a story, and discover what it is they want or need from books."[17]

Because Beverly wanted stories that were funny ("Low," 290), because Mrs. Bunn advised her to "Make it funny" (*Yamhill,* 186), and because Cleary finds that "[f]unny or sad, or even funny and tragic, describes my view of life," she has emphasized humor ("Laughter," 558). Believing that "comedy is as illuminating as tragedy," Cleary also is aware that her readers "may be frightened or discouraged by tragedy in realistic fiction" ("Laughter," 558). The world of Cleary's books is one in which a boy's lunchbox alarm keeps his lunch safe but proves noisy to disarm, in which talcum powder turns the white spots on a dog's coat pink, in which a girl's first kiss is interrupted by a gopher-bearing cat, and in which a little girl crowning herself with cockleburs discovers that uncrowning herself is not quite so easy. Though some of the humor in Cleary's books is slapstick—Ribsy dumping paint on his owner, Ramona giving herself and Howie an unexpected blue bath— most of it is more subtle, for Cleary has noted that "children laugh because they have grown," because they have grown past the embarrassment and can see their younger selves in perspective ("Laughter," 562). Readers close to the problems Cleary's protagonists encounter may not find them funny, but as they resolve the dilemmas of their childhoods they are able to enjoy the humorous aspects of the growing up of Henry and Ramona and Ellen and Leigh; "the best humor," Cleary reminds us, "leaves room for growth" ("Laughter," 561, 562). This humor may be the main reason for Cleary's continuing popularity, a popularity she never has actively sought. Children love humor, Cleary notes, and they long for it "in a world grown grim" ("Laughter," 563). Humor captures the early reader, helping her or him to realize that "reading is a worthwhile experience": "Over the years the first books to catch the imagination of children who have escaped the reading circle and are ready to discover the pleasures of reading have been simply written humorous books" ("Laughter," 562). And more experienced readers enjoy looking back on and feeling superior to their earlier, less mature selves. Like the books Cleary cites in an article on humor, her own works reward more than one reading, amusing and delighting readers who are "discovering fresh insight" each time they reread a book ("Laughter," 563).

The real popularity of Cleary's work lies both in their timeless qualities and in the way Cleary has responded to her readers. In print since 1950, *Henry Huggins* seems as fresh for young readers now as it did then. Dealing with the ordinary fears and pleasures of childhood, which do not change, Cleary's works are timeless in their depiction of the inner life of a child and in what will entertain that child. On the other hand, Cleary has responded to the changing world of her readers by expanding the reality she presents. Moving from Henry Huggins, who lives with two parents in a suburban house and deals only with the problems he gets into himself, to Ramona Quimby, who lives with two parents but is aware that parents can divorce and deals with her father's layoff and the tight economic times that follow, to Leigh Botts, who lives with his divorced mother in a tiny cottage and is beset by loneliness, Cleary has kept the situations contemporary even as she emphasizes the unchanged essentials. Henry is as much a product of his time as Ramona is of hers and Leigh is of his, but they share the same needs for love and acceptance, and they all struggle with the confusing process of growing up, as Beverly Bunn did. Drawing on her own ordinary life and the lives around her, Cleary shows her readers that growing up is never easy, but it can be funny.

2

A Boy and His Dog

As a young reader in Portland, Oregon, Cleary longed for stories "about American children in moderate circumstances who lived with two parents in plain square houses on fifty by one hundred lots in a medium-sized city and who walked a few blocks to a red brick schoolhouse like the one I attended . . . [and who acted] like the children in my neighborhood who were only moderately well-behaved and who were often naughty" ("Writing," 8). As an adult librarian in Yakima, Washington, she found herself fielding requests from young readers for—as boys from a local parochial school put it—"books about kids like us" ("Regina," 23). The result, published in September, 1950, was *Henry Huggins,* the first of six works about an ordinary boy and his dog, both of whom find themselves getting into most unordinary situations.[1]

A Dog and His Boy

Henry Huggins

Henry's first story seems to have been written in that half-hap-hazard way in which many first books are produced. Having spent the years of World War II as an army librarian, Cleary found herself with more time for herself after she and her husband moved to Berkeley, California—time, and typing paper in the linen closet. Now, she remarked to her husband, "I'll have to write a book":

> "Why don't you?" he asked.
> "Because we never have any sharp pencils," I answered.
> The next day he brought home a pencil sharpener and I realized that if I was ever going to write a book, this was the time to do it. ("Writing," 10)

The book was begun 2 January, the date on which all her subsequent works would be begun ("Early," 25). Cleary had intended to write "a book that was to be a girls' story about the maturing of a sensitive female who wanted to write" ("Regina," 23). What came out was somewhat different, for she found herself "remembering the boys of St. Joseph's and the children who had once come to Saturday afternoon story hour and my own childhood reading" ("Regina," 23). Cleary, at a table in the spare bedroom, "began a story based on an incident that had once amused me about two children who had to take their dog home on a streetcar during a heavy rain. This turned into a story about a boy who would be allowed to keep a stray dog if he could manage to take him home on a bus. When I finished the chapter I found I had ideas for another chapter and at the end of two months I had a whole book about Henry Huggins and his dog Ribsy" ("Writing," 10). Cleary sent the finished work to William Morrow and Company "because I had heard that Elisabeth Hamilton, who was then editor, was one of the best and because I had once heard an author remark that Morrow was kind to authors" ("Writing," 10). The work—then titled "Spareribs and Henry"—was accepted six weeks later (Reuther, 441), and Cleary realized her ambition to be an author.

Henry Huggins set the episodic tone of most of Cleary's work for younger children, though in this book the chapters are more loosely connected than are those in Cleary's later novels. This is because, Cleary admits, "when I began *Henry Huggins,* I did not know how to write a book, so I mentally told the stories to that remembered audience and wrote them down as I told them. This is why my first book is a collection of stories about a group of characters rather than a novel" (Fitzgibbons, 168). The book concerns Henry's growing relationship with Ribsy, the dog he finds on the street, and also his solutions to the problems of everyday life, which, in Henry's case, mysteriously exaggerate themselves.

Henry is the type of boy to whom nothing much seems to happen—until he meets Ribsy. Just getting Ribsy home after the two first meet involves a hair tonic box, a melee on a bus, and the police. Suddenly, life is exciting. The weekly trip to the pet shop for Ribsy's horsemeat leads to Henry's buying a pair of guppies on sale; and, since guppies beget guppies beget guppies, Henry soon has a roomful of jars of tiny fish. He is surprised and relieved to learn that the pet shop owner will take them in exchange for enough credit to buy a tank and a pair of fish that do not breed in captivity. Distracted by Ribsy as he and Scooter McCarthy toss Scooter's new football back and forth, Henry throws the ball into the back seat of a passing automobile and must buy a replacement, which costs $13.95 (plus 41¢ tax). Catching night crawlers for neighbor Mr. Grumbie proves to be the key, and, with his parents' help, Henry comes up with the necessary 1,331 crawlers. Even better, the driver of the passing automobile returns Scooter's ball, leaving Henry with money to buy his own football.

Ribsy comes to Henry's rescue after Henry gets the part of the little boy in the school's Christmas pageant; teased about the sappy role, Henry is wild to get out of it but cannot until Ribsy manages to knock a can of indelible green paint on Henry's head, leaving him to play the Green Elf instead. Ribsy himself becomes a pale pink dog at a dog show. After a thorough bath, Ribsy is still wet when he and Henry arrive at the show, and so when Ribsy takes a nice, long roll in a flower bed, he ends up muddy. When he sprinkles talcum powder on the white parts of Ribsy to re-whiten them, Henry finds that the powder itself is pink—and so is Ribsy. However, after a memorable show in which Ribsy entangles Henry in the leash, refuses to obey commands, and involves Henry in a dog fight, Henry and Ribsy go home with a silver cup for the "most unusual dog" in the show.

As a result of Ribsy's picture's being in the paper, another boy claims him as his own runaway. Henry feels sorry for the boy, but he cannot give up Ribsy; finally, the boys decide to let Ribsy choose. Ribsy picks Henry, to the delight of Henry and the entire neighborhood, because neither the neighborhood nor Henry's life would be the same without him.

Both young and adult readers apparently felt as enthusiastic. "Probably no reviewer of children's books has forgotten the excitement and fun of reading the first of Beverly Cleary's Henry Huggins books in 1950," May Hill Arbuthnot later recalled.[2] Reviewers also expressed that excitement, praising the humor and simplicity of the work. "This story of Henry Huggins and his dog, Ribsy, is written for younger boys and girls but we defy anyone under seventy not to chuckle over it," said one,[3] while another emphasized that "there is not a dull moment but some hilariously funny ones in the telling of Henry's adventures at home and at school."[4] Most important, Cleary began to receive letters from her young readers.[5]

Readers' responses to the work point up Cleary's success in presenting the everyday concerns of everyday life: "reality twisted to the right into humor rather than to the left into tragedy" ("Laughter," 558). The emphasis of the book is on Henry's misadventures, which arise naturally out of things of everyday life: finding a stray dog, keeping guppies, attending a dog show, acting in a school Christmas pageant. It is real life that shapes Henry's adventures, and while these everyday situations are taken to the limits, it seems logical and inevitable; the ultimate events are not forced but, rather, grow naturally. Trying to carry a lively, adult dog like Ribsy onto a city bus naturally is difficult, and the resulting slapstick is the natural outcome of a panicked dog on a crowded bus; guppies are programmed to multiply, and a softhearted boy naturally would have hundreds to care for before a few weeks pass.

These events are inevitable because of Henry's personality. Though the episodic, action-filled chapters leave Cleary little room for characterization, Henry emerges as a believable boy who is not above ridiculing girls or arguing hotly with his friends and accustomed to taking care of his own problems—whether it is earning money to replace a friend's football or getting out of playing a sappy role in a Christmas pageant. Henry's allowance for several weeks goes for fish supplies, and the pet shop owner is impressed with Henry's success with the hundreds of tiny fish. Earnest and responsible, Henry seems the sometimes-hapless pawn of absurdity: he never instigates trouble but is somewhat passive. After all, it isn't *Henry's* fault that guppies reproduce so quickly, or that an automobile races past just as he throws a football, or that the city transit authority allows only boxed dogs onto buses. But Henry is not passive for long. Once things begin to happen to him, he takes charge and solves his own problems in a way that is logical to a young boy. Need to have a dog in a box? Fine. Put him into the biggest box possible. The box needs to cover the dog? Fine. Wrap the dog in paper and put him into a shopping bag. Need to clean a dog that has rolled in the mud? No problem. Use a little talcum powder on the white parts, and hope the fact that the powder is pink will not show in the bright sun. Henry's middle name seems to be "perseverance."

Tested throughout the book, Henry's skill at persevering seems to grow stronger by the last chapter. The rules of the transit authority prove too much for him in the first chapter, and he must be rescued by the police; even Henry finally cracks under the strain of taking care of hundreds of guppies. But he is unswerving in his attempts to earn money for Scooter's football, to get out of playing the little boy in the Christmas pageant, and to win a prize for Ribsy in the dog show. This strengthened perseverance stands him in good stead in the book's final chapter, when his relationship with Ribsy is threatened. Episodic as the book is—as we have seen, Cleary called it "a collection of stories . . . rather than a novel"—it takes as its theme the growing bond between the boy and his dog. The last chapter works to reaffirm their relationship, as Ribsy chooses Henry over his old master in a tense but hilariously undramatic scene. Stopping, lying down, sighing, and biting a flea, Ribsy chooses Henry in a way that is realistic and that repudiates melodramatic scenes in other works too numerous to mention. It is the kind of scene few of Cleary's readers will experience firsthand, but it is firmly rooted in reality.

It is just this rooting in reality that soon set up a puzzle for Cleary: while her adult readers found Henry's adventures humorous, many of her younger readers found them "'funny and sad.'" ("Laughter," 558). It was years before Cleary realized what they meant. Planted in everyday life, Henry's adventures strike a bit too close to home for some of her young readers to find humorous; too young to put Henry's problems in perspective, they do not always see the humor in his troubles. It is those who can feel superior to their younger selves who laugh at Henry, and this is mostly adults and older children ("Laughter," 561). This dichotomy has remained for almost all of Cleary's works.

Henry Huggins not only introduced readers to Cleary's style of humor and view of real life; it showed them a large cast on which Cleary could base subsequent books. From Henry and Ribsy to Scooter to Beezus and Ramona Quimby, all are introduced here; the cast is large and varied enough to support the thirteen works Cleary would set on Klickitat Street.

Henry and Beezus

Though Cleary's next book was *Ellen Tebbits,* she "continued to have ideas about Henry Huggins" ("Writing," 10); and on 2 January Cleary began her next book about the boy and his dog. Though the book still focused on Henry and his relationship with Ribsy, Cleary brought forward two children who had been minor characters in the earlier work and gave them new emphasis: Beatrice (Beezus) Quimby and her preschool-age sister, Ramona Geraldine Quimby. *Henry and Beezus,* published in 1952, paved the way for Cleary's Ramona series, so popular in the 1970s, for in this work Ramona begins to show her true colors.

At the center of *Henry and Beezus* is Henry's desire to own a bicycle, which he cannot afford. The lack of both bicycle and funds is emphasized in the first chapter, when Ribsy steals a roast the neighbors are planning to barbecue. Henry can only look on in envy as Scooter McCarthy chases Ribsy on his bicycle and rescues the roast. More determined than ever to get his own bicycle, Henry also now must pay for the chewed-up roast.

Finding forty-nine boxes of bubble gum dumped by a businessman who has gone out of business leads Henry into his own business. But selling the gum at school soon becomes a problem: the principal outlaws gum chewing on school grounds, Henry's customers demand more than the one flavor he has, and Henry finds himself reducing the price until he is giving the gum away and has given up keeping track of delinquent accounts. Henry, too, goes out of business, dumping the gum, with Beezus's help, exactly where he found it earlier.

Beezus also helps when Henry gets into trouble by teaching Ribsy to fetch. Scooter, who will pay Henry to take his paper route while he goes to Scout camp, suddenly finds that the papers he has delivered are vanishing: it turns out that Ribsy, enthusiastically practicing his new paper-fetching skills, is fetching the neighbors' papers as well. Inspired by Ramona's squirting of everything in sight with her water pistol, Henry and Beezus "untrain" Ribsy by squirting him with water each time he goes after a newspaper.

Henry believes his moment will come—he will finally get a bicycle—at the police auction of bicycles, but in reality his troubles have just begun. He and Beezus are accompanied by Ramona, who is pretending to be a windup toy and who must be wound up what seems like every five minutes. Ramona's demand for food leads to Ribsy being tied to a parking meter and getting a ticket, which an amused policeman "fixes" for Henry. Once they get to the noisy, crowded auction, it looks as if Henry must leave without his bicycle, for he cannot get in a bid, and Ramona, bored, announces loudly that she is going to throw up. Quelling her with a sisterly threat, Beezus must later go up front to claim her when, having gotten lost in the crowd, Ramona is held up by the auctioneer. Here, though, Beezus can bid, and she bids $4.04 for a bicycle—but a girl's bicycle, not a boy's. Henry tries to make do

by tying a broomhandle in the appropriate place, but this subter-
fuge does not work, for his new bicycle has too many structural
faults.

The opening of the Colossal Market provides the neighborhood
with free entertainment in the form of samples and doorprizes.
Even Henry wins a prize—$50 worth of work at the market's
beauty salon, which he doubts he will ever live down. However,
when Beezus offers to buy a coupon, Henry realizes that his prize
has value after all; and he sells the coupons for almost enough
money to buy the fancy red bicycle he has coveted. At last he can
pass Scooter with calm assurance.

The Henry of *Henry Huggins* is growing up, and in this second
Henry Huggins book Cleary emphasizes the ways in which Henry
is expanding his relationships and his world. Having created a
neighborhood full of children for Henry to play with, Cleary emphasizes his growth by showing him in action with his friends.
Where the first book focuses on the growing bond between Henry
and Ribsy, the second highlights Henry's relationships with his
peers, particularly Beezus and Ramona. The increased mobility a
bicycle provides is important to a child forging ahead into the
wider world.

Still responsible and persevering, Henry continues to fall into
one troublesome situation after another. Working to alleviate his
bikeless state, Henry rarely anticipates the somewhat-exagger-
ated, but always natural, outcome of his actions. But who could
predict that a dog taught to fetch the evening paper would fetch
every paper in the neighborhood? Or that simply selling bubble
gum could get so out of hand? Still beset by events, Henry, nevertheless, does not let himself be defeated by them; he takes charge
of the situation as best he can.

But this time Henry has help. Whereas in the first work he was
able to take care of his problems himself, in the second he often
finds himself calling upon Beezus. It is Beezus's and Ramona's
wagon that Henry must use to transport his bubble gum from and
to the empty lot; Ramona's squirting of everything in sight with
her water pistol inspires him in his quest to untrain Ribsy. Beezus

tells Henry of the bicycle auction; Beezus bids for Henry's bicycle; Beezus makes up for the fact that it is a girl's bicycle by showing him that the coupons he wins in the last chapter are more valuable than he thought. Henry is often reluctant to have Beezus's help, for she is, after all, only a girl, interested in gardenias and in having her hair waved. But having proved his independence in the earlier book, he now learns to accept the aid of others, at the same time forging more complex relationships with his peers.

Complex is the word when dealing with Ramona, who provides much of the book's humor. In love with slugs and with getting her own way, yelling when she does not get what she wants, and embarrassingly blunt, Ramona is the typical bratty younger sister, descendant of many a bratty younger sister in earlier works for children—the kind of character whom we would rather read about than know. Here, she is not so much a character in her own right as she is an impediment to Henry: she must be placated before he and Beezus can pick up his bubble gum; pretending to be a windup toy, she runs down at inopportune moments when Henry is impatient to be at the bicycle auction; demanding food, she is the reason Henry ties Ribsy to a parking meter and gets a ticket; and her bored announcement that she is going to throw up almost gets them sent home before Henry can bid on a bicycle. She is both hilarious and irritating in her unpredictability. Older sister Beezus, used to these difficulties, takes them in her stride, giving in to Ramona or quelling her with sisterly threats; only-child Henry, who is most emphatically *not* used to them, has no such defenses and must deal with Ramona by dealing with Beezus. In her first presentation, Ramona is dominated by Beezus, but her liveliness shines through; and it is easy to see why she eventually became protagonist of her own series.

Focused on Henry, this work introduced another of Cleary's most enduring characters. But, more importantly, it presents its readers with a character who succeeds in growing up. Dealing with Beezus, earning the money for his bicycle, Henry is definitely moving into the larger world—a movement Cleary emphasizes in the later works about Henry Huggins.

Henry and Ribsy

After *Henry and Beezus* came *Otis Spofford,* but Cleary continued to have ideas about Henry and his dog, and on 22 September 1954, *Henry and Ribsy* was published. The book sprang from an idea Cleary's father had that "it would make a funny story if Henry and his father took Ribsy salmon fishing and Ribsy was so frightened by a salmon flopping around in the boat that he jumped out and tried to swim away" ("Writing," 10). Inspired by incidents of her daily life, Cleary found that *Henry and Ribsy* "was an easy book to write and I had a good time writing it" ("Writing," 11).

Just as funny as the first book, *Henry and Ribsy* is equally episodic. The work emphasizes Henry's attempts to keep Ribsy out of mischief to earn a promised trip salmon-fishing. The trouble begins with Ribsy's theft of a policeman's lunch right out of the police car; Mr. Huggins extracts from Henry a promise to keep Ribsy out of trouble until salmon season. Excited by the prospect of catching an enormous fish, Henry agrees and then realizes what a job he has landed for himself.

The promise even complicates taking out the garbage, for Ribsy defends the garbage so ferociously that the garbage collectors skip the Hugginses's house. When Ribsy growls at Scooter as he wheels Henry's bicycle out of the garage, Henry realizes that Ribsy is protecting his bicycle and has been protecting the garbage. Because Ribsy did not "protect" the garbage until Henry took it out, he bargains with his father to take over clipping the edges of the lawn, which is a harder job but which will make it difficult for Henry and Ribsy to get into trouble.

After Henry's mother helps him out after a disastrous home haircut, Ribsy helps him pull his loose canine teeth. Now Henry discovers a new talent: spitting double through the holes in his mouth. His care to keep Ribsy out of trouble almost comes to nothing when Ramona gets revenge for Ribsy's stealing her ice cream by putting his bone into her lunchbox. Following Ramona closely, Ribsy ends up at the bottom of a jungle gym on the school playground, with Ramona screaming at the top. The sight convinces two PTA members that Ramona has climbed the gym out of fear. After a confusion created by Ribsy's barking, Ramona's howling, a spontaneous game of catch, and the PTA mothers trying to decide what to do, the school principal—a friend of Ribsy—takes charge and gets Ramona down.

Ribsy gets into trouble even on the promised fishing trip, when he inadvertently helps Mr. Grumbie's hooked salmon escape before jumping into the river. Henry's chance to catch a fish vanishes, for he and his dog are put ashore. His humiliation deepens when he realizes that Scooter is out fishing, too, and sure to catch a salmon. Strolling along the beach, however, Ribsy finds a fish for Henry: a Chinook salmon trying to swim up a shallow stream, when Henry holds on to long enough to be rescued by a man attracted by Ribsy's barking. The man clubs the salmon and helps Henry carry it back. Henry's salmon weighs twenty-nine pounds, and his triumph is complete when he learns that Scooter has caught nothing and that Mr. Grumbie has caught a fish to replace the one he lost.

Henry and Ribsy delighted both reviewers and its intended audience. Reviewers enjoyed the humor: *Booklist* said it was "better, if possible, than its predecessors" and praised its "natural characters and . . . unhackneyed, genuinely funny situations,"[6] while *Publishers Weekly* called it "one of Mrs. Cleary's most hilarious books."[7] Yet another reviewer felt that this work "has more real child humor than some of the earlier Cleary books have had."[8] The young readers voted to give it the Young Readers' Choice Award of the Pacific Northwest Library Association in 1957.

After emphasizing the relationship between Henry and his peers in *Henry and Beezus,* Cleary refocuses in *Henry and Ribsy* on the relationship between Henry and his dog. As before, the situations Henry finds himself in are not of his own making, and he sometimes seems to find himself the pawn of circumstance; but once again, he takes charge and solves his problems himself. Having introduced the idea in the first book that having a pet is not easy, Cleary returns to this topic in the third book, focusing on the difficulties of keeping a lively dog out of trouble—the kind of trouble only a Huggins could get into. Difficulties seem to follow Ribsy as they do Henry: the lawn he chases a cat across is the one freshly seeded yard in the neighborhood; like his owner, Ribsy has his own problems with Ramona. As in earlier books, Cleary allows these humorous problems to grow naturally out of the situation. But the problems the two encounter strengthen their bond.

Having set up the trouble Ribsy can get into as her major theme, Cleary does not allow anything to distract her readers from this problem. Though this work takes Henry farther afield than the earlier two works and though we see him interacting more than before with those around him, Cleary uses this broader scope to focus on his main problem with Ribsy.

Henry always has interacted with the children in the neighborhood, but now Cleary makes his interaction part of his main problem. The neighborhood children spread the story of Ribsy's growling at the garbage collector until it is exaggerated beyond recognition. Ramona may have been a pesty little obstacle in *Henry and Beezus,* but here she is a real danger to Henry's fishing trip when she takes Ribsy's bone in retaliation and ends up screaming at the top of the jungle gym with Ribsy below in what looks like a classic case of a child's fear of a vicious dog. Even Mr. Grumbie, during a memorable day fishing with Ribsy and Henry, manages to cause them as much trouble as Ribsy causes him. But Henry's love of his dog is solid, and trouble from other sources does not dent it. In spite of the problems Ribsy causes, their relationship emerges stronger than ever.

As in *Henry Huggins,* the two support and help each other, though more in this third book than in the first. Henry defends Ribsy from all critics, from his parents to his neighborhood friends to the ladies of the P.T.A., as he struggles to keep Ribsy out of trouble or to undo the trouble Ribsy has caused. This can be difficult when Ribsy threatens the garbage collectors or seems to threaten Ramona in front of the P.T.A. For his part, Ribsy helps Henry in more ways than before. In *Henry Huggins,* he had merely accidentally dumped paint on Henry at an appropriate moment. Now he incidentally saves Henry from a chore by proving that he will guard the garbage from all comers if Henry takes it out, he plays tug-of-war with a piece of string and thereby pulls

Henry's canine teeth in an appropriately doggy and dramatic way, and—after their disastrous morning of fishing—finds for Henry a salmon even bigger than those Henry had dreamed of catching. Without meaning to, Ribsy shows Henry tangible expressions of his devotion. While their relationship has never been one-sided— Henry counts on Ribsy's love as much as Ribsy counts on Henry— it seems to become more equal here; the boy whose favorite song is a dog food jingle has a dog worthy of such devotion.

Henry and the Paper Route

The next Henry book was not published until 1957, after Cleary had published her first adolescent novel, *Fifteen,* and the first of her series of books about Ramona Quimby, *Beezus and Ramona.* Though three years had passed between books, Henry has aged only one year: in *Henry and the Paper Route* he is ten, and his interests have widened to include having his own paper route.

When the book opens, Henry decides to take a paper route. Undaunted though he is a year too young to have a route, Henry sets off to talk Mr. Capper—who is in charge of the routes—into giving him the route. Henry's professionalism loses its edge when he ends up with four rummage-sale kittens in his jacket, and an amused Mr. Capper asks Henry to come back in a year or two.

At home that night, Henry has another problem, for his parents and Ribsy object to having four kittens in the house. Henry decides to solve both problems with ease: he will sell subscriptions to the newspaper, offering a free kitten with each subscription; and the list of new subscribers will persuade Mr. Capper to give him a route. This does not go as planned, however, and Henry ends up giving the kittens to the local pet shop owner to sell. The house is quiet that night without the kittens; Mr. Huggins sends Henry to buy the most audacious of the four, Nosy, who quickly settles into the household.

More determined than ever to get his own route, Henry folds papers for Scooter once a week. The week that Henry's school starts a paper drive, Scooter has Henry deliver the papers for him one evening; Henry seizes this chance to advertise the paper drive by enclosing an advertisement in each newspaper. The advertisements' success causes problems, for Henry receives many calls, and the magazines and newspapers soon fill the Huggins's garage and overflow into the driveway. Bundling the paper is less fun than collecting it, and hauling it to school is even less fun. Though Henry's room wins due to his efforts, next time he will not advertise: it was too successful.

Henry's eleventh birthday is wonderful, especially since now he is old enough for a paper route, and the new family who has moved in might include a boy. Then Scooter gets the chicken pox, and Henry must take his route. That day he finally meets the new boy in the neighborhood: Byron Murphy ("Murph"), who is building a robot and who probably is a genius. Ramona is the only child in the neighborhood who is not awed by Murph, and she imitates him, wearing sunglass frames to mimic his glasses. Scooter takes back his route when he gets well, and the route Henry had hoped to take over goes to a boy who is shifting his route to Henry's neighborhood—Murph. It is not fair, Henry thinks, that Murph not only is a genius, but he also has the paper route. On the other hand, he has humiliating battles with Ramona, who has decided to be a "paper boy" like Murph and who insists on "delivering" Murph's newspapers. Bested by Ramona, Murph gives up his route to Henry, and Ramona becomes very good—too good, Henry finds, for she is redelivering the newspapers he has just delivered. After an embarrassing fight of his own with Ramona, Henry makes a robot's head out of a box and thereby turns Ramona into a non-paper-delivering mechanical man.

Henry and the Paper Route proved as popular as the earlier Henry books, both with critics and with young readers. Once again, critics emphasized the book's humor. In 1960, children awarded it the Young Readers' Choice Award of the Pacific Northwest Library Association.

This is Henry's "breakthrough" book: in *Henry and Beezus,* he earned his first bicycle; in *Henry and Ribsy,* he took full responsibility for Ribsy and went on his first important fishing trip; now he really seems to be growing up, gaining confidence in himself and finding his place in the larger world. The determination and sense of responsibility are still there, honed by Henry's problems with Ribsy in the earlier works. The ability to find himself in outrageous situations without even trying is—to the relief and amusement of readers—also present. Henry is growing up, but in a lot of ways he is still the same old Henry.

Henry's increasing maturity shows itself on two fronts. First, and central, is his paper route. Too young to have his own route, Henry is more determined than ever after Scooter points this out to him. Scooter, two years older than Henry, has been an irritant in the earlier novels, mocking Henry's bikeless state in *Henry and Beezus* and teasing Henry about his dog and his haircut in *Henry and Ribsy*. Now his annoying inspires Henry, who is determined to get a route like Scooter's. For Henry, the route not only represents money for stamps and flashlights and the other necessities of life, but it also means growing up, and being as old and important as Scooter. It becomes even more important when it seems as if it will never happen. Mature enough at the beginning of the book to realize that he can talk Mr. Capper into giving him the route if he tries and that having Ribsy come along with him is not a good idea, Henry is young enough to load himself with four kittens that spoil his businesslike demeanor. But by the end of the work he is a boy with a paper route who has built experience in handling a route by stepping in for Scooter, and—most important—a boy who can deal with Ramona.

Coping with Ramona is the second way in which Henry displays his deepening maturity. Until now, he has been a boy who *cannot* deal with Ramona. Ramona appears as an obstacle for Henry in *Henry and Beezus* and *Henry and Ribsy,* as she and her antics make life difficult for him and Ribsy; but it is Beezus who handles Ramona in those books by cajoling, bribing, and threatening. Henry has been stymied by Ramona and by the embarrassment of the things she does. Now, having been at the center of her own book, *Beezus and Ramona,* Ramona seems stronger than ever as an unpredictable character who must be dealt with; now that she is older, she causes trouble in more complex ways than before. But now Henry finds his own way to handle her by outwitting her. It is not the kind of solution that would have occurred to Henry earlier; growing in maturity, Henry is also growing in his ability to judge other people. Handling Ramona is pushing Henry into maturity.

The Henry at the end of the work is a more confident character who is finding his place in the world. At the beginning, he is intimidated by Scooter, Ramona, and Murph. By the end of the work, he has learned not to be cowed by any of them. Scooter will always be older than Henry, but Henry gets one up on him by using the paper route for the advertisements that lead to success in the paper drive. By the end of the book Henry has a paper route of his own, just like Scooter. Ramona he learns to outwit. Outwitting Ramona, Henry even learns not to be intimidated by Murph, the genius who not only plays chess but is building a robot and has a paper route. Witnessing Murph's embarrassing failure with Ramona, Henry also sees Murph at his worst and realizes that the genius is not all-powerful; managing to outwit Ramona, Henry accomplishes what even the genius could not. In the process he gets the paper route he has worked for, but this job is the least indication of Henry's growth.

Henry and the Clubhouse

Readers had to wait five years for the next Henry book. The adolescent works *The Luckiest Girl* and *Jean and Johnny,* a novelization of "Leave It to Beaver," and the historical novel *Emily's Runaway Imagination* were published before *Henry and the Clubhouse* came out in 1962. Having created the progressive plots of the adolescent novels, Cleary brought her newly honed skills to her works for younger readers: though the action of *Henry and the Clubhouse* slices neatly into the even-length chapters comfortable for young readers, the book itself is much more unified than were the earlier books. But one thing has not changed: Henry still gets himself into trouble without even trying, usually because of five-year-old Ramona Quimby. As Henry book followed Henry book, Ramona's role in each grew. Finally, in *Henry and the Clubhouse,* she is the focus of Henry's trials and tribulations.

First, however, there is the problem of the paper route. During a bumpy ride to the dump in the Grumbies's old bathtub, Henry realizes that he will be late delivering his newspapers and may lose his paper route as a result. Having telephoned his mother to have someone fold his newspapers, Henry is horrified to find her delivering the newspapers herself; his father is stern about Henry's responsibility to his route.

Henry's main problem, however, is that he has not sold any newspaper subscriptions. An idea to build a doghouse grows when a neighbor tears down his garage and gives Henry enough wood to build a clubhouse, complete with windows. Soon he and Murph are hard at work. Henry's attempt to sell a subscription to a new neighborhood family fails when Ribsy and the new dog, Ranger, decide to resent each other and start a fight; Ranger chases Ribsy down the street, and Henry feels that perhaps this is not a good time to sell a subscription. He tries again the next day, but Ranger chases him away.

Halloween arrives, and Henry still has not gotten past Ranger. Trick or treating is fun, especially after Henry receives a stuffed owl: at the new neighbors' house, Henry watches in amazement and satisfaction as Ranger, terrified of the owl, cowers beneath a chair; he takes this chance to sell a subscription, though his satisfaction is marred when the new customer calls him "Harry Higgins." Ramona is Henry's next problem when he collects his money: left to watch Ramona, the three Kelly children, and the Kelly dog while Mrs. Kelly gets money, Henry cannot stop Ramona from opening the lid of the washing machine in time for it to spray dirty water everywhere. Escaping, he must return because he forgot the money.

Ramona is a bigger problem once the clubhouse is finished. After the girls pull pranks because the boys refused their help, the boys get a padlock, which Ramona locks behind Henry one day when they are alone. Waiting for his parents to come home, Henry remembers his paper route and must tell both Ramona and her sister the club's secret password before they will use the club's hidden key to rescue him.

Henry's problems with Ramona take a new turn after he gets her to stop bothering him on his route. Knowing of Ramona's infatuation with the host of the local cartoon show, Henry writes to him for help and watches in satisfaction as he speaks directly to

Ramona and tells her to leave Henry alone. Awestruck, she promises. Awestruck, she also follows Henry everywhere; though she does not interfere, she is embarrassing, carrying a smaller version of his delivery bag, and, one snowy day, correcting a client who calls Henry "Harry." Henry must even pull her home on the sled before finishing his route. When a glowing letter to the editor praises the way he helped Ramona, Henry realizes that good old Ramona has been responsible for his moment of fame.

In this last work, which is completely from Henry's point of view, Cleary shows us a Henry clearly on his way to becoming an adult. While he still finds himself getting into impossible situations, he also evinces a new maturity, especially in the way he sees Ramona. Henry is not perfect; he still fails to think ahead about the possible outcome of his actions. There is, for example, his ride in the Grumbies's old bathtub, a bumpy but entertaining ride that must be cut short because Henry has forgotten about his paper route. The well-built clubhouse owes its sturdiness to Murph's planning, for, left to his own devices, Henry would have simply started to build without thinking of how it should go together. Also, many of Henry's clubhouse difficulties stem from his typical eleven-year-old-boy's dismissal of girls. But most of Henry's problems in the book stem not from lack of foresight but from those around him. It is Ranger's hostility toward Ribsy that gives Henry trouble as he tries to sell the new people a subscription to his newspaper; Henry comes close to being late delivering papers because Ramona locks him in the clubhouse. As ever, he is usually in trouble not of his own making, and, as ever, his determination sees him through.

Many of these problems stem from one source: Ramona, who is now five years old. Once presented as an obstacle for Henry to get around, in this work she still represents an obstacle, but now Henry begins to understand her and his place in her life. She is still an irritating little force, locking him in the clubhouse, opening a washing machine during the spin cycle while he is supposed to be watching her and her friends, seeming to accuse a possible new customer of setting forest fires, and trailing after him with her own bag for delivering newspapers. But by the end of the

work Henry comes to see her less as some cosmic force of provo-
cation than as what she is, a lively little girl eager for his attention. Though Henry's mother assures him of this description of
Ramona, he does not believe her until the end of the work. Then,
displeased because of all the trouble she has caused him and
pleased because she has told Mrs. Peabody Henry's real name,
Henry finds himself feeling sorry for Ramona as she stands tired,
cold, and pathetic in the deep snow. Seeing her suddenly as the
small child she is, Henry finds himself helping her, though he
does not want to. Henry receives an immediate reward in the
form of a letter of praise from a customer and his father's resulting pride in him, but having found compassion even for Ramona,
Henry is clearly on his way to real maturity.

Though *Ramona the Pest* would not be published for another
six years, *Henry and the Clubhouse* is important in Ramona's career as an independent character. Identifying with Beezus in *Beezus and Ramona* and with Henry in the earlier Henry Huggins
books, the reader cannot be blamed for viewing Ramona with little sympathy. But now, seeing her as a small child eager for Henry's attention, it is easier to feel sympathy even for a child who
locks another person in a clubhouse. Sympathy is just what we
come to feel for Ramona in her own series. Then, too, Ramona has
some of her best scenes in this work, as she interviews herself
with a cardboard-tube microphone and, especially, in her infatuation with Sheriff Bud.

Cleary uses this chance to get in her say about the burgeoning
influence of television. While television is not mentioned in
Cleary's earlier works, by 1962 its impact was being felt in American culture in general, and Cleary satirizes its influence and the
commercial-saturated cartoon shows. Sheriff Bud's program, in
which he seizes every opportunity to insert pitches for Nutsies
and for Crispy Potato Chips, is the essence of avaricious advertising; even Henry's letter provides an opening for a potato chips
advertisement. Wearily and warily listening as her daughter is
directly asked for help by a character on television, Mrs. Quimby
informs her, "Whatever it is, I'm not going to buy it" (160). Ramona proves the perfect recipient of all this advertising, en-

thralled by what she sees on the television. Enamored of television commercials, she repeats them everywhere, sternly informing Mrs. Peabody that only she can prevent forest fires, singing the Crispy Potato Chips song when asked to do a trick on Halloween, and joyously reciting the Nutsie candy bar commercial word for word in honor of the candy bar she receives. Searching for a hero, Ramona finds one through most of the book in Sheriff Bud, whom she imitates by wearing disguises; she shifts her allegiance to Henry primarily because he can communicate with Sheriff Bud.

Though *Ribsy* was yet to be written, it is possible to see in *Henry and the Clubhouse* the appropriate winding down of the Henry Huggins series and the beginning of the Ramona series. Here, Ramona comes into her own as a believable and lively force of energy. Once a boy to whom nothing much happens in the first book, Henry now has become more confident and ready to find a place in the larger world, a responsible and determined boy who somehow gets himself into surprising difficulties—and gets himself out of them as well.

Ribsy

The Henry books came full circle with the last one, published in 1964, after Cleary's fourth novel for adolescents. In *Ribsy,* the most popular dog on Klickitat Street is the focus of his own adventures. Cleary already had written part of a scene in *Henry and the Clubhouse* using Ribsy's point of view in the scene of his fight with Ranger. Now she devotes half a book to Ribsy's feelings and thoughts as, in his own version of *Lassie Come Home,* a lost Ribsy makes his way back to his boy in a reaffirmation of the love between the boy and his dog. However, as a child, Cleary did not want "to read about a noble dog who died in the last chapter after a long journey home on bleeding paws ("Regina," 23), so Ribsy's journey has a few twists to it that never would have occurred to Lassie.

Ribsy's troubles begin with a flea, a new car, a Pomeranian, and a shopping center parking lot. His collar must be removed so he can get the flea; the automatic window of the new car opens when he accidentally triggers it barking at the insolent Pomeranian; and the parking lot confuses scents so that Ribsy jumps into the wrong car. The Dingley family is startled to find him here, but they take him home until someone claims him. Home is on the outskirts of town, far from Klickitat Street, and Ribsy is miserable.

So is Henry, who begins a search for his dog. Given a bath by the Dingleys, Ribsy hates his new smell and seizes the first chance to run away from it, though he cannot outrun or get rid of the scent. As Henry, miserable, advertises for Ribsy, Ribsy is finding the world a frightening, uncongenial place. A lonely widow adopts him for a while, and life with her is pretty comfortable for Ribsy. But he longs to run with the boys he sees playing, and doing tricks for the widow's little club is humiliating. He is a dog, not a person, and he wants to do dog things. When the club leaves, Ribsy bolts.

Hearing from the Dingleys, Henry runs his advertisement for three more weeks. Ribsy, meantime, is in the city, scrounging for food and looking for Klickitat Street. For a time he is the unofficial mascot of the second grade. But now that Ribsy has been gone for a month, he is getting used to being lost, finding much to enjoy in his new life. One day he finds his way into a football stadium during a game, joining the players at a critical moment and tripping the quarterback about to make a touchdown. Joe Saylor, grabbing Ribsy, sees a chance to be important and claims Ribsy as his; after the game, Ribsy follows Joe home. Henry, seeing Ribsy's picture in the newspaper, calls Joe, who lets him talk to Ribsy on the telephone. Ribsy is off again, into the night, looking for Henry.

Henry is confused, unaware of what has happened at the other end of the telephone conversation; Ribsy is confused, recognizing Henry's voice but unable to find him. In front of an apartment building, he meets Larry, a bored latchkey child who tries to smuggle Ribsy into his apartment—an operation that goes awry when Ribsy's barking draws the attention of the building's manager. Then Larry tries to smuggle Ribsy *out* of the building but must hide him on a cold, uncomfortable fire escape. Frantic, Ribsy barks for attention and is answered by Henry, who has talked his parents into searching Joe Saylor's neighborhood. Soon Ribsy is off the fire escape and in Henry's arms. All are happy: the reward is enough for Larry to buy a new ball, and Ribsy has come home.

Reviewers enjoyed this work just as much as they did the first Henry book, emphasizing the humor of this work, as they had of all the others. "The characters are real, the dialogue is lively, the humor is unquenchable," wrote the reviewer for the *Bulletin of the Center for Children's Books,*[9] while *Horn Book* called Ribsy's adventures "an exceedingly fast-moving, varied, and original sequence of adventures in being lost" with "high comedy and pathos."[10]

In its reaffirmation of the relationship between Henry and Ribsy, *Ribsy* neatly parallels the first Henry book, *Henry Huggins;* in both works, the two characters' belonging to each other is tested and affirmed. In *Henry Huggins* it is Ribsy who must decide to belong to Henry in the book's climactic scene, whereas in *Ribsy* Henry's determination to belong to Ribsy gets as much emphasis: Ribsy's journey home is paralleled by Henry's efforts to find his beloved dog, and their reunion owes more to Henry's determination than it does to Ribsy's, for it is Henry who finally finds Ribsy, not the other way around.

Using alternating points of view, Cleary presents the reader with both searches, emphasizing Ribsy's. Ribsy's point of view not only helps advance the plot but adds a layer of humor and emphasizes Ribsy as a lively personality. In many of Cleary's other books—most notably, the Ramona books—the humor works on two levels, with the child reader finding something to laugh at and the adult reader laughing at something else. *Ribsy's* humor works on two levels, too, as the reader understands from a human viewpoint what Ribsy sees from a dog's-eye view and enjoys the difference. Thus a football game becomes for Ribsy a gathering of yelling, hotdog-eating children around a smooth, green field where boys chase a football in a kind of dog paradise; hearing Henry's voice over the telephone is confusing, for no Henry is in sight.

Using Ribsy's point of view also emphasizes his ordinariness. Having seen Ribsy only from Henry's point of view in the first four books, the reader gained insight into him in the scene told from his point of view in *Henry and the Clubhouse*. Now, privy to many of Ribsy's thoughts in a work told mostly from his viewpoint, the reader sees him as very much his own dog, a vital personality and an ordinary dog. Intolerant of squirrels and more than tolerant of boys, hotdogs, and balls to chase, Ribsy is very much the everyday dog no brighter or more loyal than any other—the kind of dog who could lose his master's scent in a big parking lot and who must take up with the humans he meets in order to survive more comfortably. Ribsy's devotion to Henry is never in question, but even a loving dog can get used to being lost and—while not happy—can be comfortable in his aimless wandering. Cleary makes it clear to the reader that this is not a dog who is obsessed with crawling home to wag his tail feebly and lick his master's hand, but, rather, a dog reacting to a wide, complex world full of excitement and adventure. Like Henry, Ribsy is acted-upon more than the actor: he finds himself led by his appetite and his search into most of his adventures. But, like Henry, Ribsy needs determination to get out of his difficulties (though it is Henry's determination to find his dog that leads to the final happy ending).

This ending highlights the bond between the boy and the dog as it emphasizes that Ribsy's place in the family is both real and secure. At the beginning of the book, Henry's parents are reluctant to allow a wet Ribsy into the new family car. But they become as caught up in the search for Ribsy as Henry is, and by the time they find the dog, it is clear that Mr. and Mrs. Huggins have come to think of Ribsy as part of the family. Having found each other in the first book, Ribsy and Henry re-find each other in the last. Ribsy's place in the Huggins household is thereby confirmed, and he rides in the Huggins's new car, along with the rest of the family.

An Ordinary Boy

The popularity of the Henry books was assured from the start, and that popularity has not dimmed. Beginning in 1964, the Henry books were translated into Swedish, with German, Dutch, and Finnish editions to follow; Norwegian, Danish, and Japanese editions followed in the early 1970s, and a Chinese edition of *Ribsy* was copyrighted, though never published. The books were made available in Great Britain in the late 1970s. The works were the basis of a series of television programs that ran in Sweden, Denmark, and Japan in the 1970s.[11]

In the United States, the Henry books have been in print since 1950; in 1979 Henry was one of the rather limpid-eyed paper dolls featured in *Cutting Up with Ramona*. Their audience has accepted them wholeheartedly. "Henry is almost a catalyst," librarian Margaret Novinger found. "Give one book to a youngster and he will be back to finish the series" (Novinger,73). Cleary herself noted that "many boys write to me. Their most frequent comment is that one of the Henry books . . . was the first book the boy enjoyed reading" (Roggenbuck, 60). Since the first eight-year-old girl wrote to Cleary soon after publication of *Henry Huggins*, scores of others have written fan letters to their favorite author, describing their families and their lives ("Dear," 22; "Writing," 11).

What readers are responding to is Cleary's presentation of the events of an ordinary life: the "little everyday experiences that do not seem important to adults, but which are so terribly important to children" ("Writing," 11). Cleary's skillful blend of the stuff of ordinary life and her understanding of children make Henry an "Everychild," whom we watch grow through the trials and triumphs of daily life. After the first book, Cleary worried about her presentation of a young boy: "At that time I had no children. What *had* I done? I didn't know a thing about small boys." But, reading Arnold Gesell, she "was enormously relieved to find that Henry Huggins was psychologically sound, and that I really did know quite a bit about boys" ("Writing," 10). The center of the books is Henry himself, a boy like other boys, who lives with his parents in a "square white house," and to whom "[e]xcept for having his tonsils out when he was six and breaking his arm falling out of a cherry tree when he was seven, nothing much happened" (*Huggins*, 7). Henry's life is not high drama: he does not solve mysteries or find himself in life-or-death situations. He does the things that many children do: he gets a dog and a paper route, builds a clubhouse, and makes friends. As the series progressed, Henry's friends and neighbors began to take more important parts in the action, but Henry was still their focus.

In all the books, adults and their concerns generally are kept in the background, because, according to children Henry's age, that is the proper place for adults. Since children usually are involved with their own lives and their circle of friends, adult concerns are not that important to them. "Children wanted to read about children; adults should mind their own business and stay out of the story as much as possible," according to Cleary, who, as a child, "found disappointing, even objectionable, any book in which a child accepted the wisdom of an adult and reformed"; adults "were there to be supportive when needed" ("Regina," 23). Henry's parents are supportive without being pushovers. In all the books, they are in the background, a loving stability on whom Henry can rely, but, especially in the early books, they rarely take part in the action. Bundling and delivering paper during the school paper drive, crawling in the dewy grass to catch night crawlers, loaning Henry the money he needs to buy his bicycle, climbing up a fire escape to bring down Ribsy—Henry's parents do help him when the occasion demands it. They also support Henry emotionally when Ribsy is lost, suggesting that Henry advertise in the newspaper and driving around in what might be a futile gesture to find his dog. However, they insist that Henry stand on his own feet and take responsibility for his actions. Henry must keep Ribsy out of trouble, and when Ribsy jumps out of the boat during the fishing expedition, Henry must give up his fishing to take care of the dog on land. Henry earns $50 of the $59.95 he needs for his bicycle, for his parents cannot afford to buy him a new one. Henry must take total responsibility for his paper route, collecting the money and delivering the newspapers himself—something his father makes clear to him when Henry is late one day and his mother begins his delivery route for him. Having worked hard on the school paper drive, Henry is pleased that his room has won, but he also realizes that his parents worked almost as hard as he did, and he thanks them for all they have done, "sorry that he had not thanked them sooner"; because they all helped win the paper drive, the family goes to a movie to celebrate (*Paper*, 131). Henry can depend on his parents for love and moral support, but he must not take for granted that they will help him out of his difficulties.

As a result, Henry is independent and determined, and he takes his concerns into his own hands without appealing to his parents. Having discovered how fast guppies reproduce, Henry makes their care his responsibility, and it does not occur to him to ask his parents for their advice; having lost a friend's football through no fault of his own, Henry takes it upon himself to earn the money to replace it; when he has earned $50 for his new bicycle, Henry is ecstatic that he has almost achieved his goal, and he does not think to ask his parents for the rest of the money. To an adult, the problems with which Henry finds himself contending are not earthshaking; they are, nevertheless, important for Cleary's audience, not just because they are Henry's, but because they are the readers'. Henry deals with the matters of everyday childhood: trying to be grown up and learning to be responsible, relating to friends and neighbors, occasionally having difficulties with school and adults. Impatient at being too young for his own paper route, Henry attempts to seem grown up enough to impress the district manager into giving him one; the two months he must wait to be old enough for his own route seem endless. Taking responsibility is a major matter in the works, as Henry is responsible not only for Ribsy but for himself and his paper route.

A major subject of the books is relationships and the inherent difficulties therein. Henry must cope with the tantrums and hero-worship of preschooler Ramona, with the fact that Beezus—though a good friend—is "only" a girl, and with the awe-inspiring genius of Murph. Henry has the kind of problems with school and adults with which almost any child can identify. He is embarrassed by being chosen to play the little boy in a "dumb"

Christmas pageant—something adults cannot understand. He is nonplussed by how to tell an adult customer that she is calling him by the wrong name. All these problems may seem small, but they loom large in the average child's life, and they are the kind of problems that every child must solve ("Laughter," 557).

The problem-solving is appropriate, for Cleary had set out to write about ordinary children solving ordinary difficulties, and much in the works is from everyday life. Keeping in mind the boys of St. Joseph's who only wanted funny stories about ordinary children, Cleary tried to oblige and found she had "a collaborator . . . a rather odd, serious little girl, . . . who sat . . . reading for hours, seeking laughter in the pages of books"—herself as a child ("Laughter," 557). What that child wanted to read about was "children, preferably children in my own neighborhood, as they were, not as they should be in the opinion of adults. An avid reader of all sorts of books, . . . I wanted most of all to read about problems children could solve themselves" ("Regina," 23). These are the kinds of problems Henry faces. Having been "brought up to believe that if you wanted to do something, you went and did it," Cleary gave Henry the determination and imagination with which he tackles his problems and usually solves them ("Perfectionist," 25).

In the Henry books, as in almost all her work, Cleary used the stuff of ordinary life. Some of that stuff is from her own childhood: that "collaborator" within Cleary has kept her "from writing down to children, from poking fun at my characters, and from writing an adult reminiscence about childhood instead of a book to be enjoyed by children" and has provided some of the material in the works ("Laughter," 10). Cleary's childhood was "bounded by the experiences of an average American child and I have been fortunate enough to make stories out of the ingredients such a childhood provides—trips to the beach or the mountains, classroom experiences, neighborhood play, family relationships" ("Writing," 11).

Henry himself is a "composite of boys Cleary had known as a child."[12] The Christmas pageant that he is so desperate to get out of in *Henry Huggins* was Cleary's fourth-grade pageant, complete with line of tin soldiers being knocked over by a basketball cannon ball (*Huggins*, 98; *Yamhill*, 107, 108). The solution to Henry's problem with that pageant already had appeared in "The Green Christmas," a story Cleary wrote as a freshman in high school (*Yamhill*, 186–87); the story provided not only the plot, but the title of the chapter. Having decided that Henry should get a bicycle at the end of *Henry and Beezus* but unable to figure out how, Cleary saw the solution in a newspaper story "of a raffle in which someone had signed a ticket in the name of the Little Sisters of the Poor. They had won fifty dollars worth of beauty work at Elizabeth Arden. Suddenly my problem was solved"; Henry, also winning coupons for free beauty work as a prize, would sell his coupons for almost enough for his bicycle ("Regina," 26). *Henry and Ribsy* having evolved from a suggestion by Cleary's father ("Writing," 10), Cleary also found inspiration in the events of her own life for many of its scenes:

> We had our car lubricated and it occurred to me that Henry would like to ride up on the grease rack and a dilemma could easily develop if he was in a car on the grease rack and his dog on the ground. A neighbor remarked that her son disliked taking out the garbage and I was reminded that the dog next door always barked furiously when the garbage men came. Of course Ribsy would feel that the garbage men were trying to steal the garbage Henry placed in the can every day because he would think it was Henry's garbage. A dog eating a small girl's ice cream cone was the inspiration for another chapter. ("Writing," 10–11)

Henry's capture of a salmon with his bare hands was inspired by one of Cleary's cousins, who once caught a salmon the same way ("Writing," 10).

For some readers, the books may be "dated," for life-styles have changed since 1950. These differences show up in small details. In *Henry and Beezus*, Henry wears a "genuine Daniel Boone coonskin cap with the snap-on tail" of the kind popular in the 1950s (the authenticity of which Cleary skewers rather neatly and subtly) (10). In the same book, he wears a beanie. In *Henry Huggins,* the reader may wonder why Henry's copy of the Christmas play is a blurry carbon instead of a photocopy (85). Critics have begun to question Mrs. Huggins's role: she does not work outside the home, and some have found her stereotypical. Having noted that Henry and his friends "are exclusively white, middle-class children," one felt that "Henry's mother is something of a stereotype, always cooking and keeping the house neat—though she did help Henry pick up night-crawlers."[13] Mrs. Huggins also helps Henry deliver his papers, as Cleary has noted ("Regina," 24); however, Mrs. Huggins's embarrassingly awkward throwing also belongs to the stereotype (*Clubhouse,* 28–30). Cleary points out that the reader has no idea what Mrs. Huggins does when she is not directly involved in Henry's problems and wryly notes the zeal with which textbook editors attempt to "modernize" fiction to be included in a textbook:

> When Henry telephones his mother to ask if he can keep the dog he has found, Mrs. Huggins must not say in one editor's reader, "I don't know dear. You will have to ask your father," a line I felt was funny because we have all heard a version of it so many times from both male and female parents. The editor informs the author that this line does not show Mrs. Huggins as a strong person. The author mulls this over. Must every female in fiction be a strong person? . . . And is poor Mrs. Huggins really weak because she suggests her husband should be consulted, is she stalling a bit to give herself time to consider the situation, or is she considerate? Should not a father be consulted before a dog is added to the family? But wait. Farther down the page Mrs. Huggins relents and tells Henry he may keep the dog if he can bring it home on the bus. Here another thought occurs to the author but apparently not to the editor. Just possibly Mrs. Huggins is a weak person because she gives in to her son. Should the author point this out to the editor? . . .

> Another textbook editor will allow Mrs. Huggins to say
> to Henry, "I don't know dear," but crosses out, "You will
> have to ask your father." He apparently feels that con-
> sulting Henry's father would make Mrs. Huggins a weak
> role model for girls. But might not girls, observing that
> Mrs. Huggins does not consult Mr. Huggins about a dog,
> grow up to become wives who add dogs to their families
> without consulting their husbands? Will this make them
> strong or overbearing? The author wonders about a gen-
> eration of unwelcome dogs and their effect on the divorce
> rate. ("Regina," 24–25)

Though the works were written in the 1950s and early 1960s,
children still respond to them, for the spirit of the books and the
trials of childhood remain contemporary; as Cleary has pointed
out, what she is essentially writing about—growing up, with all
the attendant problems and exciting times—is not dated and
never will be. What children see when they read the books is a
boy in a loving, supportive family and neighborhood, which they
enjoy reading about and sometimes long for. Some readers have
written that they wish they could live on Klickitat Street; one boy
feels that Henry has "such nice neighbors." Others read Cleary's
books "when they are feeling sad" (Fitzgibbons, 170). Cleary notes
that "as with real mothers, [readers] seem to take [Mrs. Huggins]
for granted, although once in a while a child remarks that Henry
has a nice family. However, two letters come to mind. A nine-year-
old girl wrote, 'Mrs. Huggins is a great mother to a family there
all good together they make the story seem good' [sic]. A boy once
asked me to write a book 'and have Mrs. Huggins go to the hospital and then come home again so they could be a family again.'
One wonders what lay behind this sad little letter" ("Regina," 25).

Henry's world is, after all, secure. He does not worry about
crime or divorce, for these things do not seem to exist in his neighborhood. When he finds bubble gum boxes stacked in a vacant lot,
no one suggests that it might not be safe to chew the gum; when
Ribsy is lost, no one hints that he might have been struck by a
car. Henry's parents are loving to each other and to him. Henry's

neighborhood is a fairly enclosed one: he has his parents and his dog to love; he has his paper route; and, especially, he has many friends. As a child, Cleary had enjoyed the "Our Gang" movies, which "were about neighborhood children playing together"— something she wanted to read about in books (*Yamhill*, 104). In the Henry books, she gave children such a neighborhood. As one critic noted, *Henry Huggins* laid the foundation of more books about the children of Klickitat Street (Roggenbuck, 57). As book followed book, more emphasis was put on these other characters, as Henry grew into the wider world. The foundation had been laid for what is perhaps Cleary's most popular series: the Ramona books.

3

Forever Ramona

"We hope that Mrs. Cleary will write a whole book about Ramona very soon," the reviewer for *Publishers Weekly* wrote at the end of a review of *Henry and Ribsy* (131), and Cleary obliged in 1955, launching the career of one of her most popular characters. Ramona Geraldine Quimby and her older sister, Beatrice, already had appeared in almost all the Henry books, with the antics of temperamental preschooler Ramona providing both tension and comedy; Ramona had threatened to take over *Henry and the Clubhouse* and *Henry and the Paper Route*. It seemed inevitable that as lively a character as Ramona should become the center of her own series. In the course of the seven Ramona books,[1] however, Ramona became something more, as the works themselves presented the experience of ordinary family life in ways different from the Henry Huggins books. While Henry often concerned himself with the outer trappings of growing up—getting a bicycle, getting and keeping a paper route—Ramona deals more with inner matters—feeling grownup and getting along with teachers and other children—and with the often-complex relationships between the members of a loving family.

The Works

Beezus and Ramona

The first book in the Ramona series, however, focuses on Beezus. Written during the period when Cleary was writing books about Henry and the other children of Portland, Oregon, *Beezus and Ramona* is more or less of a piece with them, with Cleary giving Henry's good friend a book of her own. This work also introduces the age-old difficulty between siblings that would crop up in later Ramona books with realistic regularity.

Beezus's biggest problem in life is Ramona, her exasperating four-year-old sister. For example, there is the great book debacle: tired of rereading the same book, Beezus takes Ramona to the library, consoling herself that the boring work they check out can at least be returned. Ramona has other ideas, however: that is, "writing her name" in it in crayon squiggles to make it hers. When they pay for the book, an understanding librarian points out that, while they certainly have bought the book, it belongs to Beezus, who had checked it out; and Beezus will read it to Ramona only when Beezus wants to!

Ramona is twice as exasperating during Beezus's weekly art class, interrupting both the class and Beezus's struggle with her unimaginative muse. Trying to be innovative and imaginative, and refereeing an altercation between Ramona and the boy from whom she has stolen a lollipop, Beezus orders Ramona out of the class. Triumphant, she then draws her own picture of Ramona's invisible pet lizard, a green dragon with a lemon drop eye and lollipop spikes down its back, breathing pink cotton candy. Warmed by praise, Beezus realizes that she, too, has an imagination.

Tantrums are not unusual in the Quimby house, so Henry and Beezus ignore one of Ramona's until they hear her pounding on the bathroom door, with Ribsy, Henry's dog, barking inside; somehow the dog locked himself in after she put him into the bathroom and shut the door. Though Mrs. Quimby unlocks the bathroom door with a nail file, Beezus cannot forgive Ramona for spoiling her time with Henry and guiltily realizes that she does not like Ramona one bit; and sisters, like her mother and her aunt, are *supposed* to like each other.

The feeling resurfaces when Beezus watches Ramona one afternoon and finds her, after a frantic search, in the basement, taking just one bite of apple after apple, for the first bite of an apple is always sweetest. Advice from the girls' aunt, a teacher, to ignore Ramona results in a chagrined Ramona's being unusually good the rest of the evening. The Quimbys have applesauce for dessert. Then, one rainy Saturday, a party arrives out of nowhere: children whom Ramona had invited the day before. The makeshift entertainment includes applesauce, a parade, and a tantrum by Ramona. Afterward, Beezus and her mother learn that Ramona had organized the party because she knew no one would let her; Beezus realizes that she, too, had felt that way when she was younger. All the family can do is wait for Ramona to grow up.

However, on Beezus's birthday, her anger toward Ramona comes into full bloom when Ramona ruins her sister's birthday cake not once, but twice. Sorry for herself for having such an impossible sister, Beezus feels guilty for not loving Ramona—normal feelings, she is assured, for siblings are not supposed to love each other all the time. Hearing of the sibling troubles of their aunt and Mrs. Quimby, Beezus realizes that that is just the way with sisters. Suddenly, her birthday is just as beautiful as her storebought birthday cake, and Ramona is not exasperating at all.

Though the book is Beezus's, it was Ramona who entranced reviewers, and, it seems, readers as well. "Ramona Quimby, the strong-willed four-year-old . . . now has a whole book in which to try the patience of well-behaved big sister Beezus," exulted the reviewer in *Horn Book,* going on to note that "[w]earing the rabbit ears she constructed at nursery school, Ramona moves purposefully through her world, leaving destruction and distraction in her wake." *Publishers Weekly* ignored Beezus almost completely, calling the work a "new and, of course, hilarious book . . . which concentrates on the antics of Beatrice Quimby's 4-year-old sister, Ramona": "Adults will be able to follow the infant logic that leads

Ramona into her various escapades, but to the 9-and 10-year-olds who will read and love this book she will doubtless remain a nasty little villain in homemade paper rabbit ears, determined to spoil everyone's fun."[3]

It is, of course, Beezus's book—her name appears first in the title and the story is told from her point of view—but Ramona dominates it, as she had most of the later Henry Huggins books. The reader comes away from the work with a strong image of staid, responsible Beezus at odds with her lively little sister, but there is a stronger image of four-year-old Ramona wearing bunny ears and riding her tricycle into the coffee table, Ramona writing her name in purple crayon on all the pages of a library book, Ramona inviting a party of preschoolers to the house, Ramona baking her doll in Beezus's birthday cake. Like Henry, Beezus is the hapless victim of circumstances, not actively creating the situations she finds herself in but doing plenty of reacting. Unlike Henry, Beezus finds herself in situations that do not arise from *her* actions: for Beezus's fate has a name, and it's Ramona.

The reader sympathizes with Beezus and her trials and enjoys every moment of them. There is, of course, the humor of the situations and the scrambling by all around Ramona to set things right. There is also a fascination with the terrible that keeps one turning pages: what will Ramona do next? Will she *really?* For the child whose younger sibling is a Ramona, there is Beezus with whom to commiserate—here, at last, is someone who understands. After all, *nobody's* younger sister could be worse than *this*. And Ramona *is* a terror, wiping her paint-covered hands on the cat, throwing eggs—shells and all—into the mix for Beezus's birthday cake to see what will happen, locking Ribsy in the bathroom to punish him for taking her cookie. In this last work presenting Ramona from another's point of view, it is very hard to love her.

This unlovability is precisely the point. Having created Ramona in *Henry Huggins* and given her such irritating qualities in *Henry and Beezus* and *Henry and Ribsy,* in *Beezus and Ramona* Cleary uses these traits to make a point about growing up and about the nature of sibling relationships. Siblings cannot be expected to love each other all the time, Cleary tells her readers, but growing up will alleviate some of the difficulty.

Cleary sets up an important contrast between Beezus and Ramona. Sensible, responsible Beezus, age nine, watches her younger sister and tries to keep her out of trouble; even the frightening furnace in the basement does not deter her from searching for Ramona when she thinks she is lost. Not as imaginatively open as Ramona, Beezus watches her sister drag the string that leashes Ralph, Ramona's invisible lizard, and has trouble making up her own imaginary animal for art class. Irrepressible Ramona, five years younger, *is* irrepressible because she does not listen to people, or listens to all the wrong things. Scoldings about what she should and should not do are not Ramona's idea of what to listen to; legends about gold at the end of the rainbow *are*. With the single-minded intensity of a preschooler, Ramona gives in to a vivid imagination that turns marshmallows into powder puffs and the figs in fig cookies into chopped-up worms; asked in the rhetorical fashion of parents what sort of punishment is appropriate for a girl who has invited her own party as she has, Ramona immediately comes up with several that are both cruel and unusual. Though Beezus comes to realize that she has just as much imagination as Ramona, the contrast remains, serving to set the girls apart.

Aware of her responsibilities to Ramona and to the family, Beezus also feels guilty about how she really feels about her younger sister. So frustrated at times is Beezus by what Ramona does that at times she does not love or even like her—definitely, thinks Beezus, not what a sister is supposed to feel. She feels she must be a terrible person; Beezus is, however, only a normal one, Cleary points out. No one could actively love someone like Ramona all the time; having witnessed Ramona in action, the reader has a chance to take Beezus's place and judge just how lovable Ramona is. Besides, sisters never have gotten along all the time: Mrs. Quimby and her sister provide a case in point. Set up by Beezus in the first chapter as the ideal of sisterly devotion, they are revealed in the final chapter as sisters who may be devoted to each other now but certainly were *not* so loving while they were growing up. Like Beezus and Ramona, they were different from one another as children. The differences have remained, but as adults they have grown very close.

Growing up is the key. To the child having Beezus's problems in real life, Cleary offers the comforting thought that Ramona's growing up will solve most of the problems. Mrs. Quimby offers her an example: Beezus herself, who may have been quieter than Ramona but who did some of the things Ramona has done. Growing up, Beezus has changed; so have her mother and her aunt. Surely even Ramona will change for the better.

Ramona the Pest

Like the reviewers of *Beezus and Ramona,* readers seem to have focused on Ramona, for Cleary found herself fielding requests for "a whole book about Ramona," a request she ignored at first, for she "still believed what we had been taught in library school: Children did not want to read about characters younger than themselves; and girls would read about boys, but boys would not read about girls. Gradually I saw that these generalizations did not hold if children found books funny" ("Laughter," 561). But, listening to her own children reminiscing at ages nine or ten about being younger, Cleary "noticed that nothing was so funny to them as their memories of kindergarten and nursery school. . . . I began to understand that children would enjoy a book about a younger girl because they would recognize and enjoy feeling superior to their younger selves" ("Laughter," 561).

Ramona the Pest gestated for fifteen years (Reuther, 443); it appeared in 1968, after Cleary had published eleven works that included the last of the Henry books, her four adolescent novels, and the first book about Ralph, the motorcycle-riding mouse. In the fifteen years, Ramona has aged only one: the book chronicles the ups and downs of the new, grown-up, five-year-old Ramona, who knows that she is *not* the pest older children call her and who is eager to catch up with her sister by going to school.

The ups and the downs start immediately. There is trouble with the "gift": told by Miss Binney where to sit "for the present," Ramona does, not rising until recess, when Miss Binney finally learns the reason behind Ramona's behavior and learns to be more careful about what she says to her kindergarteners. Then there is the curl problem, with Ramona "boinging" a classmate's corkscrew curls. Even resting is a problem: snoring to show how good she is resting, Ramona sets the pattern for very noisy resting when others snore, too.

Show and Tell is also a problem. Howie, loaned a stuffed rabbit by the Quimbys, is so unenthusiastic about it that Miss Binney must enthuse for him and gives him a new red ribbon for the bunny. After a quarrel, he gives it to Ramona for the pleasure of taking off one of the wheels of her tricycle, thereby turning it into a two-wheeler.

Kindergarten is exciting, and Ramona works hard, learning to print her name, with a "Q" after it which she turns into a cat with whiskers and ears, which she reluctantly erases after Davy is scolded for taking her advice to turn the "D" in his name into a robin. The first day Howie and Ramona walk themselves to school, they find something wrong: the class has a substitute teacher. Betrayed by Miss Binney, Ramona hides behind trash cans in the schoolyard, to be found during recess and taken by the understanding principal to class and introduced to the strange teacher. Boot trouble occurs when Ramona must wear Howie's old, brown boots to school—as if boots were meant to keep your feet dry and not to show off. These are replaced when Ramona's new shoes are too big, by new, red *girl's* boots, perfect for slogging happily through the mud of the construction site across from the school, until she gets stuck and must be rescued by Henry Huggins. At Halloween, Ramona is the baddest witch ever in a rubber mask so frightening that Ramona feels braver inside than outside it. But, to Ramona's dismay, no one knows who she is behind the mask; during the Halloween parade, she carries a sign with her name printed on it.

Ramona is growing up: she has a loose tooth, and one day she walks to school by herself. Great excitement and admiration result when her tooth comes out; she gives the tooth to Miss Binney to keep safe. Rapt with love of Miss Binney and with the glory of losing a tooth, Ramona boings Susan's curls and is in trouble again after truthfully answering "no" when Miss Binney asks if Ramona can stop boinging Susan; Ramona is sent home until she can stop. Ramona is sad, for Miss Binney does not love her any more, and she cannot go back to school. Besides, her tooth is still at school. The next few days, Ramona wants to go to school but cannot since her teacher does not like her; instead, she spends boring and lonely days waiting for Miss Binney to forget her. Finally, Howie brings a letter from Miss Binney: her tooth is taped to it, and Miss Binney has made the "Q" of Ramona's last name into a kitty cat. Jubilant that her teacher likes her, Ramona will return to school tomorrow!

Reviewers responded immediately to the humor of the book, pointing out the discrepancy between the age of its heroine and the age of the probable readers. "Writing a book about a five-year-old that older children will enjoy is an art," asserted the reviewer in the *Saturday Review,* "and in this story Beverly Cleary has created a comic and endearing character in the irrepressible Ramona."[4] *Horn Book,* calling Ramona "a spirited, resourceful, and determined heroine," noted that "eight- or nine-year-old children who can look back with the superiority of middle age upon their kindergarten days will smile knowingly at Ramona's first encounters with school life. . . . Ramona did not submit to the process of education without a struggle, and the skirmishes, vividly described, will remind the young reader of the child he once was (or wished he had dared to be!)."[5] Pointing out the nostalgic response of the child readers, the reviewers waxed a little nostalgic themselves, revelling in the humor of scenes such as those where Ramona thinks she will receive a present from Miss Binney and Ramona's "abortive attempts to be the best rester in class" (*Saturday Review,* 38). Children were just as enthusiastic, giving *Ramona the Pest* the Georgia Children's Book Award, the Nene Award, the Sequoyah Children's Book Award, and the Pacific Northwest Library Association Young Reader's Choice Award.

Ramona the Pest may have been so titled because in the earlier works Ramona is, indeed, a pest, as Henry points out in the course of his dealings with her. But in the course of the book, the title becomes, at least as far as the reader is concerned, an oxy-

moron: Ramona may appear to be a pest, but seeing her actions
from her perspective we see that she really is a lively little girl.
Cleary does the same thing in *Otis Spofford,* where she shows us
the bully from *Ellen Tebbits* from his own viewpoint and so en-
gages the reader's sympathies. In *Henry and the Clubhouse,*
Cleary shows us Ramona as less of an obstacle and more of a very
small child; Beezus, in *Beezus and Ramona,* empathizes for a moment with her younger sister. Now, having written all the Henry
Huggins books and free of the need to keep the reader sympathetic to Henry's point of view, Cleary shows us a little girl growing from a pest to a wonder of a kindergartener.

As in her other works, Cleary emphasizes the humor of exaggerated situations arising naturally from daily life. And exaggerated is the word, for who but Ramona could get into trouble
wearing new boots or could become a kindergarten dropout? Like
Cleary's other hapless protagonists, Ramona does not mean to get
into such difficulties; they just happen. But now, together with
these difficulties Cleary emphasizes the difficulties of childhood
and of growing up as Ramona worries about getting along with
her teacher and the other students, frets about being a failure,
and finds so much confusing about what grownups say and do.

Cleary clearly presents a child's-eye view of life, from the bore-
dom of long shopping trips and the intolerable nosiness of adults
like Mrs. Wisser to the seductive charm of new red boots and the
fascination of Susan's long corkscrew curls. The etiquette problems of whether "acting big" in kindergarten is worse than being
a pest are treated with appropriate seriousness. *Ramona the Pest*
and the later Ramona books allow Cleary to focus on the feelings
one has growing up: feeling stupid compared to others, being
thought too young to merit attention or to have one's feelings re-
garded by adults, and feeling like a failure. Also, there is the difficulty of understanding adults. "Sit here for the present," Mrs.
Binney tells Ramona, but no gift is forthcoming. The "dawnzer
lee light" turns out to have nothing to do with electric lights. And,
Miss Binney does not seem to expect an honest answer to the
question of whether or not Ramona can stop pulling Susan's curls.

Ramona's problems with Miss Binney are the same kind of problems she has throughout the book. Where Henry's problems mostly relate to events such as getting a bicycle or keeping a paper route or taking care of his dog, Ramona's arise from growing up and from difficulties with others. Ramona gets stuck in deep mud in her new boots and must be rescued by a disgusted Henry Huggins in a classic scene, but her more important problems stem from her new relationships. In the earlier books, Ramona's main relationships are with her family and the other children of the neighborhood. Now, in kindergarten, she is moving into a world of more complex relationships as she must deal every day with others her own age and with an adult outside the family—her teacher, Miss Binney. The difficulties she has in the book reflect this: she must try to keep from boinging Susan's curls and she must deal with the anxiety of an unexpected substitute teacher. Ramona must prove that—contrary to what Beezus and Susan call her—she is *not* a pest. But, most important, Ramona must get along with Miss Binney, whom Ramona is so eager to please. Ramona's inspiration to add whiskers, ears, and a tail to the Q of her last name falls victim to Mrs. Binney's scolding Davy for making the R in his last name into a robin. Ramona mourns dropping out of kindergarten at the end of the book not because she regrets boinging Susan's curls, but because she has disappointed Miss Binney, who obviously does not like her any more; it is Miss Binney's acceptance of Ramona that brings a happy ending. Ramona the kindergartener has tangible proof that she is not a pest.

Ramona the Brave
The next Ramona book was not published until 1975, after the publication of two books written from an animal's point of view: *Socks* and *Runaway Ralph. Ramona the Brave,* however, was the first of four Ramona books published in consecutive years, as Cleary brought her lively little creation from age six to age eight.

Kindergartener Ramona the pest is now first-grader Ramona the brave, who proves her courage by defending Beezus. Beezus is furious, and Ramona is shaken to see her mother's amusement and herself as Beezus sees her: a nonheroic little girl. But Ramona *is* brave, when she looks at her favorite picture in a book: a deliciously scary picture of a gorilla. On the first day of school, Ramona feels big when she looks at the kindergarteners in their separate classroom, but small when she enters the main school building with the other students, although it is pleasant to greet old friends. This pleasantness does not last beyond Show and Tell, when Ramona tells her classmates about the hole that has been "chopped" in the side of her house, in preparation for the addition of another bedroom. The other students do not believe her, and literal Howie denies it, since the men had only pried off the siding, not chopped a hole. Now Mrs. Griggs, the teacher, and the class will think she is a fibber.

Soon, Ramona envies the carefree kindergarteners on the playground. Making owls out of paper bags for Parents' Night is spoiled when Ramona sees another student copy her owl and be praised for it; everyone will think she copied from Susan, instead of the other way around, so she throws her own owl away. Worse, the afternoon of Parents' Night, Ramona, owlless, grows ever more miserable and angry and finally cannot stop her hands from crushing Susan's owl. Fleeing her conscience and the school, she runs home. To Ramona's humiliation, the next day she must apologize to Susan in front of the entire class. Ramona feels that Mrs. Griggs does not understand, and she wants to run and run and never come back.

The days plod by, rainy and dull and unchanging. Ramona dreads school, feeling that Mrs. Griggs does not like her, and she dreads sleeping by herself in her dark room, where "something" wants to grab her. Things reach a crisis when the progress reports come out: Ramona is doing well but must learn self-control and not be so interested in other students' schoolwork. Ramona, who has been helping slow-learner Davy, feels the injustice of this assessment and of her parents' comments. Cheered by Beezus's defense of her, Ramona cannot go on being afraid of the dark; she hides the gorilla book under a couch cushion, and when she gets back into bed, the "something" under it does not grab her; she is safe.

The next day, brave Ramona is ready for anything, except the large German shepherd that growls at her as she walks to school a different route. Throwing first her lunchbox, then her shoe at the dog, Ramona must run to school in one shoe and a sock. Oddly, Mrs. Griggs understands her explanation. During reading, there is an interruption: the dog's owner has brought Ramona's scarred shoe to school. Ramona agrees with the school secretary: she *is* brave, "just about the bravest girl in the first grade."

Reviewers greeted Ramona's second book all to herself with the same enthusiasm with which they had greeted the first, emphasizing her difficulties being a big, brave first-grader and Cleary's skill in presenting a lively six-year-old with a mind and imagination all her own. Although the reviewer in *School Library Journal* called Ramona "professional pest and loudmouth extraordinaire" who is now "trying hard to mend her brattish ways" and is "semi-reformed" though still "naughty,"[6] most reviewers saw Ramona as she sees herself: a little girl trying hard to grow up, sometimes misunderstanding and misunderstood. *Horn Book* called her "one of the most endearing protagonists of children's fiction," and "uncannily real little girl" whose "impetuousness and fierce sense of justice . . . embroil her in inevitable clashes with the teacher";[7] while the reviewer for the *Bulletin of the Center for Children's Books* emphasized that she is "as convincing a first-grader as a fictional character can be, trying to be compliant but too independent a child to be conforming."[8] Praising Cleary's "intuitive accuracy" at portraying the "jumbled feelings" of a child and her "infallible perceptions of the world from the other side of seven," (*Horn Book*, "Brave")[9] reviewers also noted the nostalgic pleasure the book's intended audience would receive from it. "Having already weathered similar emotional storms, middle graders will read about Ramona's fear of the dark, first-day-at-school jitters, etc. with a relish that is part sympathy and part superiority" (*School Library Journal*, "Brave").

In *Ramona the Pest,* Ramona proves that she is not a pest; proving that she is brave in *Ramona the Brave* is more difficult. Now a big first-grader who looks with easy superiority at the babyish kindergarteners, Ramona must deal courageously with a misunderstanding teacher, with fears of the dark, with her conscience and, finally, with a huge German shepherd. Her troubles are still those recognizable to any child, and these problems still seem to get out of hand in a way that is both natural and humorous. But now, older, Ramona seems to be connecting with the world in new ways: more self-aware, she begins to see herself as others do, as if from the outside; and a bored and unhappy Ramona begins to look on the younger kindergarteners not with superiority, but with the nostalgia familiar to people even older than she is.

Most of Ramona's problems still stem from her relationships with others, which is appropriate for a character whose first incarnation was as obstacle for another Cleary character. Davy's reading problems add to Ramona's difficulties with her teacher; Susan's copied paper-bag owl leads to more trouble than Ramona could have predicted. Intensely involved with her family and with those around her, Ramona seems to look to others for her sense of security and identity. Realizing that neither Beezus nor their mother has thought that she was brave in the first chapter makes Ramona feel like the silly little girl they consider her; after the principal's secretary remarks on how brave she was to face the huge dog, Ramona feels forced to agree. It is Mr. Quimby's invocation of Ramona's "spunk" that gives her the courage not to be afraid of the dark and not to be so afraid of the dog that she cannot act.

What her teacher thinks is still important to Ramona, for a teacher is a mighty figure to a child Ramona's age. But for the first time, Ramona is conscious that her efforts to please Mrs. Griggs seem not to be working; Mrs. Griggs is the first person Ramona is conscious she cannot get along with. Placid, stolid, and a bit repressive, Mrs. Griggs is not the ideal teacher for emotional, imaginative Ramona; even quiet Beezus did not really enjoy having her as a teacher. Someone who could force a child to apologize to another child in front of a whole classroom could not possibly understand the whole story behind the crushed owl; there is a hint that Mrs. Griggs has not quite understood Ramona when, at the end of the book, she studies Ramona, stops herself from quoting the well-worn rules, and allows Ramona to do what she has asked to do. Once again, the approval of a teacher is essential for a happy ending to Ramona's story; but it is approval bolstered by that of Beezus's teacher, the wonderful Mr. Cardoza, who not only has honored Ramona by knowing her name but who treats her as an equal, not as a funny little girl. Growing up is widening Ramona's circle of relationships.

Several times in the book, Ramona seems to step outside herself and see herself as others do. After Beezus tells her version of the events in the park, Ramona suddenly seems to see herself "as if she were standing aside looking at herself" (19); laughed at by a disbelieving class of first-graders when she tries to tell about the hole chopped in the Quimby house, Ramona again has this confidence-shaking experience (67). Also, in a scene Cleary would repeat in later books, Ramona sees reflected in a mirror a stranger, a distorted image: one that does not reflect what she feels herself to be, but someone else. Fleeing Susan's crushed owl, Mrs. Griggs's anger, and her own conscience, Ramona cries after scraping her knee and sees in the mirror "a stranger . . . who did not look at all the way Ramona pictured herself" (95). This girl, unlike Ramona, does not look like the kind of person everyone would like, but Ramona wants the girl to like her.

For the first time, Ramona begins to worry not just about whether or not others approve of her but whether or not her conscience approves; guilt inspires Ramona's nighttime monsters almost as much as the dark does. Learning to know herself inside out, Ramona begins to understand that others, seeing her outside in, know her differently and cannot always understand that, really, she is a nice person. What she needs to do is reconcile the two images—the inside Ramona and the outside Ramona—which is a difficult process for someone much older. The notion of Ramona's seeing herself from the outside is oddly appropriate for a character who is first seen through the eyes of others, in the Henry Huggins books and in *Beezus and Ramona*. Ramona is a character who we come to know from the outside in, and, seeing Ramona as she sees herself, the reader, too, must reconcile the two images.

Ramona and Her Father

Readers did not have to wait long for the sequel: "Ramona and the Three Wise Persons," a chapter from *Ramona and Her Father* was published in the December, 1975, issue of *Family Circle;* and the book itself was published two years later. The book was a reaction to "didactic books that are supposed to help a child understand problems"; Cleary felt that

> children who must endure such problems want to read about children who do *not* have the same problems. . . . I feel it is presumptuous of adults to feel they can offer solutions in fiction to troubled children. . . .
>
> Children turn to books for comfort. They tell me so, and letters of children who long for fathers influenced me, not to try to solve the problems of a fatherless child, but to write a book, partially drawn from my own childhood, in which a loving father was a central character. ("Regina," 24)

Ramona and Her Father deals in a realistic but comforting way with the problem of a parent's layoff and with the resulting tensions, emphasizing that no family's life is perfect. One payday in September, Mr. Quimby is laid off. Suddenly, there are many changes in Ramona's house, especially in Mr. Quimby, who is now at home instead of Mrs. Quimby. Preoccupied by the family's financial problems, Ramona takes to heart Mr. Quimby's comments about how much money a child actor in a commercial probably makes: she practices being in commercials. But practicing gets her into trouble, especially when she crowns herself like the boy in the margarine commercial, with a crown of burdock burrs. Removing them is a painful business, but Ramona is heartened that her father prefers having a lively girl like her to an actress.

As autumn progresses, everyone but Ramona seems cranky. When a neighbor gives the Quimbys a gigantic pumpkin, everything is normal for an evening while Mr. Quimby carves the most frightening jack-o'-lantern ever. That night, however, Picky-picky eats the pumpkin in lieu of his cat food, and Ramona has new worries: angered by Mr. Quimby's insistence that the family cannot afford a better cat food, Beezus points out that *he* can afford to smoke and that smoking is bad for him. A campaign to stop Mr. Quimby's smoking seems fruitless. Then one day Ramona comes home to a locked house; sitting on the back porch in the cold, she thinks frightening thoughts about her fears that she has driven her father away and about the scary things from which he must protect her. Relieved when he finally comes home, Ramona is also relieved after a cosy afternoon to find that he will try to stop smoking. Unfortunately, stopping makes Mr. Quimby even crosser. But Ramona and Howie make tin-can stilts and have a wonderful time clanking around on them; clanking and singing at the top of her lungs make her forget her troubles, and the afternoon the two finally count down from 100 bottles of beer on the wall to zero is a most satisfying one.

December arrives, with its Christmas pageant. Ramona volunteers to be a sheep and volunteers her mother to make the costume. The next days are trying for Ramona, especially since her mother is too busy working to make the costume and her father is nagging and sneaking an old cigarette. Though she just wants her family to be happy, Mr. Quimby explains, no family is perfect; they just have to work at it. While Ramona feels lucky to have the family she does, she also wishes her mother would sew the costume; instead, Ramona must be a sheep in old flannel pajamas. The other Quimbys are cheerful because Mr. Quimby has found a job, but Ramona refuses to be a sheep printed with pink rabbits. Caught up in the preparations, she is miserable, for now she cannot back down. The Three Wise Persons save the day, calling her "adorable" and disguising her with a mascara-painted nose. In her imperfect costume, Ramona glows in the love of her imperfect family in a moment of perfect happiness.

Ramona and Her Father charmed reviewers as much as the earlier Ramona books had, though reviews emphasized not so much the humor but the strong sense of family life Cleary had woven around the theme of a family crisis. Calling the book "true, warm-hearted, and funny," the reviewer in *Booklist* noted that Cleary "catches a family situation that puts strain on each of its members, despite their intrinsic strength and invincible humor,"[10] while the *Bulletin of the Center for Children's Books* pointed out that, despite the Quimbys' problems, "life goes on. In any household containing Ramona it could hardly do otherwise."[11] Especially, Cleary's style came in for commendation, with reviewers praising her "impeccably authentic dialogue and exposition" (*Bulletin,* "Father"); the skill with which she "delineates the contemporary family with compassion and humor, unerringly suggests the nuances of suburban conversation, and develops as memorable a cast of characters as can be found in children's literature";[12] and Cleary's "uncanny gift for pinpointing the thoughts and feelings of children right down to their own phraseology—while honoring the boundaries of clean, simple writing" (*Booklist,* "Father"). In 1980 the book gained international attention by being listed on the International Board on Books for Young People Honor list and won a Garden State Children's Book Award, the Young Reader's Choice Award, and the newly instituted Texas Bluebonnet Award.

With this work, Cleary begins to focus not just on the child growing up, but on the family. Earlier works such as *Beezus and Ramona, Jean and Johnny, The Luckiest Girl, Sister of the Bride,* and *Mitch and Amy* had emphasized family dynamics as their protagonists struggled with sibling rivalry or the nuances of parent–child relationships. But Ramona's family had been more or less in the background of her stories, as she moved into the wider and exciting world of school. Now, with school not quite as much an adventure Cleary begins to emphasize the Quimby family as a whole, though Ramona is still the focus. As in the earlier works, Ramona's problems stem from her relationships with others; now, however, these problems do not involve her teacher and her peers as much as they do her family.

Seen up close, it is a family in the midst of change, with the dynamics of family relationships growing more complex. Cleary shows us a family under stress, and in the process Mr. and Mrs. Quimby begin to emerge as people as well as parents. When Mr. Quimby loses his job, Mrs. Quimby begins to work full time; both clearly worry about Mr. Quimby getting another job and about paying the bills. In Mr. Quimby, Cleary shows her readers a father ever more tense and unhappy as he waits for another job offer: his increased gloominess and increased smoking reflect his tension, as does the way he now quotes his grandmother as if her maxims hold the key to happiness. Impressed when her father explains to her about his smoking as if she were an adult, Ramona—and the readers—begin to see him not simply as a parent but as a person in his own right. The rest of the family is also changing: Beezus is growing into rebellious adolescence; even Picky-picky, the family cat, seems grouchy all the time because of old age and because of the cheap cat food the Quimbys now buy. On the fringe of these changes, Ramona mostly watches and hopes things will improve; she feels at times as if she is the only family member unchanged by their new situation. Watching Beezus question their parents' authority and behavior, Ramona also responds to the Quimbys's new situation by worrying about the family—especially her father—as she has not before. With Mr. Quimby at home most of the time, Ramona begins to interact with him more. He becomes the focus of some of her deepest worries: Ramona worries about her father's smoking, about whether or not he will get a job offer, and about whether or not he has left her and the rest of the family when he is late coming home one afternoon. In *Ramona the Brave,* she had begun to see herself as others do; now Ramona begins to extend her sympathies and empathies to others.

Cleary also takes this chance to point out that even such a stressed family is not a failed one, if its members work at making the family loving and whole. Realizing the economic impossibility of getting all she has asked for on her Christmas list in the first chapter of the book, Ramona substitutes one item: a happy family. Throughout the book, she despairs of ever getting one: Ramona's plans to become a rich child actor on commercials and thereby make her family happy fall through. But this does not matter for, Cleary points out, the Quimbys already *are* a happy family. Ramona must realize that, though her family seems unhappy and imperfect, things are not that bad. No family is perfect; no one is perfect. The Quimbys are not the smiling family Ramona draws at the beginning of the book, but this does not mean they are unhappy. In the family's closeness and the respect with which the Quimbys treat each other lie what are important. They may not be perfect, but the best they can do is work at it.

Presenting her readers with the portrait of a family in flux does not keep Cleary from exploring the sense of childhood as a confusing time of misunderstanding and being misunderstood that she had set up in earlier Ramona books. Again, Ramona comes to see herself from the outside and understand that others do not see the real her. Practicing to be in commercials, she begins to see herself as a cute child with fluffy, blonde hair, an image suddenly replaced with reality after she embarrasses herself with her teacher. But a greater epiphany comes at the Christmas pageant, where—as she had in *Ramona the Brave*—Cleary uses a mirror to show Ramona an outside view of herself that she must reconcile with her own, inside view. Having earlier felt that she is the only one unchanged by the family's new anxieties, Ramona is, ironically, again the only one unchanged by the family's good fortune, sulkily attending the Christmas pageant as a pink-rabbit-covered sheep. Mourning her family's indifference to her problem, Ramona sees her distorted image reflected in a glass Christmas tree ornament—big-nosed and tiny-eyed—and thinks that it does not show the real her; she is really a nice person, but nobody seems to understand (175).

Cleary wisely does not dwell on this moment, but she uses it to hint that the inside and the outside of a person don't always mesh, just as the inside and outside of a family don't, either. For a moment during the Christmas pageant, Ramona seems to achieve perfection. Cheered by the attention of the eighth-grade girls who paint her sheep's nose with mascara, in the magic of seeing her sister and her friends transformed by the pageant, Ramona basks in the pride of her parents, and all seems well; the members of the Quimby family are happy and together. At the beginning of the book, Ramona has made a joyful "yeep" unto the Lord, since "yeep" seems about as joyful a noise as she can think of; now she tries a joyful "baa" and is squelched by a pageant shepherd, but no matter. In this moment of perfection, even a silent tail-wagging is enough.

Ramona and Her Mother

Because "parents deserve equal time," *Ramona and Her Father* was followed by *Ramona and Her Mother* in 1979. The latter, like the former, was written "in rebellion against the portrayal of family life in many contemporary children's books" ("Regina," 25). Having focused in *Ramona and Her Father* on the fact that no family life is perfect, Cleary points it up again in the later book, also emphasizing the loving supportiveness of the Quimby family: "All children . . .long to have their mothers say they love them, so this became the theme of *Ramona and Her Mother*" ("Regina," 25), as Ramona feels lost in her mother's busy life and longs to be called (like Beezus) her mother's girl.

The action of the story opens hard on the ending of *Ramona and Her Father;* Mr. Quimby has gotten a job, so the Quimbys celebrate at a New Year's Day brunch for the neighbors. Willa Jean, Howie's little sister, is exasperating as usual, and to her horror Ramona hears her parents reflect that Willa Jean was just like Ramona at the same age; Ramona knows better. Plus, Beezus got to act like a grownup and was complimented by their mother, while Ramona never got a chance and had to deal with Willa Jean. She wishes that someone had complimented her and called her her mother's girl, as they had Beezus. One rainy Saturday Ramona gets a chance to be her mother's girl as they sew and talk together. But Ramona's sewing project turns out badly and her disappointment is overwhelming, especially as she feels left out of Beezus's and their mother's activities. Mourning in the bathroom, she gives in to a desire to squeeze out a whole tube of toothpaste, forgetting her sorrows in the process. When Mrs. Quimby discovers what she has done, Ramona must put the toothpaste in a jar to use herself and thus is even excluded from the family toothpaste.

One February day, everything goes wrong, culminating in a quarrel between Mr. and Mrs. Quimby, after which, though the girls are shocked, their parents are oddly cheerful. The next morning all is normal; Mr. and Mrs. Quimby explain that grownups—especially tired grownups—are not perfect. Nevertheless, Ramona orders them not to quarrel again. The next family quarrel is between Mrs. Quimby and Beezus, who refuses a home haircut. A professional cut is no better, for Ramona is given a cute pixie cut and twelve-year-old Beezus ends up with a forty-year-old's hairstyle. However, things settle down: when Beezus washes her hair, she looks like the old Beezus again, for her new cut is not much different from her old one; and Ramona soon forgets about her own hair.

Ramona feels especially cozy the night she wears a new—not hand-me-down—pair of pajamas. She feels not so cozy when she wears them the next day under her clothes. The day drags on and Ramona feels warmer, until her teacher extracts a confession. The cozy feeling returns with her teacher's understanding, when she gives Ramona a sack for her pajamas. But Ramona leaves her pajamas at school, and when the teacher calls the next day, she makes "a great big fuss" over the betrayal of her secret. Now it all comes out: nobody loves Ramona and everyone loves Beezus. Overriding Beezus's big-sister complaints, Ramona threatens to run away, and Mrs. Quimby helps her pack. With the suitcase too full for Ramona to budge, she understands: Mrs. Quimby cannot get along without her. Their talk is revealing. The call had been about Ramona's nose-twitching, for she has been pretending to be her mother's little rabbit. Comforted, Ramona tells about the pajamas and learns that her teacher had called her a "little sparkler," which she adds to the end of her name, now written in grownup cursive!

Though they did not dismiss the book's humor, reviewers emphasized Cleary's delineation of a young member of a "perpetually normal family."[13] Noting that the work was less a cohesive novel than a series of incidents, reviewers focused on the maturing Ramona, "a wholly delightful personality" now "at a particularly difficult time: too young to be given the freedom or the responsibility her older sister Beezus has, too old to be treated indulgently, as is obnoxious little Willa Jean Kemp."[14] The reviewer in the *Chris-*

tian Science Monitor reminded readers of Ramona's new maturity: "When Beverly Cleary first introduced the irrepressible Ramona Quimby . . . she presented a classic four-year-old pest adept at making life miserable for older sister Beezus and neighbor Henry Huggins. Ramona has now, many books and years later, matured into a sadder but wiser seven-year-old who has every intention of redeeming her troublesome past."[15]

Cleary's style and presentation of the small details of daily life and growing up also came in for praise. One reviewer noted that Cleary "writes in a deceptively casual and conversational style, she has a fine ear for dialogue, and her family scenes are vividly real and funny" (*Bulletin,* "Mother"). Another explained that, while Ramona's actions may sometimes be irritating, "Ramona is hard to dislike. So skillfully has Cleary presented the viewpoint of a child coping with strained family relationships in difficult times that it is easy to sympathize with Ramona's attempts to be grown-up even when they fail." The reviewer went on to emphasize the way that Cleary presents the little realities of daily life: "The author's gift for nuances and realistic detail give a genuine picture of suburban family life right down to the meals cooked in a Crock-Pot, trips to the shopping mall, and the ever-pervasive influence of TV commercials. As always, Cleary chronicles the experience of being young with [compassion], humor, and insight" (*Monitor,* "Mother"). In 1981, the book won the American Award for children's fiction in paperback and the Garden State Children's Book Award.

Ramona and Her Mother presents a Ramona still learning new ways to relate to her family as she struggles to become closer to her mother. As in *Ramona and Her Father,* Cleary focuses on interaction with one parent while showing a family working through the kind of changes every family goes through, and, as in the earlier work, she shows us the focal parent as a person as well as a parent. Now, however, Cleary begins to point up Ramona's growing maturity by showing us just how far she has come.

At the heart the book is Ramona's desire to be identified with her mother, and essential to this desire is a longing to have her

growing maturity acknowledged. Having been considered her father's girl for so long, Ramona now longs to identify with her
mother, a longing mixed with a desire to be considered grown up,
like Beezus, and, to be, like Beezus, "her mother's girl." The problem is Ramona's age, and the problem surfaces in the first chapter, with the introduction of four-year-old Willa Jean Kemp. Willa
Jean had appeared in the first Ramona book, *Beezus and Ramona,* and in every work since then; but now Cleary uses her not
just as obstacle for Ramona as Ramona was obstacle for Henry
Huggins, but as guidepost for a Ramona on the way to being an
adult. Used to being compared unfavorably with twelve-year-old
Beezus, Ramona is not prepared to be compared unfavorably with
Willa Jean, whom she considers messy, crumby, and pesty. But
this is precisely what happens, and as Cleary shows that her heroine is at an awkward position between Willa Jean and Beezus,
she also reminds her readers of just how much growing Ramona
already has done.

At age seven and a half, Ramona finds herself positioned between Willa Jean and Beezus, too old to act like the former and
too young to act like the latter. Expected to entertain Willa Jean
during a brunch the Quimbys give for the rest of the neighborhood, Ramona watches wistfully as Beezus helps their mother
and serves the guests. At the same time, Ramona resents the fact
that irrepressible Willa Jean can do as she likes. Having planned
to look generous and responsible as she cares for messy, crumby
Willa Jean and proud of the fact that she is getting grown-up
front teeth, Ramona feels big and awkward beside an angelic
Willa Jean dressed in pink ruffles and smiling with tiny, perfect
baby teeth. At the same time, Ramona finds herself very attracted to Willa Jean's teddy bear; longing to act as grown up as
Beezus, Ramona is still young enough to love a teddy bear. But
stuck caring for Willa Jean, who is both spoiled and difficult to
control, Ramona longs to be impressing the adults with her growing maturity, as Beezus is.

Instead, Ramona finds herself being identified not with Beezus
or with Mrs. Quimby but with Willa Jean, directly as her parents
reminisce about Ramona at the same age, and indirectly as she

unconsciously mimics Willa Jean. Having arranged for Willa Jean to pull out a whole box of facial tissues just as Ramona has longed to do, Ramona herself gives in to this sort of impulse and squeezes out a whole tube of toothpaste. But it is the direct comparison that offends her. Having already been identified with Willa Jean at the party, Ramona resents this further identification, for she knows that although she may have done some of the things the adults laugh about, she never was such a pest as Willa Jean. The reader, however, knows different, having seen Ramona at work in earlier books. Cleary plays off this knowledge to allow us a laugh at Ramona and to show how far she has come. Like Ramona's parents, the reader can reminisce and, watching Ramona, be reminded of the Ramona of the Henry Huggins books and just how much she has grown.

But Ramona can see only that she is not as grown up as she would like to be, and part of not being grown up is not being her mother's girl and not feeling as valued as Beezus. Ramona is not simply feeling sibling rivalry: she feels left out, especially when making slacks for her stuffed elephant proves impossible, while Beezus's skirt turns out so well. At times, Ramona's efforts to win her mother's praise do reflect sibling rivalry, for Beezus interprets her siding with Mrs. Quimby during Beezus's campaign for a professional haircut as being "goody-goody"; Ramona later feels secretly pleased and guilty when her haircut turns out better than Beezus's. At the end of the book, Ramona realizes that she never really doubted her mother's love; feeling set aside by Beezus's competence and by Mrs. Quimby's full-time job, she has needed to have her mother's love verbalized. Mrs. Quimby, helping Ramona to pack for running away from home, makes it clear that she could not do without her younger daughter any more than she could do without her older daughter. Ramona's happiness is complete.

Ramona Quimby, Age 8

Ramona Quimby, Age 8 appeared in 1981, two years after the previous Ramona book. Now twice the age she had been when her readers met her in *Henry and Beezus,* Ramona is determined to shed forever her old image and is equally determined to act her new age and to let her family know that they can depend on her. For life in the Quimby household is different: Mr. Quimby takes college classes during the day while he works part time; Beezus is now in junior high school; and Ramona must ride a school bus to another elementary school, where she has a new teacher and a new class.

The first day of school is exciting; Mrs. Whaley is unlike any teacher Ramona has had before. On the problem side, Mr. Quimby studies hard and is often tired from taking classes and working; Ramona is not sure that she likes Mrs. Whaley and resents being nice to pesty four-year-old Willa Jean Kemp every day after school. She deals with Willa Jean by standing on her dignity as a third grader to get out of playing. But Mrs. Whaley is another matter. One day Ramona cracks her hard-boiled egg open on her head—and finds her hair full of raw egg. While rinsing her hair in the office, she overhears Mrs. Whaley call her a "show-off" and a "nuisance," and Ramona's humiliation deepens.

Mrs. Quimby apologizes for the egg mixup, but, angry with Mrs. Whaley, Ramona is angry with almost everyone else, too. When supper's tasty and unusually tender meat turns out to be tongue, the girls' protests lead to them making the next night's supper themselves. Cooking is a bit of a challenge—especially without a recipe—but supper is a success. The two girls, though, get out of the way before their parents, who have volunteered to wash the dishes, see the state of the kitchen.

The supper debate has cleared the air at home, but school is different: anxious not to be a nuisance to Mrs. Whaley, Ramona comes to dread school. Then one day she throws up in class, the biggest nuisance of all. Since she is well enough to be grouchy, Ramona finds her sickness tiresome; there is nothing good on television but the commercials. Assigned to "sell" a book to the rest of the class after her return, however, she takes inspiration and imitates a cat food commercial. Emboldened by Mrs. Whaley's approval and safe behind her cat mask, Ramona tells her teacher what she had overheard and feels better to hear that the words had not meant what they seemed to.

But Ramona feels better only at school. At home, the whole family is cross one dismal, rainy Sunday; finally, Mr. Quimby gets exasperated and they go out to eat. Because Mr. Quimby has ordered the family to have a good time, some things go unsaid that might have been stated under other circumstances. When it comes time to pay the check, the Quimbys learn that their meal has been paid for by an eccentrically dressed old man, because they are such a nice family. Embarrassed at first, they realize that they *are* nice, though not all the time, for no one is nice all the time. Ramona feels good about being part of a family that sticks together, and she feels good about the family's happy ending to its Sunday.

Ramona Quimby, Age 8 pleased reviewers as much as it pleased children, earning starred reviews in both *Booklist* and *School Library Journal* for the way in which Cleary presented the humor and realities of contemporary life. "No doubt about it, *Ramona Quimby, Age 8* gets better with every year," one reviewer declared after noting, perhaps wryly, that "Cleary has brought her 'nice sticking-together family' into the 1980s. She's taken the best from the 60s and 70s—she's freer now (viz., neighbor Willa Jean Kemp's playmate Bruce 'doesn't wee-wee in the sandbox') and more feelings-centered. And, she's done it without sacrificing any of the decency or laughter that makes the Quimbys a favorite happy family. As if answering critics of her 'perfect' family, Cleary puts the Quimbys under real pressure and lets the strains show."[16]

The reviewer in the *Christian Science Monitor* pointed out that the Quimbys "have their share of contemporary challenges: her mother works full-time and runs the household on a shoestring budget . . . so that her father can return to college."[17] Another praised Cleary's "unrivaled knack for juggling ordinary happenstances and catching the unexpected effect," as well as her "insights into child and adult behavior," which "are sharp as well as funny, with the episodes adding up to a convincing, comfortable family portrait."[18] *Horn Book* agreed, pointing out also that "it is one of the author's enduring gifts to make the small miseries of childhood seem like high tragedy and to turn everyday occur-

rences into comic adventures."[19] Though not ignoring the humor
in the books, a reviewer pointed out that "Ramona's believable
adventures always have an instructive purpose in Beverly Clear-
y's caring hands. She deals with such young concerns as getting
ill in class and worrying about parents losing jobs" and that "one
of the many strengths of this book is author Cleary's quiet en-
couragement of reading" (*Monitor*, "Age 8"). In 1982, *Ramona
Quimby, Age 8* was a Newbery Honor book.

Once again, the emphasis is on change, not just in the Quimby
household, but elsewhere as well. Most of the changes concern
education: Mr. Quimby is going back to college to earn a degree
in teaching; Beezus has entered junior high school; Ramona is
taking the bus to a new school in a new neighborhood; even Willa
Jean enters nursery school. There also are the changes Ramona
and Beezus are going through; Beezus seems responsible for
much of the family tension because she is an adolescent. In this
time of upheaval, great stresses are put on Ramona and the rest
of the family; Cleary emphasizes once again that an imperfect
family can still be a happy family.

Having seen Ramona identified with Willa Jean in *Ramona
and Her Mother*, the reader of *Ramona Quimby, Age 8* watches a
Willa Jean who seems more and more what Ramona was at the
same age: opinionated and intent on getting her own way. In the
earlier book, Willa Jean already had ruined Ramona and Howie's
checkers game as Ramona used to spoil Beezus's and Henry's
games in the Henry Huggins books. Now Ramona is expected to
be the main playmate for a four-year-old whose idea of entertainment is repeatedly enacting her own version of the wedding of the
frog and the mouse. But Willa Jean is not really like Ramona at
that age: she does not have as lively an imagination, and she most
definitely is petted and indulged by her grandmother, unlike Ramona. Whereas Ramona was only interested in interpreting the
world in her own terms—shutting Ribsy in the bathroom for taking her cookie, worshipping Henry and Sheriff Bud, pretending
to be a windup toy—and thereby got into other people's way by
accident, Willa Jean is downright bossy.

But Willa Jean is not Ramona's only problem. In a new school among new students, with a teacher unlike any other she has had, she is eager to please this all-important adult. Pleasing Miss Binney had been paramount in kindergarten; pleasing Mrs. Griggs had been important in the first grade. Though Ramona wanted to please her second-grade teacher, their difficulties had not been dramatic; Ramona's pleasure at being called Mrs. Roger's "little sparkler," which inspired her to add sparks to her new, cursive signature, is based more on the feeling of closeness she has with Mrs. Rogers than it is on the teacher's approval of her. With Mrs. Whaley, Ramona's teacher problems come to the fore again. Unsure of her standing with Mrs. Whaley anyway, Ramona is devastated when her teacher seems to call her a "show-off" and a "nuisance." Now Ramona worries about being a nuisance and works to avoid it, embarrassed at throwing up in class not just because it is embarrassing, but because now she is being a nuisance again. As always, Ramona takes care of her own problem; safe behind her cat mask and behind the success of her book report, Ramona confronts Mrs. Whaley herself and gets a heartening response.

As in *Ramona and Her Father* and *Ramona and Her Mother,* Cleary focuses on family relationships, on the stresses of growing up and of raising a family on a small income, of too much work and not enough time. Beezus, who is moving into adolescence, begins to criticize her parents more and more; Ramona, in third grade, demands accuracy and perfection from everyone. Cleary emphasizes Mr. and Mrs. Quimby's problems, too; having seen each as the person behind the parent in their respective books, the reader is prepared to understand that parents have bad days too and that they can act silly: the balding Mr. Quimby still can slap his graying wife on the bottom, to their daughters' shock and amusement. Beezus and Ramona criticize their mother's cooking and discover how difficult cooking can be when they must make supper themselves. Cleary shows Mrs. Quimby worrying about bills and Mr. Quimby studying after putting in many hours at school and at work. As she had shown her audience that an imperfect family can be a happy family in *Ramona and Her Father,* here Cleary shows than an imperfect family can be a nice family as well. No one is nice all the time, but they work at it; the Quimbys enjoy each other's company and stick together, and the effort of being consciously nice to each other in the restaurant reminds them how close they are when they work at it.

Ramona, of course, is convinced that she is nice all the time. As her reflections in the mirrors in *Ramona the Brave* and *Ramona and Her Father* have shown an outer Ramona different from the inner Ramona, so her outside does not always reflect her inside: sometimes her niceness is a bit "curdled." But this realization leads her out again to her family. Having empathized with them all through the book, worrying about her father disliking his difficult job and wanting her mother to be happy, Ramona now realizes that, just as *she* is always nice, even when that niceness is curdled, so others may be the same. Going into a new grade is one way to tell that she is growing up; the less tangible ways—the ways that count—also prove it.

Ramona Forever

It was 1984 before the next, and last, Ramona book was published. Having published the third book about Ralph S. Mouse, *Dear Mr. Henshaw,* and *Lucky Chuck,* and having won the Newbery Award for *Dear Mr. Henshaw,* Cleary was perhaps ready to finish her books about the Quimby family and turn to other things. It is clear to readers that *Ramona Forever* is the last work about the Quimbys. It is a book of transitions and conclusions, emphasizing that an ending is only another beginning, as the Quimby family goes through drastic changes.

The changes begin when Howie's uncle, Hobart Kemp, comes to visit from Saudi Arabia. Ramona quickly decides she does not like Hobart, and from there the afternoon goes downhill, ending with Ramona's realizing suddenly that Howie's grandmother does not like her. Resolved that she will not be looked after by someone who does not like her, Ramona lets it all out at supper; their parents will let Beezus and Ramona look after themselves for a week to see how things work out.

For the first two days, it is fun to be in the quiet house alone. On the third day, a quarrel develops, with both girls unable to apologize. The death of the family cat oddly brings them back together: they bury it to keep their mother from being upset. Ramona finds herself able to apologize, and the girls forgive each other. They also learn what they had suspected: Mrs. Quimby is pregnant. Realizing that she will no longer be Mrs. Quimby's baby, Ramona thinks that maybe she would rather have another cat.

In the next weeks, many plans are made, for Mr. Quimby will get his teaching certificate several weeks before the baby is due. A discussion with her mother assures Ramona that she will still be loved; being the middle child, she will be in the middle of Mrs. Quimby's heart. At last, Mr. Quimby is offered a less-than-ideal job; the rest of the Quimbys, however, feel that if one school wants Mr. Quimby, then perhaps another will, too.

Another big change occurs next. Hobart and Ramona's Aunt Beatrice will be marrying and moving to Alaska, where Hobart has a job. Hobart insists on planning the "real" wedding he wants, with Ramona and Beezus as bridesmaids, ordering dresses as casually as he later orders ice cream cones. The wedding is beautiful, despite a few hitches, most notably when Hobart loses the ring while getting it off the pillow; and Ramona must find it. The reception is most satisfying: the girls have Howie tie their shoes to the bumper of the bride and groom's car, Ramona makes peace with her new uncle Hobart, and Beezus catches the bouquet. A lovely day ends with pizza.

The postwedding letdown is emphasized by Mr. Quimby's failure to find a teaching job: instead, he must take a job managing a grocery store. Then Roberta Day Quimby is born. Sitting alone in the hospital lobby because she might carry some disease, Ramona has an attack of itchy, germy-feeling "siblingitis." But when she meets Roberta, Ramona falls in love with her and realizes how much she herself has changed: growing up is hard work, but she herself is doing a wonderful job of it!

"Happy days, Ramona is back!" trumpeted the review in *Booklist,* and other reviewers followed suit, relishing the book's "laugh-out-loud scenes, memorable characters, and keen perceptions."[20] Reviewers also seemed to grow nostalgic as they reviewed Ramona's growing maturity, emphasizing that Ramona, who once acted like Willa Jean, had matured into an equally interesting middle child: "[Ramona] still exhibits the contradictory behavior and the conflicting emotions that have made her so human and endearing; but these attributes are now tempered by self-restraint. Howie's younger sister carries on Ramona's uninhibited ways while Ramona knows that 'she had grown past Willa Jean's kind of behavior, which had been fun while it lasted.' Appreciative readers may experience similar conflicts—cheering Ramona's coming of age but also suffering a twinge of regret."[21]

But, reviewers emphasized, "Ramona, dancing in front of the three-way mirror, watching all the Ramonas dancing into the distance, thinks, 'forever me.' And Ramona *is* forever, in all her clownish, exuberant, tender good nature"; "Ramona will remain Ramona—forever."[22] Reviewers noted that *Ramona Forever,* in its depiction of daily life, emphasizes more than Ramona's growing maturity. "Sandwiched between all the laughs and hustle-bustle are some realities that give the story depth," the reviewer in *Booklist* stated, "most notably Mr. Quimby's inability to find a job as a teacher. . . . Mr. Quimby's decision to take a job as a grocery store manager has an understated poignancy that is balanced by the great happiness he finds in his growing family" ("Forever," 63). The *Christian Science Monitor* focused on the family and its relationships, emphasizing that the relationship between Beezus and Ramona, "in all its variableness . . . becomes the glue of the story. Or, in a larger sense, it is the family love that binds, for the Quimbys, with all of their give and take, speak to us in their most laughable, human way of love" ("Forever," B5).

The final Ramona book emphasizes the Quimby family changing more than ever: Mr. Quimby finishes his degree; Roberta Quimby is born; Picky-picky dies of old age; and Aunt Beatrice marries Howie Kemp's Uncle Hobart. It also focuses on Ramona working to find her new place in the family and to understand family members as well as trying to find her new place as a more grown-up person. More importantly, the book shows Ramona clearly growing up.

Focusing on the family, Cleary gives Ramona problems that arise naturally out of family relationships rather than out of outside events; Ramona's teacher and schoolmates do not even appear in this novel. Ramona has problems with Willa Jean and with Mrs. Kemp, coming to realize with some astonishment that not all adults like all children and also that she is a grown-up role model for Willa Jean. Most of Ramona's difficulties stem from her problems in finding her new place in the family: as middle child, as younger sister to an almost-teenager, and as niece-in-law to a man she does not like. She learns to accept and to deal with each situation. Mistrusting Uncle Hobart, Ramona is unwilling to admit him to the family but finds herself overridden by her aunt and also finds herself learning to tolerate and even to like him; her outgrown shoes dance behind the honeymoon car in an odd sort of blessing. Beezus's sensitivity and self-consciousness about her looks combine with the stresses of the two girls taking care of themselves and lead to the worst fight the Quimby girls have ever had. Ramona unwittingly hurts Beezus's feelings; making up after Picky-picky's death brings them closer together than before.

The arrival of Roberta Day Quimby is important, with Ramona having some of the same sibling problems Beezus already has had and, most importantly, with Ramona realizing just how far she has progressed. Having shown us Beezus and Ramona's sibling difficulties through the whole series, Cleary now shows us these problems beginning anew, with Ramona as older sibling and— just as difficult—in the place of middle child. No longer the baby of the family but not the oldest, either, Ramona frets over her new position, so like the awkward position she had found herself in, between Willa Jean and Beezus, in *Ramona and Her Mother*. Unable to see the new baby at the hospital because Ramona might be "germy" does not help. But Mrs. Quimby informs Ramona that she will have a new position as middle child, in the middle of Mrs. Quimby's heart; and Mr. Quimby's hug ends Ramona's attack of "siblingitis."

Seeing Roberta especially makes Ramona realize how far she has come. Though she has been identified with Willa Jean in earlier works, Ramona has not had a sense that she has grown because she does not have a sense that she was ever like that—not really, not such a pest. Watching Roberta, cross-eyed and uncoordinated on Mrs. Quimby's lap, Ramona realizes that she, too, was once like that; she also realizes how much hard work goes into growing up. The reader, too, can look back and realize how much hard work has already gone into Ramona's growing up and how much she has changed from the four-year-old who so distracted and distressed Henry Huggins. The reader can agree that growing up *is* hard work, that Ramona is right that she is succeeding wonderfully at growing up.

Cleary, too, agrees, showing us a Ramona who takes charge of Willa Jean and sees Willa Jean—her own personal obstacle—as Henry Huggins once was persuaded to see Ramona—his obstacle—as what she really is: a young child uncertain about the world but trying to conquer it. Secretly envying Willa Jean for doing what Ramona would have liked to do as she sits on the accordion for a glorious moment full of ghastly noise, Ramona nevertheless knows that she has grown beyond such things; her thoughts about Willa Jean in the face of Mrs. Kemp's wrath are as uncharitable as Henry's thoughts about Ramona usually are in his works. But Willa Jean shows Ramona her important place in Willa Jean's life by calling her on the telephone; Ramona realizes that, to Willa Jean, she is a confident grown-up when she takes charge of Willa Jean during Uncle Hobart's wedding shopping trip. Willa Jean may be a nuisance, but first she is a young child.

Cleary uses reflections again to show us a protagonist who is very much her own person. In *Ramona the Brave* and *Ramona and Her Father,* such reflections had been distorted, showing a Ramona who is very different on the outside than what she feels like on the inside. Now, however, whirling in front of the mirrors, mirrors, mirrors in the bridal shop, Ramona sees her reflections go on forever, growing ever tinier, but undistorted, herself: "Forever me," she thinks (116). Reflected and reflected, the mirror images show us a many-faceted child who is at last a unified "one."

An Ordinary Girl

From the beginning, Ramona seems to have been one of Cleary's most popular characters. Ramona's adventures have been translated into Japanese, Spanish, Chinese, German, Dutch, French, Danish, and Norwegian. Her adventures were made available in Great Britain beginning in 1966. The reviewer of the British edition of *Ramona the Pest* in 1974 was less than indulgent with Ramona, noting that *Ramona the Pest* "contains a great deal of acute observation of five-year-old behaviour," but that Ramona—"the American counterpart of Dorothy Edwards' 'Naughty Little Sister'"—"appears to us, as American products sometimes do, more brash, noisier, less appealing. . . . Ramona is a credible and realistic presentation of a five-year-old child. Perhaps it is part of that realism that she is not over-endowed with charm."[23]

Later reviews, however, seem to have been kinder, calling Ramona "that likable explosive little individual" and contending that Cleary's "picture of the transition from being an important top Infant to a small, insignificant member of a Junior school is delightfully recognizable for children anywhere, despite the American terminology."[24] In 1979 *Cutting Up with Ramona* featured liquid-eyed paper dolls based on Beezus and Ramona; *The Beezus and Ramona Diary,* which included illustrations and scenes from the Ramona books, appeared in 1986. In 1984 Ramona appeared on posters for the American Library Association, proclaiming that "Libraries Are Forever!" in a take-off of the title of her last book. In 1988 American public television aired a ten-part series of half-hour shows based on *Ramona and Her Mother, Ramona Quimby, Age 8,* and *Ramona Forever.*

Of course, the readers—of some surprising ages—responded. When producers of the television series polled their potential audience, they found that "without question, when we interviewed children about their favorite books, they all mentioned Ramona.

She was *definitely* the most popular character of all."[25] But the books appeal to a far larger audience than originally intended. From letters, Cleary has realized that *Ramona the Pest* "has proven to be one of my most popular books with children from kindergarten through junior high school" ("Laughter," 561); and *Publishers Weekly* "heard from mothers that their home-for-the-holiday college-student offspring were making off with the December [1975] issue of *Family Circle*. The would-be lawyers, the political science majors and the beginning filmmakers were all eager to read the adventures of 'Ramona and the Three Wise Persons,' a feature supposedly for children" ("Beverly," *Publishers,* 54).

Child and adult readers alike respond to Cleary's apt, clear presentation of the trials and triumphs of contemporary family life as well as the trials and triumphs of a lively little character whom many readers feel akin to or think they know. Writing simply and economically, Cleary has produced books that appeal to the young child who is struggling through problems like Ramona's, as well as the older child who can enjoy the humor of the situations because she or he has grown beyond them; adults can rekindle the sense of childhood and can see Ramona's situations from the point of view of the adults around her.

Ramona, whose exploits and perceptions link the books, is, (like Henry Huggins) an Everychild who asks the questions and thinks the thoughts that many of us have done or would like to have. Cleary has noted that some of her readers have written that their younger siblings were like Ramona; some wrote that they themselves felt like Ramona ("Dear," 22); in her troubles and doubts and joy in growing up, Ramona is the ordinary American child growing up in the twentieth century. She is a character we learn about outside in. Seen from Henry Huggins's point of view in the Henry books, she is the essence of the bratty little tagalong, following Beezus everywhere and often leaving the older children frustrated and bewildered. Pretending to be a monkey, announcing in a crowd that she is going to throw up, taking Ribsy's bone because he ate her ice cream, Ramona is embarrassing in a way familiar to children with younger siblings. The point of several of

Henry's adventures seems to be to find a way around Ramona, and the major triumphs of *Henry and the Paper Route* and *Henry and the Clubhouse* come when he has learned to deal with her. In *Beezus and Ramona,* seen from Beezus's point of view, Ramona is still a brat: she throws a party without asking the family; spoils Beezus's birthday cake, not once but twice; crashes her tricycle into Henry and Beezus's checkers game; and locks Ribsy in the bathroom as punishment for eating her cookie. Beezus must focus not on Ramona, but on her own feelings about a frustrating little sister. With publication of *Ramona the Pest,* readers saw Ramona's character from the inside, and though many of her exploits might make the reader unsympathetic to her, seeing Ramona's actions from her own point of view creates an unexpected sympathy.

Having seen Ramona at age four in the Henry series, the reader watches her grow to age eight, from a small child dependent on others to a child on whom others can depend and who realizes how hard growing up is and how far she has come. The six-year-old afraid to sleep by herself in the dark and even more afraid to admit it because that "would be the same as saying she was failing at the job of growing up" in *Ramona the Brave* (127) has become the more confident eight-year-old twirling with a thousand other reflected Ramonas and realizing that she is "winning at growing up" by the end of *Ramona Forever* (182). While the emphasis in the Henry books is on the outer trappings of growing up, the emphasis here is more internal. Henry deals with the outward signs of maturity—getting a bicycle, taking responsibility for Ribsy and for his paper route—and his triumphs are in getting those things. Ramona's struggles are internal, and so is much of the action of the books; their episodic nature emphasizes their focus on character, for each chapter is an incident melding with other chapters into a character study of an active, imaginative little girl. The outer signs of growing up—going to another grade in school, riding a bicycle, having her own room—please her because they prove how grown up she is becoming. Her problems are not with getting these outer trappings of maturity, but with teachers, other students, her family, and herself. Desperate for

Miss Binney to like her, kindergartener Ramona mourns when her teacher is firm with her. The turning point of *Ramona the Pest* comes when Ramona realizes that Miss Binney does like her; she has similar misunderstandings with later teachers. Uncertain when her parents—lost in their problems—seem not to love her any more, Ramona must be reassured. Most of all, she struggles in the books to feel grown up, like a person and not a nuisance. Very aware of the contrast between the mature Ramona going off to kindergarten and the "little" children who stay home, in *Ramona the Pest,* she is equally aware of the contrast between the mature Ramona going off to first grade and the "babies" going to kindergarten, in *Ramona the Brave.* But she will never catch up with Beezus, no matter what, and Ramona often feels misunderstood by the people around her, who do not realize that she is trying to act grown up, trying to be reasonable, that she really is a nice person, though sometimes her niceness "curdles." The five-year-old who knows she is not a pest in *Ramona the Pest*—no matter what older people say—is the eight-year-old who feels her teacher thinks she is a nuisance in *Ramona Quimby, Age 8.*

In the course of emphasizing the emotional trappings of growing up, the books forge their own emotional bond with readers of all ages by dealing with the stuff of everyday life, especially the typical fears and problems of childhood that make children feel small and insignificant. Fears of the dark, of big dogs, of driving a parent away by not being good, of not being loved, of a parent's dying, of making a teacher angry: these are worries familiar to Cleary's readers, no matter what their age. Reluctant to write for children of nine or ten about a younger child, Cleary realized that there is nothing funnier to children than "their younger selves," and so they can "laugh at Ramona because they used to act like her or because they have a little brother or sister exactly like her" ("Laughter," 561–62). So the books provide a humorous sentimental journey for their readers: for the main readers older than she who enjoy looking back on their own younger selves, and for the adults enjoying a sense of déjà vu from Ramona's fears of the dark or her reading the newspaper by filling in the blanks between words she knows with Zs. The books are circular, as the reader—

and an often-bewildered Ramona—watch Willa Jean Kemp indulge in the same kind of behavior Ramona did at the same age, even to destroying the checkers game between Howie and Ramona as Ramona had destroyed a checkers game between Henry and Beezus. So even the reader close to Ramona's emotional age can laugh when in later books Ramona is compared with Willa Jean: with the pleasure of recalling the way Ramona had behaved in the Henry books, as well as in the first of the Ramona books, the child looks back on Ramona and her earlier exploits much as do the adults in the book. There is humor, too, in Ramona's waxing nostalgic in *Ramona the Brave* about the carefree days of kindergarten, for the reader of *Ramona the Pest* remembers just how "carefree" those days really were. Often there is subtle humor: Miss Binney's frozen smile after Ramona earnestly asks after a reading of *Mike Mulligan and His Steam Shovel* how he went to the bathroom while digging the basement of the town hall (*Pest*, 23); or the description of Ramona's father, who "could run fast for a man who was thirty-three years old" (*Brave*, 51). There is also, as David Rees has pointed out, the scene in which Ramona watches three girls dress for the nativity play:

> "Are you Jesus' aunts?" she asked.
> The girls found the question funny. "No," answered one. "We're the Three Wise Persons."
> Ramona was puzzled. "I thought they were supposed to be wise *men*," she said.
> "The boys backed out at the last minute," explained the girl with the blackest eyebrows. "Mrs. Russo said women can be wise too, so tonight we are the Three Wise Persons." (*Father*, 176–77)

"The use of the word 'Persons' and 'Mrs. Russo said women can be wise too'," Rees points out, "are neat bits of satire, well above the heads of eight-year-olds, but, no matter—they will still be laughing at the remark about Jesus's aunts" (Rees, 100–1).

Concerning themselves mainly with tracing Ramona's growing maturity, the books also concern themselves with ordinary family life and family situations, emphasizing that things do not always go right for even the best family. The Quimby family deals with common problems: money troubles, relationships, the little incidents of daily life. It is not a perfect family, for Beezus and Ramona bicker in all the books as siblings always have, and the parents occasionally fight as well; twelve years old in the last book, Beezus begins to test the limits of parental authority. Life in the Quimby household is not perfect, either. There are money problems after Mr. Quimby loses his job, and the family cannot often afford little luxuries such as going out to eat or getting a professional haircut. Mr. Quimby does not really like the succession of jobs he gets; when he finishes his college degree, he does not get the teaching job he wants and instead becomes manager of a supermarket. On top of the family's monetary woes comes another child. On a memorable day in *Ramona and Her Mother,* absolutely nothing goes right, from the car breaking down to Mr. and Mrs. Quimby quarreling in front of their horrified daughters. Though only-child Henry Huggins realizes after his parents help with the paper drive that his parents are individuals just as he is, it is an isolated incident; the nuances and pressures of family life do not absorb him. Ramona, intense and emotional and part of a more complex family structure, is much more involved with her parents and is witness to more examples of her parents acting like ordinary people. Concerned that her father will die from smoking, she launches an antismoking campaign; she wants her father to like his job and yearns for her parents' love and for recognition that she is, indeed, her mother's girl. Concerned with the family's economic problems, Ramona decides to make lots of money starring in commercials and practices toward that end. She and Beezus are very disapproving when their parents fight, for parents are supposed to be perfect, and fighting is not dignified—especially when it ends with one parent swatting another with a pancake turner (*Mother,* 113).

As Cleary points out, this is what family life is really like; it is not supposed to be perfect. Grown-ups are not perfect, especially when they are tired. Mothers occasionally want to sit in the sun and blow the seeds off dandelions. Fathers get grouchy when they give up smoking and occasionally sneak a cigarette. One just does the best he or she can. That is the theme of almost all the books. As Ramona learns to do the best she can to succeed at growing up, so the Quimbys do the best they can to be a happy family, for family relationships can be difficult. Especially in the later works, the complexities of family relationships are important, with both girls learning to deal with sibling rivalry and Ramona realizing that her family loves her very much, though they may not always show it. Just as Beezus realized that she does not always have to love Ramona in *Beezus and Ramona,* Ramona must realize that even after her mother has another baby, she will still be loved, in *Ramona Forever.* Both girls struggle to get along with each other, recognizing that, although it is nice to get along, there are still so many things to disagree about. At the end of *Ramona Quimby, Age 8,* the family works to be pleasant to each other in a family restaurant, and the conscious attempt soon relaxes. Family life, Cleary reminds the reader over and over in the Ramona books, is not perfect: though the Quimbys are a "nice family," they are not nice all the time; the important thing is that they stick together (*Age 8,* 188).

This strong sense of everyday reality is appropriate, for, as she had in the Henry books, Cleary used much from ordinary life. Some of it may have come from her own readers' suggestions[26]; but, though Cleary has maintained that "I had the same feelings, but I didn't do the same things Ramona does" (Herron), the Ramona books use more of her own childhood than do her other works, perhaps because creative, impetuous Ramona has much in common with her creator. Like Beezus, in *Beezus and Ramona,* Cleary embroidered a potholder picturing a smiling teakettle (*Yamhill,* 119). Like Ramona, Cleary had early realized that "the first bite of an apple tastes best," and so would take only one bite out of each apple before tossing it aside (*Yamhill,* 23–24; *Beezus* 94). Cleary named her doll "Fordson-Lafayette," after a tractor and a town, because she thought the names were pretty (*Yamhill,* 80), while in *Beezus and Ramona,* Ramona owned a doll named "Bendix" and, later, in *Ramona the Pest,* another named "Chevrolet"; when the family is naming the new Quimby in *Ramona*

Forever, Ramona likes "Aston Martin" as a name. Ramona's favorite place to read—as Cleary's was—is by the furnace outlet. Though Cleary actually tried to walk around the world (*Yamhill,* 30–31)—where Beezus only thought Ramona meant to—Ramona goes after the pot of gold at the end of the rainbow in *Beezus and Ramona,* as Cleary herself had (*Yamhill,* 32); Cleary's walk around the world was stopped by her boots becoming weighted down with mud, which may have inspired a similar scene in *Ramona the Pest.* The relationship between "small, impetuous, and quick" Cleary and her "large, good-natured, and deliberate in thought and movement" cousin Winston seems to be of the same nature as that between mercurial Ramona and stolid Howie (*Yamhill,* 45). Like Ramona, Cleary made stilts out of coffee cans and shouted "Pieface!" at other children, played Brick Factory, was puzzled about the "dawnzer lee light," and chased a little boy on the playground because she loved him (*Yamhill,* 71, 76, 95). Like Ramona, Cleary had misunderstandings with her teachers, including the devastating experience of being called by one (with amusement) a "nuisance" (*Yamhill,* 100–1).

Written twenty years after the Henry Huggins books, the Ramona series cannot help but seem more contemporary and presents a grittier reality. The reader is surprised to realize that Ramona, age eight in 1981, was just four years younger in 1952. Like the Henry books, the Ramona books reveal the time period of their composition in small details: Beezus wants to have her hair cut so it looks like the skater's on television, the girls enjoy gummy bears, and the Quimbys use a crock-pot. But the relationships and emotions the books explore are timeless. In the small details, such as Ramona's drumming her heels on the wall of her room to show her family that her spirit is not broken, the realities of having one's hair washed in the kitchen skin, or the nuisance value of someone who throws up in school, there is a strong sense of the everyday that has remained the same for generations. Cleary notes that

> when *Ramona and Her Father* was published, I was astonished to have several librarians remark that I had

finally written about contemporary problems. I had? I feel I have been writing about small problems contemporary to children all along. And fifty years ago my father, like Ramona's father, lost his job through a merger, tried to give up smoking and became irritable, which made me fear he might not love me. A man's loss of livelihood, grimmer in those days before unemployment insurance, comes under the heading, not of contemporary problems, but of universal human experience which is the proper subject of a novel, adult or juvenile. ("Regina," 24)

For, after all, it is Ramona and her family that form the books' focus. Though "many children tell [Cleary] Ramona should be spanked" ("Newbery," 435), more feel free to laugh at her, seeing themselves or the way they were, assured that if the little demon of Klickitat Street could "win at growing up," so could they. In the adventures of an ordinary Oregonian, readers could find laughter and themselves, as they could in the adventures of the ordinary children who enliven the pages of Cleary's other works.

4

Other Lives

As Margaret Novinger has noted, "[s]omeone has said that every good writer crates his world, peopled by his characters in the time and place in which he sets them"; the world that Cleary has created in her works, "bounded by childhood and humor," is not "a large and majestic world . . . neither is it a slight nor insignificant one" (Novinger, 72). It is, however, a well-peopled world. In short stories, picture books, an historical novel, and several works of modern fiction, Cleary has chronicled the adventures of ordinary children: from Oregonians Ellen Tebbits, Otis Spofford, and Emily Bartlett; to twins Mitch and Amy Huff and Jimmy and Janet; to that quintessential American boy, Theodore (Beaver) Cleaver. As in the Henry books and the Ramona books, the emphasis in these works is on the ordinary lives of children: lives full of fear and happiness and humor and the triumphs of growing up.[1]

The Whole Gang

Ellen Tebbits
Having set out in her first book to write "a girls' story about the maturing of a sensitive female who wanted to write" ("Regina," 23), Cleary had produced instead a humorous book about a boy;

her second book, *Ellen Tebbits,* published 5 September 1951, is a girls' book, though not about a sensitive would-be writer. Instead, it emphasizes the sometimes-funny, sometimes-touching aspects of being nine years old and having a best friend.

Ellen Tebbits and Austine Allen meet in dance class. Ellen has a big secret: her mother makes her wear woolen underwear, and in her anxiety to change in private, Ellen insults Austine. Her apology during class stands her in good stead when the long underwear she has rolled under her clothes begins to slip and her discreet hitching is imitated by Otis Spofford, the dancing teacher's son; Austine's engineered collision with Otis finally gets him out of the room. Even better, Ellen learns that Austine, too, is wearing woolen underwear. The two girls realize that they can be good friends.

Ellen's only problem with third grade is that the teacher never asks her to clap erasers, which must mean that she does not like Ellen as much as she does the others. Ellen seizes a chance to impress her teacher by bringing to class a flowering beet for science. It is a long, muddy, beet-juicy process, with Ellen tearing her dress to boot. But Ellen's state helps, for she and Austine are chosen to clap erasers: it is such a messy job that the teacher did not think to ask tidy Ellen to do it. After Austine learns that Ellen has actually ridden a horse, Ellen has new best-friend problems, for the story grows as it spreads, as does Ellen's discomfort. An outing is her downfall, for they rent horses to ride, and Austine proves the more adept rider; Ellen finds herself—on horseback—in the middle of a stream. Her troubles on horseback, however, are kept between her and Austine, like the underwear, because they are best friends.

At the end of summer, Ellen has a wonderful idea: the best friends will wear matching dresses made by their mothers, though Austine's mother does not sew a well as Ellen's. The result is predictable: Ellen's is lovely, but Austine's leaves much to be desired, including a sash. Austine seems to take comfort in untying Ellen's sash until finally, her sash yanked once too often, Ellen turns and, horrified, finds herself slapping Austine. Convincing herself that Austine started it, Ellen is more unhappy

when Austine finds a new friend. The school play compounds her
unhappiness. As substitute rat in "The Pied Piper of Hamelin,"
Ellen must fill in on the night of the open house. This is fun until,
at the end of the play, she is pushed onstage, an unwanted par-
ticipant in a Maypole dance. Unable to find her way back when
her mask slips, to the delight of the audience Ellen gets tangled
in the streamers. As she is helped offstage by Austine, Ellen decides she is forgiven, only to overhear that Austine did not know
who the rat was. If it had been Ellen, Austine would not have
helped because of the slap; it was Otis who had yanked the sash
that last time.

Ellen knows she must apologize, but things have gone on too
long. Then she and Austine are sent to clap erasers during class.
Suddenly angry at herself and Austine, Ellen yanks Austine's
sash and accidentally tears it off, leading to tears and apologies
all around; their friendship is sealed when each reveals that her
mother has made her put on winter underwear. Ellen and Austine are best friends again.

Reviewers noted that reserved Ellen Tebbits was very different
from Henry Huggins: the reviewer for *Booklist* felt that *Ellen Tebbits* was "not so funny, perhaps, as the author's first book *Henry
Huggins*,"[2] while *Horn Book* noted that "[t]o me the book seems a
bit contrived and not quite so good as *Henry*"[3]; another critic
thought that the book "lacks some of the spontaneity of *Henry
Huggins*."[4] However, all agreed that the book seemed humorous
and genuine. "Ellen is a real girl and her adventures full of zest
and interest," wrote the *Horn Book* reviewer, noting that because
of the success of *Henry Huggins, Ellen Tebbits* would "have a
warm reception"; *Booklist* felt that girls would be entertained by
the book, for the "humor and incidents . . . are entirely childlike"
(*Horn Book*, "Ellen"; *Booklist*, "Ellen"). A later critic noted the
"sympathy and humor that makes [Ellen's adventures] fun to
read" (Eakin, #259). The reviewer for *Publishers Weekly* gave the
book a warm reception, predicting that it would "be a favorite
with many young readers" and recording that the chapter in
which Ellen appears as substitute rat "is one of the funniest incidents I have read in a long time."[5]

And *Ellen Tebbits is* a funny book. The struggles of quiet, re-served, believable Ellen to maintain her composure as she perches on a boy's bicycle and clutches an enormous beet, as she plays an out-of-place rat, or on a horse taking advantage of her inexperience gain their humor from that reserve and from the way such events develop naturally from her activities. Having shown her deftness in presenting real life in *Henry Huggins,* Cleary expands her presentation in *Ellen Tebbits,* focusing on El-len's adventures with her friends at school in scenes familiar to her young readers. The pleasure of clapping erasers and the value of Scotch tape in repairing torn clothing are recorded carefully and used in Cleary's presentation of the dynamics of a friendship.

As in *Henry Huggins,* in *Ellen Tebbits* Cleary emphasizes re-lationships—broader ones than those between Henry and Ribsy. Though only-child Henry is concerned with his relationships with peers, only-child Ellen is more so, and the thrust of the book is her relationship with Austine; her problems arise from this friendship and also from the teasing of obnoxious Otis Spofford.

Central to the book is the bond between Ellen and Austine, in which Cleary shows the reader the dynamics of friendship. Friends may be different—as quiet, tidy, and reserved Ellen is different from more impetuous Austine—but their bond is based on shared events and mutual support: Austine tells no one of El-len's troubles horseback riding and defends her from Otis several times. Despite their shared experiences and enjoyment of each other's company, it seems, at first, a mildly one-sided relation-ship, with Austine taking the more active role: she literally bumps Otis out of ballet class when he mimics Ellen; she cleans Ellen up after the great beet drama; and she takes on Otis when he teases Ellen after her dress is torn. Ellen recognizes the value of Austine's support in their relationship.

Cleary also emphasizes the value of communication in a friend-ship. Austine's unarticulated jealousy of Ellen's more perfect dress begins their problem, which is compounded when Ellen later waits for Austine to apologize while Austine also seems to wait for one. As weeks pass in silence, the two become more and more estranged, until it seems impossible for them to apologize.

Only after an equally-impetuous act by Ellen can the two communicate their anger and apologies. Support and shared experiences are important to a friendship, but communication is
essential. Shared secrets help; Cleary neatly frames the book and
the friendship in the secret the girls have in common: that their
mothers make them wear long underwear. The secret that brings
them together at the beginning of the book is the secret that ce-
ments their bond at the end.

Otis Spofford

Bad boy Otis Spofford got his own book in 1953, a year after publication of *Henry and Beezus*. The bane of Ellen Tebbits's life, in
the book about her he seems the quintessential bully. But as
would happen later with Ramona Quimby, a book from the point
of view of a prime mischief-maker serves to make its protagonist
sympathetic; having lived Otis's life with him, the reader comes
away with a deeper understanding of his liveliness and mischief.

Otis just likes to stir up excitement, especially during folk
dancing. Playing the front half of a bull in a bullfight gives him
plenty of opportunity to stir up excitement the day of the dancing,
and Otis makes the most of it. The dance is even more entertaining than planned, for Otis and Stewy—the back half of the bull—
wreak revenge on the boy who is playing the matador. But the
toreador swats the back end whenever the bull charges, and Otis
ignores Stewy's agonized protests. Though Otis's teacher promises him that someday he will get his "comeuppance," it is not
today, though Stewy and the toreador chase Otis all the way
home.

The comeuppance seems to come with spitballs. Loosing one at
the teacher, Otis receives a vague threat and simply must find
out what she will do to him; what she does is give a smile that
makes Otis nervous. After lunch, he must throw spitball after
spitball into a trashcan at the back of the room, an activity that
palls quickly. Measured out in spitballs, the afternoon drags on.
Released at last, Otis finds that a drink of water eases his dry-
ness, and a clove of garlic combats the taste of the paper. The

class's reaction is inevitable and immediate, and Otis's life is back to normal.

Otis's next bit of trouble involves two rats: one who is fed what the children eat in the cafeteria, and Mutt, who is fed junk food. Knowing that no class would prove that children should eat junk food, Otis secretly gives skinny Mutt vitamins and healthy food, so that the next time the rats are weighed, Mutt is heavier. The teacher looks so disappointed in her students that Otis is ready to confess, when Ellen Tebbits "confesses" and gets Mutt. When Ellen's mother will not allow her to keep Mutt, she brings it to Otis, who decides that Ellen is okay, even if she is neat and clean.

Insects get Otis into trouble when he and Stewy compete to find thirty insects for the local football hero, who is flunking biology; Otis finds his thirtieth—a flea—on Stewy's dog and thereby wins the competition. Stewy is not pleased.

The comeuppance comes one day when Otis is chased to school by Ellen and Austine; his humiliation is complete when his shirt is torn and his pink undershirt—accidentally put in the laundry with a red sock—is revealed. The momentum of Otis's need for excitement builds until he cuts off a hunk of Ellen's hair. The upshot is that Otis must stay after school for a week; because his mother does not yet know what happened, that afternoon will be the only time he can ice skate. Otis's fun skating is marred by his classmates' unfriendliness; and when Otis starts home, he finds that Ellen and Austine have taken his boots and his shoes, leaving him only his skates to wear. His journey home is painful in many ways, and he is scolded by his mother for chasing Ellen and Austine and for treating his skates so badly. Ellen and Austine give Otis his boots only after he mumbles a promise not to chase them any more. But Otis has his fingers crossed the whole time!

Otis's mischief made reviewers gleeful and librarians nervous. "Children who find most book heroes too good to be true will be immensely taken by Otis Spofford, a boy who likes nothing better than to stir up a little excitement—and is a master at it," the reviewer in *Booklist* wrote, going on to praise Cleary's "freshness and naturalness stemming from an understanding of children and the brand of humor that appeals to them."[6] *Publishers Weekly* called the book a "really hilarious story of a mischievous, impudent boy who is a classroom comedian, a show-off and a pest, but still very lovable" before pointing out Cleary's "devastating parody of books designed to teach American history to children. It is called 'With Luke and Letty on the Oregon Trail,' and Otis doesn't think much of it."[7] The *Atlantic Monthly* reviewer enjoyed the book's "small-boy deviltry and nonsense" and then warned that it "probably won't be endorsed by P.T.A. groups but it certainly has enough of a *Peck's Bad Boy* quality to make children between eight and twelve chuckle in secret, sympathetic glee."[8] It was not P.T.A. groups who dissented, but some librarians had enough qualms about Otis to keep the book off the shelves. Cleary, who as a child had disliked books in which the protagonist reformed, consciously created characters who "did not reform, although they sometimes got their comeuppance. . . . *Otis Spofford* was considered controversial when it was published in 1953, and some school libraries did not buy it because Otis threw spitballs and did not repent" ("Regina," 23). Otis's comeuppance seems to have been lost on these readers, as were the motives behind his actions and their effect on his readers. Paul Burns and Ruth Hines noted: "Mrs. Cleary says: 'This attitude astonished me because this type of boy is not malicious—he just likes to stir up a little excitement. There seems to be a real-life Otis in every classroom and I cannot see why anyone would object to him in a book.' Otis appeals to children perhaps because he dares to try many of the things they have been tempted to do. They enjoy the fun and mischief, but they also sense the attitudes of fair play and consideration for others that pervade the story" (Burns and Hines, 745).

Another reviewer was more sober about Otis's motives, pointing out that "Otis craves attention, primarily because he gets so little of it at home," a "serious note, which will probably be more apparent to adults than to children, in the explanation of why Otis acts the way he does" (Eakin, #266).

Having appeared as an unsympathetic nemesis in *Ellen Tebbits,* Otis becomes surprisingly sympathetic in his own work, where the reader is privy to the thought processes of a believable, lively boy who just likes excitement. Content with merely teasing Ellen and Austine in the earlier work, Otis goes farther in his own story, finally committing a terrible offense and getting his much-predicted comeuppance. But Cleary's portrait of an adventure-seeking boy is so skillful that even at Otis's worst the reader is sympathetic, blaming and understanding him in the same instant. Everyone, Cleary has noted, knows or has known an Otis, who is less interested in schoolwork than in the excitement he can stir up. He is not malicious but bored and sometimes unconcerned with his relationships with others: knowing that the results of the science project the class conducts with two rats are already a given, Otis casts about for some way to make it interesting; bored by the sappy children in the reader, Otis gets into trouble daydreaming a much more satisfactory story. Even when he cuts Ellen's hair, he does not act out of malice; he simply must know how it would feel to cut a thick hunk of hair, and he must save his pride before the other children.

Otis belongs to the long tradition of fictional bad boys, a tradition stretching back to eighteenth-century children's literature. But Cleary gives this traditional story a twist that makes it both more contemporary and more realistic. As in the traditional pattern, Otis gets his comeuppance, which is wonderfully engineered by Ellen and Austine to make him feel as frustrated and helpless as he has made them feel. But Otis emerges unrepentant, unlike other fictional mischief-makers about whom young Beverly Bunn had not wanted to read. Well aware of the tradition, Cleary abandons it in favor not only of a less didactic work, but of a more realistic character. Otis does not learn his lesson and emerge from it vowing to be good hereafter, as his antecedents have done; Otis gets his lesson, vows, and has his fingers crossed the whole time. This portrayal is more realistic for two reasons: this is *just* the kind of thing Otis would do, and a nine-year-old's repentance generally does not last long in real life. Refusing to preach to her readers, Cleary remains true to the character she has created.

Otis is a much more realistic character than those he is set in contrast to in chapter five: Luke and Letty, plodding toward Oregon in typical textbook fashion, are safely dull and educational.

Mocking these fictional characters for an audience that has squirmed through the adventures of many a Luke and Letty—or their contemporary counterparts—Cleary sets them up in direct contrast with Otis, her own fictional character. Luke and Letty are unlikely to give a parent or librarian a moment's worry; Otis the Unfriendly Indian, Otis the troublemaker, is as far from them as a character can get. As Cleary wryly noted, librarians intent on keeping "unsafe" literature out of children's hands did not buy *Otis Spofford*.

Cleary has her cake and eats it, too. Watching Otis, the reader privy to his thought processes understands how he gets into the situations he does and also understands how acting without thinking can get one into trouble. Sharing Otis's thoughts, the reader also shares his punishments, and, though Cleary glosses over the incidents by showing an unrepentant Otis, it does not negate our memory of what happened to him. Otis throws spitballs and is punished; the reader watches and remembers. Otis emerges unrepentant; and the reader secretly cheers but remembers the punishment. The same thing happens at the end of the work: we are cheered that Otis remains good old Otis, but we remember both his horror at the haircutting incident and his comeuppance. But this didacticism affects the reader unconsciously, and it is entertaining Otis that we think of, entertainingly unrepentant Otis that we remember.

"Leave It to Beaver"

Cleary wrote two books about Henry Huggins, three works for adolescents, and *Beezus and Ramona* before writing three works about another mischief-maker, one whom she had not created. It seems appropriate that an author intent on delineating ordinary life should novelize the adventures of a television character who has come to symbolize suburban normalcy: Theodore ("Beaver") Cleaver. Cleary wrote three novels—*Leave It to Beaver* (1960), *Beaver and Wally* (1961), and *Here's Beaver* (1961)—from the popular television show, which had begun in 1957. These books copyrighted by Gomalco Productions have little of Cleary in them: they lack her air of easy confidence, and she seems uncomfortable with Beaver's "gee-whiz" style of thinking and speaking that is so different from her own Henry Huggins. In novels that are almost collections of short stories, television episodes are expanded or altered or combined to emphasize family and growing up.

Mitch and Amy

Cleary drew on her own experience for *Mitch and Amy,* published in 1967; the story of nine-year-old twins, it reflected lives of her own twins, Malcolm and Marianne, in the fourth grade (Fitzgibbons, 169). Though the book emphasizes the twins' individuality, its focus is on the closeness of their relationship as the two come to realize that though they may bicker and disagree, they can, indeed, depend on each other.

Twins Mitch and Amy Huff bicker as most sisters and brothers do, but Mitch would not have life any other way. Today, he feels good because he has made a terrific skateboard out of an old skate. But Mitch's day sours when he meets Alan Hibbler, semi-professional bully, who breaks Mitch's skateboard and makes him run before throwing it at him. Sympathetic Amy lets him make instant pudding for dessert; unfortunately, he cannot read the directions on the box, so he ruins the dessert. His mother then makes him read to her for practice; the book is babyish and boring, and Amy, a good reader, cannot help but pester him in a sisterly way. Amy manages to avoid practicing math, her weak subject, until school starts.

In school, the new audiovisual equipment provides Amy's downfall. As a calm, unruffled recorded voice reads the problems, Amy, who cannot use her usual delaying tactics to count on her fingers, quickly panics. Reprieved when a fuse blows, Amy pretends to be a pioneer girl who loves to learn as she practices with her flashcards at home. Meanwhile, Mitch is having trouble with Alan, who forces him into a game of chicken on his bicycle and who swears revenge when he, Alan, is hurt. Realizing that it is wrong to ignore a bully, Mitch senses that he will soon find out if fighting a bully will make him back down.

The twins may cause trouble for each other, but they also help each other. Mitch helps Amy and her friends rinse the oversoaped kitchen floor when they earn a housekeeping badge by scrubbing it; Amy helps Mitch build a sawmill out of toothpicks for history class. Mitch, in turn, guards Amy and the piñata she has made on their way to school. This protection is unnecessary, for the papier mâché bird proves impervious even to Alan. He revenges himself by spitting into her hair, but Amy knows that there will be more run-ins with Alan. Mitch knows he must punch Alan, for a boy cannot let another get away with spitting in his sister's hair. His impending book report is a problem until Amy brings him a library book about Wild Bill Hickok, which Mitch not only can read but actually finds interesting. He feels good returning to school after the vacation, until he must confront Alan, in a fight that is broken up before anything can be resolved. Mitch has the satisfaction of knowing that he is not afraid to stand up to Alan— and so does Alan.

Meanwhile, Amy finds a friend in eccentric Bernadette Stumpf. The trouble with Alan comes to a climax when he steals cupcakes the girls are taking to their scout meeting. The climax is unexpected, for Alan inadvertently reveals that he shares Mitch's spelling problems. Amy then realizes that having a famous father must make Alan's situation seem worse. Remembering Mitch's struggles, she begins to feel sorry for Alan, especially after Bernadette trips and pins him. But the threat is over, and Amy is glad that there are two Huffs who stick together: Mitch and Amy.

What impressed reviewers about *Mitch and Amy* was the realistic way in which the twins were presented. "It is a rare author who can describe a sibling relationship with all the authority of a case study and have it emerge as a smoothly written and entertaining story," wrote the reviewer for the *Saturday Review,* who noted that "the scene in which Mother patiently hears Mitch stumble through his required daily dose, while Amy hovers nearby, unable to resist the opportunity to flaunt her superiority, will probably be long remembered—the way that children remember how Rufus M. received his first library card or Ellen Tebbits struggled to keep her winter underwear from showing beneath her tutu."[9]

The reviewer in *Horn Book* agreed, stating emphatically that "probably only a parent of twins could create so convincing a pair as nine-year-old Mitch and Amy and could write about them so realistically and so unsentimentally"; and predicting that they "will quickly find a place among the other favorite Cleary characters."[10] Also impressive to reviewers was the fact that, though Amy and Mitch had their differences, they were quick to help each other. *Horn Book* pointed out the way the twins were "passionately loyal to each other, yet frequently indulging in spontaneous bickering"; the *Saturday Review* noted the way the two "tease and squabble, compete for eminence, and defend each other when there is a common foe or a situation of external stress" (*Horn Book,* "Mitch"; *Saturday Review,* "Mitch"). The reviewer for the *Bulletin of the Center for Children's Books* escalated Mitch and Amy's hostilities: "Academically, the competitive relationship between the twins is that of a cold war, with occasional flaring of active hostility."[11] Above all, reviewers enjoyed Cleary's style and the realistic touches with which she imbued the work. "The twins' major and minor concerns . . . seem as familiar an aspect of American school life as the problems and paraphernalia of the classroom," wrote the *Horn Book* reviewer. "The author brings to her writing her usual easy humor and sensitivity to the sights and sounds of school children." The *Bulletin* praised the "ring of truth" Cleary gave to dialog, characterization, and the relationship between the characters, which had special appeal because Cleary "respects children."

Like *Ribsy, Mitch and Amy* uses an alternating point of view, though here Cleary takes the technique a step further by making each twin the focus of alternate chapters, instead of splitting the chapters between points of view, as she had in *Ribsy.* This alternating viewpoint is appropriate, for it divides the book equally between Mitch and Amy, while reinforcing their individuality.

This individuality is central to the book, which stresses the trials and joys of being nine years old while it focuses on sibling relationships. Though most of Cleary's early works have only children as their protagonists, she already had introduced sibling relationships in her works: *Beezus and Ramona* had led the way, with three of her works for adolescents incorporating the dynamics of sibling relationships into their story lines. Now, in a story about twins, Cleary explores the ways in which people who should be so much alike can be so different, and people who are so different can rely on each other so much.

Most of Mitch and Amy's problems are those facing any nine-year-old: relationships with peers, the neighborhood bully, the problems of overcoming academic weaknesses. Each must work through her or his own problems. Amy's loathing of multiplication is aggravated by the school's use of recorded test givers, and she teaches herself to enjoy learning, even if she does not enjoy the math itself. Mitch's reading troubles, similar to those Cleary herself experienced, are chronicled with sympathy and detail; he improves after learning that there are books that he can enjoy reading, as Beverly Bunn had improved with her discovery of Lucy Fitch Perkins's books. Individually, the children learn to deal with Bernadette Stumpf: while Amy makes her a friend, Mitch begins to deal with her on a budding boy/girl relationship level. Both must deal with bully Alan Hibbler, though it is more Mitch's problem than Amy's: being her brother, Mitch not only must deal with the way Alan treats him, but with the way he treats Amy. Their final fight is precipitated less because Alan has bullied Mitch through the whole book than because he has bullied Amy.

Working through their problems, the twin realize just how much they need and depend on each other. Familiar with the differences of her own twin children, Cleary emphasizes the individuality of these twins. Mitch, who is slow at reading but good at athletics, is different from Amy, who is imaginative and good at making things but slow in math. Like most siblings, Amy and Mitch bicker and pester each other: Mitch cannot avoid blowing the fluff from the dandelion Amy is about to wish on, as Amy cannot help bothering Mitch as he practices reading aloud. But when one is in trouble or unhappy, the other offers help and moral support. Amy, caught up in a game with a friend as Mitch returns home after Alan smashes his skateboard, feels the magic suddenly vanish from their engrossing play; Mitch, after an afternoon spent bothering Amy and her friends as they wash the kitchen floor, helps them rinse the inch-deep lather from the floor. Cleary frames the book in the twins' appreciation of their relationship: just as, in the first chapter, Mitch enjoys being one of the Huff twins in the last chapter, Amy also is glad there are two of them.

Picture Books

In 1960, the first of Cleary's novelizations, as well as her first picture books, were published. Even in picture books, Cleary emphasized the ordinary things of daily life, the small discoveries and splendid joys of childhood. *The Hullabaloo ABC,* published in 1960, features the adventures of a boy and girl on a farm and has as its theme the idea that a "lot of noise is a lot of fun!" Its alphabet is a noisy one, running from "A" for "Aha!," "B" for "Boo!," and "C" for "Cock-a-doodle-doo to "X" for "Exclaim," "Y" for "Yodel," and "Z" for "Zoom!" *The Real Hole,* (first published in 1960), was the first work to feature twins Jimmy and Janet, who were approximately the age of Cleary's own twins. After four-year-old Jimmy triumphantly digs his own, real hole, he and Janet disagree about its use: Janet wants to pretend with the hole while Jimmy is simply proud to have dug it. Father solves the problem by showing Jimmy that the hole he has dug is just the right size for a live spruce tree. In 1961 the next book about Janet and Jimmy was published: *Two Dog Biscuits,* in which the twins have trouble finding just the right dog to give the dog biscuits they get from a neighbor; finally, they give the biscuits to a cat which, to their mother's astonishment, crunches the biscuits right up. Originally illustrated in two colors by Mary Stevens, both works were reissued in 1986 with four-color illustrations by DyAnne DiSalvo-Ryan. In 1987 Jimmy and Janet appeared in two new works illustrated by DiSalvo-Ryan: *The Growing-Up Feet* and *Janet's Thingamajigs.* The former work emphasizes growing bigger, as Janet and Jimmy's growing-up feet are not grown up enough for a new pair of shoes, but Jimmy and Janet each get a pair of wonderful new, red boots "guaranteed" to grow with their feet. Growing up is also the theme of *Janet's Thinga-majigs,* as Janet gradually accumulates a collection of paper bags containing small treasures, which she possessively piles in her crib. When Janet and Jimmy get new big beds, however, Janet's bags will not stay in her grown-up bed, and she realizes that she is too big now to play with tiny objects: joyfully, triumphantly, Jimmy and Janet are growing up.

Though the traditional picture book audience is very young children, *Lucky Chuck* (published in 1984) seems aimed at a much older audience. Chuck, the proud owner of a wonderful, dented, secondhand motorcycle, defies the Motor Vehicle Code as he rides his bike in and out of traffic and down the center line; suddenly aware of the patrol car behind him, Chuck skids on some gravel and endures the humiliation of a ticket, a lecture, and bruises and scrapes. His adventures are narrated in the flat, simple style of a basic primer. "This is Chuck," the book intones: "He pumps gas after school. This is Chuck's motorcycle. . . . This is Chuck's mother worrying about Chuck and his motorcycle. . . . This is a rearview mirror that reflects the Highway Patrol chasing Chuck with blinking lights. . . . This is Chuck with aching bones, thinking about the wisdom of the Motor Vehicle Code and how much gas he will have to pump to pay his traffic fine."

Reviewers for *School Library Journal* and *Bulletin of the Center for Children's Books* praised the book's humor and its educational value, noting that the work emphasizes careful riding and obeying the law while telling the reader much about motorcycle riding and motorcycles; J. Winslow Higginbottom's detailed illustrations of a motorcycle on the endpapers have each part carefully labelled. Each reviewer, placing the appropriate age of its audience at kindergarten through fourth grade, also noted the style of the book: the reviewer for *School Library Journal* called it "monotonous," while the reviewer for the *Bulletin of the Center for Children's Books* noted its pattern and humor.[12] This parody of primer style, however, may seem funnier to older readers, who understand Cleary's subtlety. Both Cleary and her son had much experience with the simplistic and "babyish" subject matter of basic primers, which was a theme in some of Cleary's works; remembering her son's interest in motorcycles, perhaps when she wrote the book she had in mind the older reader tired of the simpleminded stories endemic to simple-to-read books.

Emily's Runaway Imagination

Cleary's only historical novel to date also is her most autobiographical. *Emily's Runaway Imagination,* published in 1961, is the story of Emily Bartlett, an only child growing up in Pitchfork, Oregon, in the 1920s. Emily, lively and imaginative, is Beverly Bunn; secure and well-loved, Emily is growing up in a Yamhill gold-tinted by nostalgia. Unlike Beverly, however, Emily often finds her imagination getting her into one bit of trouble after another.

Emily Bartlett has an imagination that her mother says runs away with her but that inspires her mother to start a library in tiny Pitchfork, Oregon. The town is so tiny that when Emily embarrasses herself by correcting Fong Quock, the local confectioner, the story spreads quickly; Emily will avoid him hereafter. Plans for the town library proceed, with Emily's mother having an elegant planning luncheon for the Ladies' Civic Club. The luncheon is even more memorable when it is interrupted by tipsy hogs who have eaten fermented apples, thanks to Emily: the making of her mother's party, Mr. Bartlett assures her.

Emily, who sees her runaway imagination as a horse, wishes it were one when Muriel, her cousin, visits. In love with horses, Muriel looks forward to riding one; and Emily finds herself bleaching a big, dingy draft horse into what the glow of sunset reveals as a snow-white steed. The next day it is only a clean plow horse, but Muriel is enchanted, and Emily tires of Muriel's ride around and around the barnyard long before Muriel does. A horseless carriage is another matter, and Emily has a memorable ride in her grandfather's after the clutch breaks down: each time they come to a gate, she must jump out, open it, and close it, and jump back into the automobile. When Emily's mother later admits that one must keep up with changing times, Emily reflects that, for her, it is almost too much keeping up with a tin Lizzie!

Through that busy summer, the library grows slowly and opens when books arrive from the state library. Emily reads *English Fairy Tales,* a wonderful book full of scary stories. When her cousin, June, spends the night, Emily tries to spice it with spooky stories but is halted by June's plow horse imagination. But even June's imagination rears in terror when the girls wake to a clanging and banging and a white, ghostly figure, which turns out to have no supernatural origin. Back in bed, Emily is glad that, "in a pinch," June's imagination runs away, too. In another incident, baking powder in the pie crust gives Emily a crust lighter than she had expected: the custard is on the bottom and the crust is on top! Saving herself by calling them "upside-down pies," Emily basks in praise for the flakiness of her crust.

The crops bring little this year, and hard times provide the theme of a party to raise money for books. Emily is not thrilled by wearing old clothes, and she dresses in her best, which seems a bit tight; she cannot get into her shoes, so her mother loans her an old pair of high heels. Realizing at the party that she was wrong to wear her finery, Emily is surprised to win a prize for her too-tight dress and too-big shoes. Giving her prize money to the library, Emily reflects that maybe times are not so hard after all. Fong Quock, who is returning to China, gives his house for the new library, and Emily is shamed by her avoidance of the lonely old man. She makes him a special valentine and feels doubly good: she has made up with Fong Quock and the town will have a new library, thanks to Emily and her runaway imagination.

Reviewers enjoyed both Emily and her imagination, approving of the way that this novel presents its period without overdoing the historical details. Charlotte Jackson, in the *Atlantic Monthly,* appreciated the book's "incredibly funny situations" and called it a book that would "enrapture" its audience; in the *Saturday Review,* Alice Dalgliesh pointed out that the book had "the fun that children have come to expect from this author."[13] The reviewer for the *Bulletin of the Center for Children's Books* felt that "Emily is vividly real, and the various incidents of her life are believable, humorous, and endearing. . . . [The book is] written in the artfully

artless style that marks true craftsmanship."[14] As a work of period fiction, the reviewers agreed, it shone: "The period details
lend color without being obtrusive, and the relationships and attitudes of the small town are described with a gentle affection,"
wrote the *Bulletin*'s reviewer; Dalgliesh, on the other hand, seems
to have wryly critiqued some historical fiction for children when
she noted that the book was "[a] good picture of the period, but
fortunately Emily is too lively to seem a 'period child'" (Dalgliesh,
36).

Lively little Emily is a Beverly who never had to leave golden
Yamhill for dreary Portland, a Beverly raised safe and snug in
the love of her family and neighbors. Pitchfork is peopled with
many of the inhabitants of Yamhill, though Cleary seems to have
changed a boy cousin to a girl cousin in order to give her protagonist what Beverly Bunn had yearned for: a playmate. Emphasizing the concerns of everyday life of the 1920s, this charming piece
of period fiction repudiates those historical novels that bored Beverly Bunn, who never again wanted to read a book about an Oregon pioneer girl running through the forest to warn settlers of
rampaging Indians ("Regina," 23). Cleary drew on her own experiences to emphasize that, while the trappings of daily life have
changed, the daily problems and emotions of children have not.

In fact, there is little direct mention of the period. References
to buggies and Liberty Bonds, and a visit to the general merchan-
dise store in the first chapter are the main historical indications.
Having eased the reader into Emily's time period in the first two
chapters, Cleary sets us more firmly in that period by discussing
the newfangled automobiles, electricity, and aviators—the pe-
riod-setting stuff less-confident writers would present immediately—in the next two chapters. Emily, not historical details, is
the focus of the work. Cleary uses Grandpa's tin Lizzie, her relatives' fancy new automobile, and the low-flying aviator only as
they relate to Emily, who is enchanted with these signs of progress and change. In her portrait of a young girl excited by progress, Cleary presents the reader with something more difficult to
get across, the mood of a time period. Emily, somewhat contemp-

tuous of horses and bewitched by Grandpa's tin Lizzie, excited
that Pitchfork is about to get a library like bigger, more modern
places have, and proud of her father's tractor, reflects the tenor
of her times, when anything seemed possible and progress was
nothing but good.

But this girl of the 1920s has the kinds of problems that link
her with her readers of the 1960s and later. Blessed with a vivid
imagination, Emily finds that it can be a problem—as when she
and June help each other imagine all sorts of frightening explanations for the spooky events of one night—or a blessing—as
when it inspires her mother to start a library in Pitchfork. Like
most of her readers, Emily has difficulty maintaining her dignity
in a world full of grown-ups. Like Cleary's earlier Ellen Tebbits,
Beverly Bunn herself, and most children, Emily takes herself seriously; careful of how she looks, she is just as self-conscious of
how she appears to others and dislikes being teased. She is defi-
nite about not wanting to dress humorously for the hard-times
party, and she is indignant when the ladies laugh at the tipsy
hogs. Grown-ups should understand how serious parties and
tipsy, expensive hogs really are.

In part, this self-conscious streak is compounded by Emily's
imagination, for it can exaggerate events. What Emily must discover is proportion: it is not so bad to be funny at the party when
you mean to be funny; drunken hogs are not damaged hogs. The
affectionate teasing of those who love you eventually comes to an
end. Taking action on your own part helps: when the custard pies
she bakes come out with their crusts on top instead of on the
bottom, Emily bluffs her way through the puzzlement of the people eating the pies by calling them "upside-down pies" and is complimented rather than teased. Having embarrassed herself by
absentmindedly correcting Fong Quock in the first chapter, Emily
avoids him for much of the reset of the book, hoping that passivity
will make everyone forget her gaffe. Her simple gesture at the
book's end is an apology and an affirmation of the old man's place
in her life while it also points out that taking action after a mis-
take can solve a lot of problems.

Ordinary Lives

Like Cleary's works about Henry Huggins and Ramona Quimby, these nonseries works soon were popular in the United States and abroad. *Otis Spofford* was one of the first of Cleary's works to be translated into another language (Fitzgibbons, 170); his adventures and those of Ellen Tebbits and Mitch and Amy were translated into Italian in the 1960s. Otis and Ellen may have lost something in the translation: in Italian, *Ellen Tebbits* is entitled *Il Segreto di Ellen*—"Ellen's Secret"—which could refer to the underwear she hides in the first chapter, or to any of the "secrets" she harbors in the course of the novel. The Italian version of *Otis Spofford,* according to Cleary, "had unusual illustrations which were reminiscent . . . of the illustrations in *Hans Brinker,* and created a most incredible effect" (Fitzgibbons, 170). Translated into Spanish, Mitch Huff underwent a name change when *Mitch and Amy* became *Mike y Amy*.

Written for the most part in the early 1960s, Cleary's nonseries books have a different emphasis from the series works she was then producing and planning. As Cleary showed her readers the growing-up process of Henry Huggins and planned the first book in which Ramona Quimby would appear as heroine of her own maturing process, in the nonseries works she described protagonists who are preoccupied not with growing up, but with the complexities of relationships. Though the children in these works enjoy feeling grown up, this does not have the emphasis it does in the works about Ramona Quimby and Henry Huggins. Henry was interested in growing up and acquiring the tangible signs of maturity; Ramona was interested in growing up and coming to terms with herself and those around her. In the nonseries books, it is relationships themselves that provide the focus and that give the reader a new slant on the way that other people act. In part, this deemphasis on growing up is due to the fact that the reader has no chance to watch a character mature through several books. While certain volumes in the Henry Huggins and Ramona Quimby series focus on the maturing process through which their protagonists are going, growing up is not mentioned in most of the nonseries works. It is an important part of the picture books involving Jimmy and Janet, especially of *The Growing-Up Feet*; and the theme of becoming an adult underlies *Lucky Chuck,* whose protagonist is learning both the pleasures and responsibilities of having his motorcycle license. In the works of modern and historical fiction, however, the emphasis is on relationships.

The focal relationships in most of the books are with peers, which is appropriate, for these often are the most compelling relationships for children the ages of the books' protagonists. Even in the adventures of Beaver Cleaver, Cleary has emphasized Beaver's relationships with his family (especially with his brother), sometimes altering the story to do so.

In *Ellen Tebbits,* the dynamics of being best friends come under scrutiny, with both the pleasant and unpleasant sides emphasized. The good side of having a best friend, Ellen and Austine realize, means having someone with whom to share embarrassing secrets. It also means having someone who will defend you against a bully like Otis Spofford. But having a best friend means fighting as well as sharing good times; and Cleary's detailing of the misperceptions and misapprehensions involved in Ellen and Austine's fight shows how and why things can go wrong.

Otis Spofford also focuses on friends and friendship, as Otis's need for excitement often overcomes any social graces he may possess. Always on the lookout for excitement, Otis is careless about his friends and friendships when he sees a chance for some fun. When he is overcome by the realization that as the front half of a bull he can hook the toreador in the pants during a mock bullfight, Otis ignores the fact that Stewy, as back half, is swatted each time they pass the toreador. It is Otis's need for excitement and his pride that lead him to cut a hunk out of Ellen's hair and earn the disapproval of his classmates. Otis's much-predicted comeuppance leaves him feeling misunderstood and sorry for himself, but unrepentant; Cleary makes her point about acting without thinking with much humor and with no preaching.

Mitch and Amy Huff find themselves struggling not only with each other, but with a violent bully, as Cleary explores the dynamics of twins: so much alike but so different, so close but still prone to sibling jealousy. *Mitch and Amy,* one of the longer and less humorous works Cleary has written for "middle-aged" children, presents one of the least-glamorized views of sibling relationships. Amy and Mitch bicker and irritate each other in that subtly devastating way that only the closest siblings know how to do. Amy, aware of how self-conscious Mitch is about his reading problem, cannot help feeling jealous about the extra time their mother spends listening to him read, so she cannot help doing the very things that will make him feel even worse. Mitch, bored on a rainy afternoon, interrupts Amy and her friends as they scrub the kitchen floor at intervals calculated to drive her to distraction. However, the twins support each other as only a loving brother and sister do. The strengths and weaknesses of each fit neatly into those of the other, with Mitch strong in math but weak in reading, and Amy weak in math and strong in reading. There is also the fact of their special relationship: both feel special about being twins. As a result, each helps the other overcome problems: Mitch helps Amy and her friends clear inch-deep lather from the kitchen floor, and Amy helps Mitch make the toothpick model of Sutter' sawmill; Mitch helps Amy learn the multiplication tables, and it is Amy who finds the book that interests Mitch enough to realize that reading can be entertaining. When bully Alan Hibbler threatens the two, they band together.

The main focus of *Emily's Runaway Imagination* is, of course, on the imagination. Emily's vivid imagination is both an asset and a trial: it leads to Pitchfork getting its library and magically turns a dingy-yellow plow horse into a snow-white steed for her horse-enraptured cousin; on the other hand, it gives her problems as she feeds fermented apples to the hogs and worries that Fong Quock wants to take her to China. Emily has problems with other people as well, especially with Fong Quock. Having absentmindedly corrected the man's pronunciation, Emily is too embarrassed to speak to him again, especially since the story has amused everyone in town. The climax of the book comes after Emily avoids Fong Quock as best she can while coming to realize how lonely and good-hearted he is; the valentine she gives him is as much an apology as it is a reminder for him that someone in Pitchfork is thinking of him.

Appropriately for works emphasizing the dynamics and nuances of relationships, here Cleary presents the reader with bullies who are surprisingly sympathetic and with parents who emerge from the background of the story to take increasingly active roles in the their children's lives. Not content with using a one-dimensional bully, Cleary shows hers as three-dimensional beings with motives and feelings. Otis Spofford, the essential overindulged bully in *Ellen Tebbits*, emerges in his own book as a boy who is not malicious, but just likes excitement, whose mother is too busy earning a living to make his life exciting; Alan Hibbler, the malicious bully of *Mitch and Amy*, is revealed as a boy with academic problems who is living in the shadow of his famous scientist father.

In the nonpicture books created from 1953 to 1967, there is a progression from parents who seem distant with few personal interests, to parents more fully active in their children's lives with quirks and interests of their own. Having created, in *Henry Huggins*, parents who stayed in the background, Cleary did this again in *Ellen Tebbits* and *Otis Spofford*: "They were there to be supportive when needed—the proper role, I had felt as a child, for adults. Children wanted to read about children; adults should mind their own business and stay out of the story as much as possible" ("Regina," 23). This is precisely the role played—or, perhaps, not played—by Ellen's and Otis's parents. Ellen's mother is there to sew for Ellen and make her wear long underwear; Otis's mother appears mostly to teach dancing and give Otis absentminded advice. Their fathers are immaterial: Otis's is never mentioned, and the inference from the books is that he has died or does not live with the family; Ellen's is barely mentioned. In the later *Emily's Runaway Imagination* and the later-still *Mitch and Amy*, the parents are a potent force in their children's lives, interacting with them and taking part in many of their activities. Emily helps her parents on the farm and accompanies them on outings; Amy and Mitch's parents drill them in school subjects and help them with projects and with Alan Hibbler.

The parents' individuality also comes to the fore. Just as Henry Huggins's mother seemed to stay in the background and keep house, so do the mothers of Ellen Tebbits and Austine Allen, who are described mostly in terms of what they do around the house. Ellen's mother appears to have no life outside her family and her home, and, in fact, seems a fanatical housekeeper: "The furniture was polished, the floors shone, and everything was in perfect order. Austine always felt she should be on her very best behavior, so she wouldn't leave marks on the floor or knock over a vase" (*Ellen*, 41). She also sews beautifully. Austine's mother stands in direct contrast, unable to sew and more relaxed about the house: "The furniture was old and comfortable, and there was nothing that could be easily broken. Best of all, Austine's mother did not mind the girls' making brownies in her kitchen. If they spilled cooky batter on the floor, she never said, 'Oh dear, my clean floor!' Instead, she found a cloth for wiping up the batter. Ellen thought this was a nice way for a mother to be" (*Ellen*, 41).

Otis Spofford's mother must work outside the home; though she stays mostly in the background in *Otis Spofford,* her dancing instruction gives her a dimension that Cleary's earlier mother figures do not have. Emily Bartlett's mother is more fully individual, with her "spunk," with her love of poetry, books, and a good laugh, and with her own life before Emily that included an episode with a runaway horse. Emily's handsome father, occupied with the cares of being a farmer, is necessarily a more vague figure, but it is clear that he, too, enjoys having fun. In Mitch and Amy's parents, Cleary has created loving, supportive adults who, nevertheless, are very much their own people. Sometimes lovingly ironic with their children, both clearly have interests outside their children: Mr. Huff is learning to play the banjo, while nearsighted Mrs. Huff learns to identify songbirds from their songs instead of their markings and struggles to learn French cooking from a television program. Bernadette Stumpf's mother does not even appear at home, for she is busy finishing her degree at the university, which she will earn after help from her children with her homework. A woman who does not "need neatness" (*Mitch*, 205) and who finds housework boring, she also is a woman whom

Ellen Tebbits's mother could never understand. None of these parents is perfect: the perfection of Ellen's house may explain Ellen's excessive tidiness, Otis's mother may indulge him because she feels she is neglecting him, and Amy and Mitch's parents give advice that does not always work; Bernadette's mother, who allows her messy house to keep itself because she is so busy with courses, is no superwoman. But all are loving parents, which is, for a child, crucial. In this progression from parents who stay safely in the background and carry on their lives out of the view of their children to parents whose activities and complex lives are intertwined with those of their children, Cleary paved the way for the complex interrelationship between Ramona Quimby and her parents in a series written mostly after the last of these other works appeared.

Certain aspects of the novels may make them seem a bit dated—the child whose parents buy milk at the supermarket may wonder about the frozen milk inching out of bottles in *Ellen Tebbits,* and that excitement over the new audiovisual equipment may seem strange to readers used to computers in school—but, as always, Cleary emphasizes the aspects of a child's life that do not change. From Emily, growing up in the 1920s, to Beaver Cleaver, the essence of the early 1960s, and Chuck, on his motorcycle in the 1980s, Cleary's characters are ordinary children, with ordinary concerns: being taken seriously in a small town prone to joking an amusing incident into rags, trying to make up with a former best friend, keeping away from the local bully, asserting independence by racing joyfully down the highway. Like many picture books, Cleary's works about Jimmy and Janet revolve around the small excitements of a small child's life, whether getting new boots, growing out of a babyish crib, or discovering that a parent does not know everything. The ordinary lives of these children are carefully detailed. Without becoming a dissertation on Oregon farm life in the 1920s, *Emily's Runaway Imagination* is rich in the details of such a life, from judging the temperature of a wood stove by touch before baking to the jostling ride in a tin Lizzie. The details in Cleary's works of contemporary life are equally compelling, from Ellen Tebbits's math problems with sevens and nines (*Ellen,* 46) to the explosion of energy in Otis Spof-

ford's classroom the instant the teacher leaves it in *Otis Spofford*
and the dull lives of the characters who live in reading books. The
realistic imperfection of the lives of Mitch and Amy Huff is lovingly created, with the fight between Mitch and Alan that contains more wrestling than punching and the painful agonies of a
slow reader struggling through a "babyish" primer. Television, increasingly important in daily life in the 1960s, takes on new importance in *Mitch and Amy*. Having painted a devastating
portrait of television cartoon shows and their impact and com-
mercialism in *Henry and the Clubhouse* in 1962, in 1967 Cleary
presented life firmly anchored in the electronic age. Amy and
Mitch's mother uses phonograph records to learn her birdsongs
and watches television to master the art of French cooking; Mitch
is scolded for watching too much television and decides that Alan
has learned his bullying and fighting techniques from television
programs. Classroom audiovisuals provide special interest, as the
students take math tests from a recording and realize that the
television programs they watch in school are not likely to be as
interesting as the ones they watch at home; Cleary neatly plays
with the comic possibilities by having the overloaded fuses in the
temporary classrooms blow each time someone plugs in a
projector.

Cleary's use of her own experience is, perhaps, more deeply
rooted in these novels than in any of her others. "I imagine I was
very much like Ellen Tebbits when I was her age," she has written
(Fitzgibbons, 169); to Ellen, she gave the ballet lessons she herself took in Portland, Oregon (*Yamhill*, 72) and the woolen underwear that she was forced to wear when she was eleven (*Yamhill*,
116). Beverly's episode as a "substitute lilac" in third grade, however, did not end as satisfactorily as Ellen's time as substitute rat
(*Yamhill*, 99–100). Otis's spitball cure may have come from an
incident when she was in the sixth grade, when garlic-chewing
boys were forced to chew garlic in the principal's office until they
were sick of it (*Yamhill*, 122–23). The adventures of Amy and
Mitch were based on those of Cleary's own twins when they were
in the fourth grade (Fitzgibbons, 169), but Mitch's discovery that
a book can be interesting parallels young Beverly Bunn's similar
discovery (*Yamhill*, 93), and Ellen's troubles with sevens and

nines in the multiplication table parallels Beverly's own problem (*Yamhill,* 97). Malcolm and Marianne also probably provided the impetus for the first of the picture books about Jimmy and Janet. The story of Emily's adventures in Pitchfork, Oregon, in the 1920s, is, of course, the most autobiographical of Cleary's works. Cleary has recalled *Emily's Runaway Imagination* with fondness, "both because it was fun to write and because of the response from people in Yamhill, Oregon, who remember the period and can identify with the characters" (Fitzgibbons, 169). Into this book are poured the memories of Cleary's childhood: the struggle to make a living on a small farm, the love of the people around her, the excitement of the new automobiles, and the difficulties of getting a town library. Like Emily's grandfather, Beverly's owned the local general store; Beverly's mother was responsible for the start of the county library just as Emily's mother is responsible for the library in Pitchfork. Fong Quock existed in the person of Quong Hop, with whom a bachelor neighbor made a deal to sell young Beverly for a nickel ("Books"). Glowing in nostalgia, Pitchfork is Yamhill, with Emily a Beverly who never had to leave the security of the place where she was loved.

As she did in her series about Henry Huggins and Ramona Quimby, in these individual works Cleary has championed the ordinary child who, like Beaver Cleaver, is "just trying to get through till tomorrow."[15] As always, children responded, which gave Cleary a fresh look at books for children. Having learned in library school that "girls would read about boys, but boys would not read about girls," Cleary rethought this statement in light of the letters she received about *Ellen Tebbits*: "Gradually I saw that these generalizations did not hold if children found books funny. Many boys wrote telling me they had enjoyed *Ellen Tebbits*" ("Laughter," 561). It was this kind of response that led her to write the Ramona books. Laughing over the adventures of Ellen or Otis, boys and girls showed that they could enjoy a book written about characters very different from themselves, as long as it was funny. Cleary exploited this discovery further in works about an ordinary cat and an extraordinary mouse who have, basically, much the same kinds of problems their readers do.

5

A Cat and a Mouse

Just as Cleary's first book, *Henry Huggins,* was a response to the young readers she had met as a children's librarian, so her first work of fantasy, the adventures of a mouse with a motorcycle, was an answer to the needs of her own two children. *The Mouse and the Motorcycle,* published in 1965, was the first of a trilogy about Ralph S. Mouse, a tiny being with an enormous love of motorcycles.[1] Having chronicled the adventures of a mouse, in 1973, with nonfantasy *Socks* Cleary made her readers privy to the thoughts and emotions of a cat.[2] Though the works about an ordinary cat and an extraordinary mouse focus on the adventures of animals, they do not depart from the Cleary tradition: Socks and Ralph struggle with many of the problems their readers do and learn for themselves the pain and loneliness and the triumphs of growing up.

A Mouse and His Motorcycle

The Mouse and the Motorcycle

The Mouse and the Motorcycle, illustrated by Louis Darling, resulted from a reading problem, a vacation, and a trapped mouse. Having struggled with her own reading problems, Cleary was sympathetic to those of her "right-handed, left-eyed" son, Malcolm, who floundered through boring primers that seemed little help in overcoming his difficulty. As a writer who had published seventeen novels, Cleary seemed in a position to help him:

> I asked him what he would like to read about, thinking perhaps I could write a book that would help him over the hump. "Motorcycles" was the unequivocal answer, and I was stopped. Seven-year-old boys can't ride motorcycles. His sister, when the same question was put to her, for the mother of twins must always try to be impartial, answered, "A nice little animal." A nice little animal riding a motorcycle, I thought with amusement and dismissed the idea because I was not a writer of fantasy.
>
> The more our son struggled with reading, the more he pored over the illustrations of motorcycles in the encyclopedia. Could it be, I wondered, if more small boys really learned to read and to read with pleasure, there would be fewer big boys roaring along the highways on motorcycles? When I found that our library had no books on motorcycles for young boys whose reading was shaky, I began to mull over motorcycles. ("Low," 291)

It was two years, however, before the book's next element was added. On vacation in England, the Clearys found themselves among only a handful of guests in an enormous and somehow haunting old hotel. In the middle of the night, Malcolm ran a fever, but his anxious parents could find no aspirin; the next morning, after his fever was down, his parents bought him toy automobiles and a toy motorcycle: "As he played with the toys on the stripes of his bedspread, he seemed lost in some boyish fantasy of speed and danger, a small fantasy satisfying to a boy who was sick in bed and who was happily entertaining himself with dreams of cars and—most of all—of a motorcycle" ("Low," 292).

The final element appeared after the family returned home to California when a neighbor showed Cleary a mouse that had somehow trapped itself, and the book planned itself: "The thought crossed my mind that this mouse was exactly the right size to ride the miniature motorcycle my son had brought from England. A little animal on a motorcycle, a book for both my children! A story began to fall into place. The spooky old hotel must have had mice, and somewhere under a bureau or in a corner, there must have been an aspirin tablet. If only there had been a mouse to ride out into the night—" ("Low," 293). An American who had spent only five weeks in England, Cleary moved the hotel to the more familiar California Sierras, and Ralph's saga was begun.

As the book opens, someone watches as the Gridley family checks into the old Mountain View Inn. It is Ralph, a mouse in whose soul reverberates the sound Keith Gridley makes as he runs his toy cars. In Keith's absence, Ralph investigates the toy motorcycle, accidentally coasting it into the trashcan. Returning, Keith is puzzled to find his motorcycle in the trashcan; seeing Ralph, he realizes that—though it cannot possibly be—Ralph must have ridden it there. When Keith talks to Ralph, Ralph talks back: because both love motorcycles, they naturally speak the same language. After Keith is tucked into bed, Ralph is rescued and offered a ride on the motorcycle; the trick is to get onto the machine and make the "Pb-pb-b-b-b-b" sound a motorcycle makes. Ralph races around in the moonlight, ecstatic, as Keith watches.

The two agree that Keith will use the motorcycle during the day and Ralph will use it at night. Zooming around the hotel is wonderful, though Keith's mother gets a glimpse of Ralph as he returns; she will report the mouse sighting to the manager. Chastened by Keith's scolding, Ralph nevertheless complains that Keith's family is too tidy, leaving no crumbs for mice, and

Keith agrees to bring the mice whatever they want. Ralph's family, appalled that Ralph is associating with humans, is mollified by the peanut butter sandwich Keith delivers.

That afternoon, Ralph gets into trouble. Admiring the motorcycle, which is parked under Keith's bed, Ralph is almost sucked into the vacuum cleaner. Clinging desperately to the motorcycle, Ralph struggles to get away but is not strong enough to push it out of the suction; he tries to ride out instead—only to shoot into the dirty laundry when the vacuum is unplugged. Lost in laundry, Ralph is dumped into a hamper and must abandon the motorcycle to chew his way to freedom. Scolded by his relatives and by Keith for losing the motorcycle, Ralph spends a sad and lonely night watching the night from Keith's window, returning home to find his family in hysterics: the hotel housekeeper found the holes Ralph had chewed in the laundry and declared war on mice, so the family must flee the hotel for the treacherous outdoors. Ralph decides that instead the family will remain quiet and eat sparingly of food Keith brings them, for eventually the management will forget them.

At first, Ralph's plan works. But Keith becomes ill: that night, Keith is feverish, but there are no aspirin. So Ralph begins an epic search of the hotel over the objections of his family, who remember that Ralph's father had died trying to transport an aspirin in his cheek pouch. But Ralph delivers the aspirin he finds safely and in style. Having proved that he is growing up to be a responsible mouse, Ralph is a hero to his family and to Keith, who gives Ralph the motorcycle, which was found in the laundry. Keith will put it under the television in the lobby, where the maid never vacuums. Ralph will be the perfect subject of the summer-vacation essay Keith probably will have to write, impressing the teacher with his imagination.

Reviewers were just as impressed with Cleary's imagination, emphasizing the fantasy's "down-to-earth" qualities while pointing out its humor and crystalline imagination. "Although it is a feet-on-the-ground fantasy . . ., it is quite refreshing after some of the overcooked fantasies we've been having," asserted the reviewer in the *Saturday Review*.[3] *Horn Book* called it an "honest, unpretentious book, briskly matter-of-fact in style, but imaginative in plot" and noted that "amusing, realistic details worked into an ingenious pattern lend conviction" to the book.[4]

It is through these details that Cleary reminds the reader that she is writing about a mouse, while presenting Ralph as a kind of substitute boy. As she had shown the reader life from a dog's viewpoint in *Ribsy,* published the year before, so here she presents a mouse's-eye view of life. It is a slightly skewed view of the human world; Ralph sees the human world from a few inches above the ground and filtered through a mouse's senses. His is a dangerous life: Cleary's descriptions of the owl-infested darkness of night outside the inn, of the difficulties in climbing out of a steel trashcan, and of the dangers a linen pillowcase can hold make the reader aware of just how hazardous the world can be to a being measured in inches rather than in feet. It is a life in which practicality comes first: enmeshed in the day-to-day struggle to eat, Ralph and his family have little time to waste on anything not directly linked to survival.

It is essentially a powerless life. Ralph and his family are at the mercy of the hotel management and the hotel guests. While they more or less have the run of the hotel after dark, few dare to go down to the ground floor, where poison and traps may lurk. Ralph's family depends on the messiness of the hotel guests, whose dropped crumbs provide food. Their very existence depends on humans, for once the management discovers Ralph's existence, the family has a choice between traps and cats or the terrible, dangerous outdoors. Mice may seem carefree, Cleary shows us, but they are not. Their lives are hemmed in by danger and the powerlessness of the very small; it's no wonder they are as timid as, well, as mice.

Thus, part of the attraction of the book is in giving power to the powerless. Dependent on his four feet, Ralph can escape only as quickly as he can run away, and he can carry only what will fit into his cheek pouches. On the motorcycle, however, he has mobility and freedom as he zips down the hotel corridors; Ralph's world widens with the amount of territory he can now cover. Seated on the motorcycle, Ralph feels capable and independent;

this confidence carries over into his life on four feet, as he begins
to take charge after the housekeeper finds where he has chewed
through the laundry. Ralph's independence and capability contrast with the old powerlessness of the mice when he parallels his
father in transporting an aspirin tablet. Ralph's father died; the
reminder of this adds an edge to Ralph's search for an aspirin for
Keith, for the reader wonders how he will transport it without
being poisoned himself. But the aspirin incident also shows how
Ralph's situation has improved, for he has what his father did
not: transportation. Using the toy ambulance to carry the aspirin,
Ralph proves himself to his family and to Keith and shows how
far from powerlessness he has come.

Watching her son lost in playing with his toy cars, Cleary
sensed that his were dreams of speed and power; and in Ralph
she offers us a mouse who is, essentially, a substitute for a small
boy. He relates to Keith on a mouse level, but also on a boy level:
they can communicate because they both love powerful machines.
Like a boy, Ralph is in love with speed and machines and feeling
free and is beset by a mother who seems to worry too much. An
adult, thinking of those traps and cats and poisons and owls, can
sympathize with her fears, which seem overblown to the eyes of
a child. Ralph shows the determination Cleary has given all her
child protagonists. Growing up is at the heart of the novel, as
Ralph learns responsibility. In a sense, Ralph becomes Keith's alter ego as he whisks across the hotel floor on the toy motorcycle;
Keith, like Cleary's son, is too young to have a motorcycle of his
own, but he can enjoy watching Ralph. It is as if Keith were on
the motorcycle instead. For the reader, too, Ralph seems a kind
of alter ego: most of Cleary's readers are too young to ride motorcycles but, through the medium of the book, can glide with him
down the long, dark hallways, thrilling to the roar of a wonderful
machine.

Runaway Ralph

Ralph's adventures were continued in 1970, after Cleary had published *Mitch and Amy* and the first book to focus specifically on
Ramona Quimby, *Ramona the Pest*. *Runaway Ralph*—one of the

last works illustrated by Louis Darling, who died in 1970—is a
tale of the open road, the story of a mouse in search of freedom
who gets more than he bargained for.

Every night, on the stroke of nine, Ralph hears a distant bugle
playing taps from a summer camp. Nagged and pestered by his
large family, Ralph begins to look at the camp as a wonderful
retreat and resolves to run away. Ralph's independence is put to
the test that night when he must figure out for himself how to
get his motorcycle down the steps of the hotel's porch, but then
he is off to the camp, near children with peanut butter and jelly
sandwiches. Camp is not at all what Ralph had pictured: he is
challenged by the camp's watchdog and caught by one of the
camp' cats to serve as an educational tool for a litter of kittens.

In the nick of time, Ralph is rescued by Garf, a discontented
camper who puts him into a cage in the craft shop. Here Ralph's
life is quiet and safe and dull. But Garf's care is sporadic and
secretive, and the camper's songs he sings are shocking. Then
Ralph becomes Garf's "personul mowse" after the camp's director
learns that Garf does not want others feeding the mouse; feeling
special, Ralph decides to speak to Garf.

This is easier decided than done, for now Ralph and Garf are
never alone. Claustrophobic in his cage, Ralph longs for freedom
and even for the hotel and his family, but especially for his motorcycle. On a day when a camper leaves her watch in the craft
shop, the camp cat forces his way into the room when no one is
around. But when Catso finally pounces, it is on the ticking
watch, which he carries out and leaves in the bamboo. When he
is blamed for the theft, Garf retreats to the bamboo, and suddenly
Ralph hears the familiar sound of a boy imitating a motorcycle;
Garf has found his motorcycle.

Garf stays away from the craft shop until he is forced by the
director to take care of Ralph, and Garf's "personul mowse" gets
his chance to speak. Though he finally believes what Ralph tells
him about the motorcycle, Garf does not believe what he tells him
about Catso's stealing the watch. That afternoon, with everyone
away on a picnic, Catso gets into the shop and, ironically, gives
Ralph his freedom. After Ralph shows Garf the watch, the boy

finally believes him. When Garf points out that the tires of Ralph's motorcycle are too smooth for the ride back to the hotel, and the trip (all uphill) will be too far for a mouse, they strike a bargain. Ralph will return the watch so that the others will not think that Garf had stolen it, and Garf will take Ralph and his motorcycle back to the hotel.

After a long night, Ralph still has not found a way to return the watch. However, he sees his chance when the girls in the camp spread their sleeping bags to air. Chewing a hole in the sleeping bag of the watch's owner, Ralph drags the watch into the lining and, exhausted, falls asleep in the soft filling; he wakes to find that he has been made up in the bed at rest time. Captured by squealing girls, Ralph is given to Garf and rests in his pocket, secure in the knowledge that he is going home.

The sequel to Ralph's first adventures struck one reviewer as being a bit below par, though another did not agree. "It is inevitable that the sequel . . . should lack some of the impact of the first book," admitted the reviewer in *Horn Book*, "but the new story is constructed with much the same combination of simplicity, realistic detail, ingenuity, and humor that made the earlier book a resounding success."[5] *Saturday Review* noted no falling off, asserting that the book's "combination of reality and fantasy is deft, the depiction of camp life delightfully wry, and the saga of Ralph's adventures a musine triumph."[6]

Ralph's triumph is again a story of mobility and power, this time emphasizing determination and the perils of too much independence. As before, Cleary presents us with a mouse's-eye view of the world: a world in which a car's backwash holds danger for a tiny being on a toy motorcycle and the deep softness of a sleeping bag's padding provides an idyllic place to sleep. Also as before, she presents us with a mouse who is very much a mouse but also very much a small boy. He is, as Cleary's child protagonists usually are, persistent in solving his problems; despite the dangers, Ralph ingeniously gets his motorcycle out of the inn. Like any child, in love with the speed and freedom of his motorcycle, Ralph is not pleased to share his marvelous machine with the younger mice. Even his adult relatives seem to pester a bit too much. Like many a child before him, Ralph decides that the only solution to his troubles is to run away to where he can be independent.

Freedom and independence have their perils, however, especially when one is small enough to ride a toy. Captured by Garf and kept in a cage in the camp craft shop before he has been at the camp even a day, Ralph soon realizes just what a real prison is like and how free his life at the inn has been by comparison. The irony of Ralph's independence being thus curtailed reemphasizes his basic helplessness: the helplessness of the small in a very large world. In *The Mouse and the Motorcycle,* Cleary had shown us how much the mice depend on humans for food and their very survival; at the beginning of *Runaway Ralph,* she shows how difficult just leaving the inn can be for this tiny being. Having served as an educational toy for some bored kittens, Ralph now must be rescued by Garf. The tiny cage the independent freedom-seeker now inhabits is, ironically, the only place he is safe from the camp cat, which Cleary emphasizes during the tense chase through the craft shop after Catso accidentally sets Ralph free. Caged, Ralph must rely on Garf for everything, but so must Garf rely on Ralph. Accused of stealing another camper's watch, Garf cannot defend himself and must depend on Ralph to set things straight, something Ralph cannot do without the cooperation of the camp dog. Independence is good in small doses, Cleary emphasizes, but no one can be really independent from others.

Once again, Ralph finds himself relating to a boy on a boy's level, sharing a love of speed and freedom. But Garf is very different from Keith. Where Keith seems to be a happy boy content to be on vacation with his parents, Garf is not. Because his parents believe a city child should be kept busy and thus out of trouble, Garf is shuttled from activity to activity after school and on weekends; he resents being sent to camp for the summer. He never seems to have time to be alone, for the activities keep him busy, and he rarely has the room he shares with his older brother to himself. Pointing out that one cannot really be independent of the responsibility of family and friends, Cleary also notes the importance of being able to be by oneself: once Garf knows that Ralph is his "personul mowse" and has a place to go and sit, he happily takes part in camp activities. He seems to discover what the head of the camp tells him, that it is possible to be alone in his thoughts, even surrounded by other people (103). Perhaps what Ralph needs to learn is to be independent in his mind, even when he is pestered by other mice.

Ralph S. Mouse

Ralph's admirers had to wait twelve years for the final volume of his adventures. *Ralph S. Mouse,* published in 1982, is Ralph's grand finale, as he trades his motorcycle in on something considerably larger. He also has a new illustrator: in the hands of Paul O. Zelinsky, the delicate little scrap of mousedom that Louis Darling had drawn gave way to a small but sturdy little adventurer; in the illustration across from the title page, he needs only a leather jacket with the slogan "Hell on Wheels" to be the image of the motorcycle tough.

Ralph has troubles: his rough, outdoor relatives, who have moved into the hotel to escape the cold, challenge his right to have a motorcycle that he will not allow them to ride, and the motorcycle is wearing out. Worse, the dirty, mousy lobby has enraged the manager, who may get an electronic mouser. Frightened for his family and guilty because he and his motorcycle are responsible for his young relatives dirtying the lobby, Ralph has Ryan Bramble, the housekeeper's son, take him and his motorcycle to school.

School is boring and, snug in Ryan's shirt pocket, Ralph is seen poking out his head. But Ryan's teacher is the sort who admires Ralph and sees a chance to use him as an educational tool. Having introduced Ralph as "Ralph S. (for Smart) Mouse," Ryan will prove how smart Ralph is by building a maze for him to run at the end of the week with scoffing Brad helping. Ralph watches with apprehension, for Ryan has taken his motorcycle to ensure his cooperation, and Ralph worries that the maze will be too hard. Surveying the long, smooth halls so perfect for motorcycle riding, Ralph is frustrated and, finally, lonely in the silent school.

The rest of the week, he dreads Friday. Exploration fills the nights, with Ralph once narrowly escaping death by Scotch tape. Popped into a fishbowl as a visual aid, Ralph awaits his test and listens to the base libel of the students' poems, stories, and reports, including one on the destructiveness of mice, which is covered by local newspaper reporters. When it is at last time to run the maze, Ralph is limp with worry, and confused, for the peanut butter at the end of the maze is hard to smell over the other odors in the room. Running into walls, Ralph knows that he is disappointing Ryan and is suddenly angry because he *is* smart and should not have to prove it. Galloping across the top of the maze walls is efficient, if not what Ryan has in mind, but his disgust is nothing to Ralph's fury when, in the course of a fight between Ryan and Brad, the motorcycle is broken. Ralph spends a forlorn weekend missing the hotel, his family, and his motorcycle.

Monday, the students are grumpy, for the article in the newspaper made it seem as if Ralph were part of a mouse plague at school. Tired of school and of being blamed for everything and unable to face his jeering relatives at the hotel, Ralph needs a new place to live and a way to get there. He talks to Brad, who had shown an interest in motorcycling; Brad's shock at being spoken to by a mouse does not preclude his helping the mouse (after being set straight on what he sees as Ryan's rather glamorous life in the hotel). He and Ryan take Ralph back to the hotel and present him with a mouse-sized Laser XL7 sports car that looks like a dream. Ralph learns to make a new sports car noise but otherwise is speechless with ecstasy, and he uses techniques learned from the classroom to control his young relatives. Six months later, Ryan's mother and Brad's father marry, and Ralph rides every night in the lobby, giving rides to his relatives though he is the only one to drive.

One reviewer felt that the plot of *Ralph S. Mouse* was "not as interesting nor as fast moving as the previous Ralph titles," but conceded that "children will eagerly read these further adventures of Ralph and will ask for more," for "all the elements that make Cleary popular with children are present here"—a judgment with which other reviewers agreed.[7] "The story is a deft blend of realism and fantasy, quietly and consistently funny, and occasionally touching without being the least saccharine," wrote the reviewer for the *Bulletin of the Center for Children's Books,*[8] while the reviewer for *Horn Book* pointed out that "the author's ability to perceive the thoughts of children—and of mice—has not deserted her."[9] Both reviewers noted the special quality of the book's classroom scenes. The *Bulletin* called them "most diverting; Cleary captures the essence of classroom bickering and the warm relationship between a good teacher and her students" (*Bulletin,* "S. Mouse," 5). *Horn Book* agreed and noted Cleary's ability to write on two levels at once: "Full of amusing vignettes and sudden insights, the classroom is vividly set forth, with each child thoroughly individualized. The book reflects two levels of experience—an unsophisticated child's (or mouse's) and, at the same time and in some magical way, that of the adult with its hopeful, but worldly, point of view" (*Horn Book,* "S. Mouse," 648).

This last work about Ralph S. Mouse finds him still in thrall to power and mobility, still independent, and still pestered by his relatives. As before, Cleary presents us with a mouse's-eye view of our world: a world in which Scotch tape can be deadly and a padded envelope can seem a ready-chewed mouse nest. With Ralph, the reader stifles in Ryan's pocket, unable to hear much over the steady lub-lub of his heart and glories in zipping through puddles a few millimeters deep.

In her books about humans, Cleary adeptly presents scenes that an adult can enjoy on one level, while a child can enjoy it on another. Here, as she had in *Socks,* she allows the child to stand with the adult, having more experience of the human world than does the unsophisticated animal protagonist. Having little experience of the world outside the inn, Ralph is unable to explain all he sees on television and at school; and his interpretations of toothpaste commercials and classrooms are as humorous to a child reader as they are to an adult reader. Seeing teachers on toothpaste commercials, Ralph wonders where Ryan's teacher, Miss K, keeps hers; confronted with the scientific views of mice as he listens to reports during the Great Mouse Exhibit, Ralph dismisses them as base libel. In this scene Cleary sets up a playful contrast between reality and "reality," as her fictional mouse character listens in horror to the information the children have collected from books and gives it his own twist, giving the reader the "real" version. A book may say that mice are harmful and destructive, but Ralph knows that they are really just trying to survive. Also, a book may say that mice multiply quickly, but Ralph has watched Miss K multiply on the blackboard and has never seen a mouse do anything like that. From an author who the next year would point up the value of library research in *Dear Mr. Henshaw*, it is a nice little piece of satire.

Ralph is still very much the substitute young boy as he fights with his relatives and glories in speeding, but he is growing up. Though he again leaves the inn as he had in *Runaway Ralph*, it is not simply to run away from his pesky younger relatives but to save their lives: attracted by his motorcycle, they dirty the lobby and enrage the management, which threatens to demouse the inn permanently. Wishing to escape his young relatives, Ralph also hopes his action will keep them out of the lobby. When he returns, he is a Ralph more able to control the younger mice; like a child, Ralph learns a few things at school, though they are not quite the expected things. Instead of math and science, he picks up techniques for controlling youngsters from Ryan's teacher: techniques that get better results than had calling his relatives "rotten little rodents." Ralph also is growing into a more sophisticated means of transportation as well: the motorcycle a teenager would glory in is wearing out, and at the end of the novel Ralph is the proud owner of a fabulous sports car that is a young professional's dream. Having sped with Ralph down the inn's corridors in *The Mouse and the Motorcycle* and sailed down the highway with him in *Runaway Ralph*, the young reader can now vicariously zoom through the shadows of the inn in the shadow-colored Laser XL7.

It is one of the ironies of this series that this independent-minded little being is essentially helpless because of his size. At the mercy of cats and owls, Ralph also finds himself at the mercy of humans. In this work, there is no exception. The mice live in the inn under constant fear of the manager and his efforts to get rid of them; the electronic demouser could drive them out of the inn and into an equally brutal world where they are prey to an infinite number of predators. Seeking to save his relatives by leaving, Ralph must rely on Ryan to help him get away, and then finds himself at Ryan's mercy at school: Ryan will give Ralph his motorcycle to ride only after Ralph obliges him by running a maze. His prison is larger than the one he lived in in *Runaway Ralph,* but without his motorcycle for transportation it is still a prison.

Humans find independence difficult, too. Like Garf in *Runaway Ralph,* Brad is a loner who makes himself independent of those around him. Unhappy in his one-parent home, Brad does not forge many friendships at school. However, building the maze for the Great Mouse Exhibit, Brad seems to find himself enjoying his interaction with Ryan; getting a toy sports car for the great Ralph project seals their friendship. When his father marries Ryan's mother, lonely Brad gets a brother.

Socks

While Cleary was busily chronicling the adventures of a mouse, she also wrote the biography of a cat. *Socks,* published in 1973, is the story of a young cat who, unlike Ralph, does not speak with the humans in his life, but whose range of emotional responses is wide and deep. Whereas Cleary's earlier work about an animal (*Ribsy*) alternated between the points of view of Ribsy and his distraught master, *Socks* is told completely from the cat's point of view, with the reader experiencing the sometimes-confusing human world from a much different point of view.

The young Bricker couple buys Socks, and they make him right at home, allowing Socks to do as he pleases. Socks grows up loving, loved, and very determined to get his own way. Then to Socks's dismay, Mrs. Bricker's lap gets smaller and smaller, until one day Socks falls off it; his disciplining of the couple when they laugh at him fails when the Brickers put him in the basement and leave. In the next days, Socks is alone all day, dejected and confused. With the return of Mrs. Bricker, a new threat enters

Socks's life, for she carries a strange creature, which obviously is a new pet to threaten his position in the family. It seems to be a very small person. The Brickers's attention to Charles William Bricker is most annoying, for it proves to Socks that they love the baby more than they do him.

Suddenly his ordered life is completely upset; his one comfort is the baby's leftover formula. Depressed, Socks gets lazier and lazier. When Socks's weight gain is pointed out to the Brickers, he is put on a diet; Socks decides that, since the Brickers will not feed him properly, he must live by his wits. This works better in theory than in practice, for Socks's attempts to beg around the neighborhood fail. Then something lovely happens one night when the Brickers go out, leaving Charles and Socks with a sitter. Mrs. Risley is a dream: she knows how to satisfy both baby and cat, and after a contented Charles is put to bed, Mrs. Risley strokes Socks and strokes him and strokes him, until he no longer feels empty inside.

Socks's life is upset again when Mrs. Bricker's mother visits: when, in the upset household, Socks nips Mrs. Bricker on the ankle to remind her to feed him, he is abruptly shoved outside. Now comes a terrible time in Socks's life when he becomes an outdoor cat for Charles's protection. Lonely, he watches the family through the window, but loneliness is the least of his troubles, for he is bullied by the neighborhood tough cat, getting the worst of it when he must fight him. Realizing that Socks cannot care for his wounds himself, the Brickers take him into the house to care for him, finally giving him the attention he craves. Socks becomes an indoor cat again, with the Brickers keeping a strict eye on him, though he works to avoid the inquisitive child. Charles then recognizes the kitty by saying his first word: "Ticky."

Child and cat are never left alone together until one afternoon when Socks enters Charles's room and Charles shows what a big boy he is by rocking his crib to block the door. To amuse Socks, he rips the cotton out of his crib bumper, tossing it into the air for the cat to chase. Each entertains the other until Charles falls asleep and Socks, happy with such a good playmate, cuddles close against him in the crib. Seeing this comfortable little tableau through the window, Mrs. Bricker gives Socks permission to stay, and Socks sleeps deeply for the first time in a long time.

As the reviewer for the *Bulletin of the Center for Children's Books* predicted, this work has not attracted as much critical attention as have Cleary's other works, though it is popular among her young readers: "Not being child-centered, this may have a smaller audience than earlier Cleary books."[10] It seems to have attracted only a handful of reviewers. While *Publishers Weekly* noted that the story had "triteness and predictability" but would "no doubt be popular, for the prolific author has legions of fans,"[11] other reviewers enjoyed the book's humor. The *Bulletin* praised the "hilarious true-to-life episode" in which Socks "achieves the Ultimate Goal" and gets to know Charles, going on to say that the book "is written with the same easy grace, the same felicitous humor and sharply observant eye" as earlier books. Judy Staley, in *Children's Book Review Service,* simply called the book "clearly Cleary and great!"[12]

Just as Cleary had succeeded in placing the reader in Ribsy's point of view in *Ribsy,* and just as she had made the reader aware of the implications of being Ralph S. Mouse, so in *Socks* she places us in the mind of a kitten. She not only presents the world from another point of view, but shows that some emotions are not limited to only one species. Though Socks is a cat, Cleary uses his story to explore the dynamics of a changing family, with Socks as older sibling.

Presenting a character who is undeniably feline, Cleary succeeds in making this character seem a real, three-dimensional personality and makes him sympathetic even to non-cat lovers. Seeing the world filtered through the eyes of a cat, the reader gets a good sense of Socks's "catness" as the shift in viewpoint reflects a skewed world. Socks has no special knowledge of the human world around him and usually does not understand what is going on. Knowing only that he feels empty inside after the baby comes and the preoccupied Brickers pay less attention to him, Socks does not know exactly what has caused that emptiness, just as he does not analyze why he feels so good during Mrs. Risley's stroking. Like any other cat, Socks asks nothing more from life than to be loved and fed and cared for. Seeing things through his eyes, the reader sees a world bigger than usual, where the warm hood of a car makes a good place for sleeping and an old tomcat is a monster. After the first chapter, we understand what it might be like to be a kitten dropped into a mailbox, on a slithery pile in the sweltering dark. Much of the fun of reading *Socks* is not simply getting into the mind of an animal, but seeing the human world from another perspective, attempting to discern reality from Socks's experience. Reading about Mrs. Bricker's lap growing smaller and smaller, the reader suspects what is really happening. This suspicion is confirmed when the couple abruptly leaves for some mysterious place, a suspicion also confirmed in Beatrice Darwin's accompanying illustration, which shows a lonely Socks awaiting his owners in a living room with *Parents* magazine on the floor.

Though he is a cat, Socks demonstrates some of the effects of a changing family, as he becomes a substitute older sibling for Charles. Secure in the love of his owners, Socks is the pampered and undisputed ruler of all he surveys until Charles is born. Then Socks's life changes in ways parallel to the kinds of changes older siblings experience. Suddenly no longer the center of attention, Socks interprets this as being unloved by the Brickers; the visits of other people to see the baby do nothing to remedy this, for the attention to Charles is not balanced by attention to Socks. The Brickers's attempt to put Socks on a diet only exacerbates things; Socks feels emotionally locked out of the family unit. His bid for attention also is misinterpreted, as a sibling's bid for attention sometimes is—though no sibling would be physically locked out of the family as Socks is. Like any older sibling, Socks must find his own niche in the new family, his own way of dealing with the new baby and the changed situation.

Appropriately, Charles is not passive in this process: he seems to relate to Socks as younger siblings do to older siblings, enjoying Socks's company and striving for his attention. Left alone by Mr. and Mrs. Bricker, the two work out a relationship that satisfies both as it ensures peace in the family. Though on one level it is a cat story, on another level *Socks* looks at family dynamics from the outside in a way that may make it more meaningful to its young audience; watching a family cat deal with a new family member, a reader in the same type of situation can not only sympathize but learn.

Cat and Mouse

Like most of Cleary's work, the books about Ralph and Socks were soon available at home and abroad; *The Mouse and the Motorcycle* was translated into another medium when it was filmed as an episode of ABC's "Weekend Special," a Saturday morning program, in the early 1980s. *Socks* was published in a large-type edition in 1980, and Ralph's adventures were made available in Swedish, German, Spanish, and French; beginning in 1975, the works were published in Great Britain. Praising *The Mouse and the Motorcycle* in a backhanded swipe at Ramona Quimby, a British reviewer wrote that "this talking mouse seems more realistic than the same author's kindergarten pupil, Ramona" and enjoyed the "cheerful book" and "lighthearted story" in which Ralph's adventures were chronicled.[13] *Runaway Ralph* did not fare well, with another reviewer feeling it lacked depth:

The tale is a rather trivial one, made so not by the actual story which shows some originality but in the somewhat dull, pedestrian and offhand way in which it is written. There is some attempt at characterisation and interplay of feeling . . ., but one feels constantly that the author never really becomes sufficiently interested in the people involved, or in the action of the story. Imagination on the part of the author seems to stop short when feelings and reactions could have been explored in greater depth. Younger children will enjoy the story but it will leave no lasting impression, while older children who may read the book will sense the absence of the exploration of undertones which are only implied or touched upon very superficially. The illustrations too have no distinctive quality to enhance the text.[14]

But most of Cleary's fans do not read reviews, and Ralph has proved himself popular with young American readers. In 1975, Caroline Bauer noted that "motel managers all around the country are finding food purposely left in rooms just in case a mouse like Ralph might live there" (Bauer, 359); in 1979, not only were children's librarians finding *The Mouse and the Motorcycle* was the most popular of Cleary's books, but Cleary was learning from her male fans' letters that it often joined the Henry Huggins books as "the first book the boy enjoyed reading" (Roggenbuck, 58, 60).

Though the protagonists in these works are not the "ordinary children" with whom Cleary usually concerns herself, the works are not that different from her others. As usual, there is an emphasis on humor, what two critics have called "the matter-of-fact humor she does so well" (Burns and Hines, 746). Typically, much of this humor works on two levels, entertaining both unsophisticated and experienced readers. Whereas there is the simple, broad humor that appeals to the unsophisticated reader, there is also a more sophisticated kind of humor, as a cat and a mouse struggle to understand human culture. Having seen teachers in television commercials, Ralph wonders where Miss Kuckenbacker keeps the toothpaste such teachers are so excited about; he also knows that mice do not multiply as rapidly as a boy reports, for he has seen Miss K multiply with chalk on the chalkboard, and he has never seen a mouse do this (*Ralph S. Mouse*, 40–41, 85). Much of the humor of Socks's playing with Nana Bricker's wig is that emphasis on the puzzlingly–unattached hair the color of iced tea (*Socks*, 99, 107). Also, Socks's preferring overweight Mrs. Risley's plump-thighed lap over those of the fashionably thin might amuse an adult more than a child (92–93). Most important, these works about a cat and a mouse are also about the importance of family life and the difficulties and triumphs of growing up.

Ralph and Socks are learning to be grown up, in much the way Cleary's human protagonists are learning to be grown up in their own works. This is not to say that the two protagonists are not true to their species. In Ralph's preoccupation with gathering food, his dislike of feeling human skin against his paws, and his fear of owls, cats, and dogs, he is very much a mouse; Socks, curious to a fault, concerned with establishing his territory, and content to play, to be loved, and to sleep in the sun, is very much a cat. But each character has the kinds of problems and longings with which Cleary's human readers can sympathize and identify; each animal is a substitute for a human protagonist.

Socks's difficulties lie not only in growing up but in the natural shakedown occurring in any family that adds a new member. Indulged in his every whim, Socks is the unofficial master of the Brickers' house until Charles William is born: his confusion about his place in the family, his jealousy of the new member, and his struggles to regain supremacy are almost those of an older sibling. Underpetted and finally turned out of the house, Socks's happy ending comes only after he has made his peace with the new baby and has found his place in the new family configuration.

Impatient and preoccupied with the idea of speed and with the power of the machine, Ralph, especially, is very much like a young boy. In the three books about Ralph, we watch him grow from a heedless young mouse out for a good time and sometimes overwhelmed by his many relatives to a more responsible young mouse who can handle his young relatives, and, occasionally, even his older ones. The focus of *The Mouse and the Motorcycle,* especially, is on growing up, which means (for Ralph as well as for Keith) not just getting bigger, but becoming responsible. Ralph realizes this over the course of a few days. One day, unable to keep his paws off the motorcycle, Ralph is dumped in the laundry hamper, and his escape loses the motorcycle and sparks the danger his family faces from the hotel staff. The next day, having thought out how his family can escape being trapped by the management and having repaid Keith for his kindness by finding an aspirin during a treacherous search through the hotel, Ralph has proved that he can be responsible and is growing up. The difference is not physical, but mental: "Just getting bigger isn't enough," Keith tells him, "You have to learn things like not taking off down a steep hill on a bicycle when you aren't used to hand brakes. Stuff like that" (152–53). The focus of *Runaway Ralph* is on the nature of independence, which must be tempered by reality and by thoughts of others. Desperate to be on his own and away from his interfering mother, uncle, and many cousins, Ralph learns that independence has its own trials. The outside world is a dangerous and awkward place for someone so tiny, and Ralph's bid for freedom is ironically cut short by his being captured and popped into a cage, where he must depend on Garf for everything and where he watches Garf go through problems as a result of *his* independent nature. Having had a taste of what real independence can mean, Ralph opts for home, where life is less thrilling and can be troublesome, but where he is safe with his family, and again he must depend on Garf to get him there: although Cleary "cannot believe that a fantasy about a mouse who runs away on a miniature motorcycle to a children's camp in search of peanut butter-and-jelly sandwiches" teaches such a lesson, a young fan may be forgiven for writing to her that "I like *Runaway Ralph* because it taught me to be satisfied with what I have" ("Laughter," 556). At the end of *Ralph S. Mouse,* Ralph is almost adult, as he not only trades his motorcycle in for a sports car, but learns to control his troublesome little relatives. At the beginning of the book, he is beset by his cousins, who pester him for rides on his motorcycle and challenge his right to have such a machine. Having watched Ryan's teacher in the classroom, by the end of the book Ralph finds that he can use her techniques to quiet the little mice who pester him for a ride; he gets his older cousins to help him put himself and his new machine beyond their whims by declaring that rides are only for the older mice. The change in machines seems appropriate, as the motorcycle in which a teenager can delight is exchanged for the sports car of the upwardly mobile adult.

Though the animal protagonist is the focus, the works are almost as much about the humans around Socks and Ralph as they are about the protagonists named in the titles. Between the lines of the story and over the head of its protagonist, *Socks* dips into the difficulties and tensions of a young couple: the Brickers's "shabby" house is furnished in "contemporary cast-off" (33, 34); the long visit of a mother-in-law in a tiny house provides its own special tension. In Ralph's books, however, the focus is almost as much on the boys Ralph meets as it is on Ralph himself. Keith's main function in the first book seems to be to provide Ralph with a motorcycle and to spark Ralph's growth toward responsibility. Though a realistic boy who yearns to be grown up, he is relatively carefree, and his role in the book as a whole is not that important. But in the later books, the boys are more important, both to Ralph and to the thrust of the books. Kept busy by the activities encouraged by his parents and rarely allowed just to be by himself, Garf is bored by summer camp and has trouble fitting into the camp's community, hiding behind moodiness and sarcasm. While Ralph is learning that independence is not all it seems to be, the boy comes to realize that his feelings are normal and that they can and should be channeled correctly. He, too, learns something about independence when he must depend on Ralph to return the watch he has been accused to stealing. In the third book, the action affects Ryan and Brad as much as it does Ralph: new to the neighborhood and the school, Ryan worries about finding his place in both; Brad has his own troubles, for his bullying and swaggering covers the fact that he misses his mother, who has divorced his father. In the course of the novel, as Ralph realizes how much his family means to him, the two boys learn to get along together and become good friends. Ralph's books, especially, may be about the education of Ralph S. Mouse, but they are also about the education of the boys he befriends.

As in Cleary's other works, here the family unit is still the ideal, even while it is troublesome. The less-than-perfect families in the books about the Quimbys and other humans are just as imperfect in Cleary's books about animals. Ralph's family often is the bane of his life, from his nervous and fretful mother to his self-important and interfering aunts and uncles to his bratty and demanding cousins; Garf's parents seem more interested in keeping him busy than in keeping him happy; Brad's parents are divorced.

Family life does not proceed smoothly in Socks's household, for
babies are often fretful and mothers-in-law think they know best.
But the family is still the ideal. Away from the hotel, Ralph realizes that he misses his family and that he cannot get along
without it; having realized in *Runaway Ralph* that too much independence is as much a problem as too much family, in *Ralph S.
Mouse* he learns to deal with his family, taking his place in it. The
happy ending in this work includes Brad's father and Ryan's
mother meeting and marrying, though Cleary makes it clear that
life is not happily ever after, as "most of the time the boys were
glad to be brothers" (159). The thrust of *Socks* is on the dynamics
of a little family in the process of forming, with members being
added and other members finding their places in the new unit.

With this emphasis on the loving but imperfect family there
also is Cleary's usual emphasis on ordinary life. These works, not
surprisingly, do not contain many autobiographical elements, beyond the vacation, the hotel, and the toys that inspired *The Mouse
and the Motorcycle,* but this does not impair their sense of everyday life. Ralph and Socks are basically an ordinary mouse and
cat, and those around them are equally ordinary. Riding his motorcycle and talking with humans, Ralph is still a mouse concerned with food and with the depredations of owls; Socks
concerns himself with food and with keeping his feline dignity
intact. The young family of which Socks is a part is the ordinary
student family concerned with classes, money, and the new baby.
Ralph's young friends are ordinary young boys learning to make
friends, to deal with their family problems, and to take responsibility seriously. Cleary builds detail upon detail to construct a
sense of everyday reality, which is especially important in works
of fantasy and in works from an unusual point of view. Ralph's
world is that of the slightly seedy Mountain View Inn, with its
drafty rooms and dark, sticky-floored bar, the echoing and empty
school room, with the janitor's radio playing songs "about lonely
highways, broken hearts, and jail" (*Ralph S.,* 65), and the orderly
disorder of a summer camp, with its crafts and songs and boister-
ous children. From the tea-colored wig that Nana Bricker wears
to the brutality of Socks's fight with Old Taylor to Charles Wil-

liam's pride that he has learned to flip the light switch and to
entertain the cat, the everyday reality of Socks's life is equally
detailed.

With their emphasis on the lives of animals rather than on humans, these works have a contemporary feel, since mice and cats
have not really changed. It is a surprise for the reader to realize
that seventeen years lie between the publication of the first
Ralph book and that of the last; the illustrations in *Socks* are all
that point to its publication date of 1973. For as long as there are
motorcycles and lonely boys, and as long as there are new families
and cats, these works will remain contemporary, focused as they
are on the problems and triumphs of growing up—even if one is
a cat or a mouse. The progression from the happy family life of
untroubled Keith in 1965 to the stresses of that of subtly troubled
Garf in 1970 to the one-parent families of lonely Ryan and Brad
in 1982, however, points to the changing realities in the world
outside the books. "I had a father named Ralph once, but he ran
away," one fan wrote to Cleary concerning *Runaway Ralph*; another wrote, "Ralph wants to run away. That is how I feel about
my father. My father gets me mad. I want to get custody of my
mother but I am not sure. My mother is better" ("Newbery," 434–
35). The ordinary two-parent family about which Cleary wrote in
the Henry Huggins books was being joined by the just-as-ordi-
nary one-parent family, as the American divorce rate increased.
The boys in Ralph's books reflect that change in the ordinary life
of Cleary's readers and point the way to a different kind of Cleary
family: one with only one parent. Perhaps unconsciously responding to the letters about *Runaway Ralph*, Cleary had presented
her readers with the one-parent human families of *Ralph S.
Mouse* and paved the way for the one-parent household of aspir-
ing writer Leigh Botts.

6

Dear Mr. Henshaw

Publication of *Henry Huggins* in 1950 marked the beginning of the special relationship between Cleary and her readers, as readers wrote her letters about her books and themselves. These letters from fans have helped Cleary to keep track not only of readers' responses to her works but of the readers' own concerns—important for a writer seeking to chronicle the adventures of children. The letters have allowed Cleary to respond to her readers' needs and demands: writing the Ramona books, for example, after demands for "a whole book about Ramona." But never had Cleary responded as directly or as effectively as in the Newbery Award-winning *Dear Mr. Henshaw,* which acts, itself, as Cleary's letter to her fans, while it documents the changes in ordinary life-styles.[1]

Dear Mrs. Cleary

Beginning with the first letter, from an eight-year-old girl after *Henry Huggins* was published ("Dear," 22), Cleary received thousands more, from 75 to 300 pieces a day during the school year— letters dutifully written as part of a class project or out of love of the books ("Dear," 25). Each decade has produced its own kind of letter. In the late 1950s, Cleary began to receive more and more questionnaires, on such questions as "Where do you get your ideas?" "What is your favorite food?" "How much money do you make?" and asking for "tips on writing." Cleary idly wondered what would happen if she sent questionnaires back to her readers; the 1960s saw an upsurge of didacticism, with children pressured to find the moral of the story or to "tell an author what they don't like about a book or how it can be improved" ("Dear," 22). Pressure on the author began in the 1970s, as children began to demand answers, informing Cleary that their grades depended on her answer: "I have to write and you have to answer. . . . If you don't answer, I get a bad grade" ("Dear," 22).

But always, children told Cleary about themselves: the children of the 1950s revealing to her that "'We have a new Mercury that spits on the windshield.'. . . 'May 12 we got ink in our inkwells.'. . . [or] 'My grandmother raises popcorn'" ("Writing," 11). Over the years, Cleary has noted a diversity of others:

> a crop-duster's son in South Dakota; children who dislike living in mobile homes; a lonely little girl whose father is stationed in the Philippines and who has brought her friends with her in books; a child whose family built a log cabin in the woods and who lives without electricity; children of all races—I know from the pictures they enclose—who write as children, with no mention of color; blind children whose teachers translate their braille letters; brain-damaged children whose brave letters are barely intelligible; wealthy children who write of horses, swimming pools, and the latest video equipment; poor children—one girl wrote a happy letter listing her Christmas presents: pajamas, a sweater, and a toothbrush; inner-city children who wish they could live in Henry Huggins's neighborhood; boys and girls who live in children's homes . . .; farm children, who almost always write interesting letters; a girl who wrote that she read my books in cars, trucks, and jeeps; refugee children, who write meticulous letters and whose teachers

enclosed notes describing the terrors the children have survived to reach the United States or Canada; . . . children who hate reading; children who say they can't get enough of reading; happy children, grieving children, exuberant children, sick children. ("Newbery," 432)

Though Cleary had noticed an increasing surface sophistication in her readers ("Newbery," 434), she also noted that their "deepest feelings remain the same." Her readers enjoy books they "can understand"; they want pets and they want teachers who like them; they note that their siblings could use improvement; and, most important, they "want to love and to be loved by two parents in a united family" ("Newbery," 433). For there has been an increase, too, in letters "filled with sorrow": "parents were divorced, a father had been murdered, children who were alone after school were sad and frightened" ("Dear," 23). "Another child tells me, 'My parents are devvorst. My dad is the kind of person who never wants to be around kids.' Many children say they remain with their mother, but their pets live with their father. A girl confides, 'I wish I could sue my parents for malpractice but I know I can't so I just try to forget what they do.'" ("Newbery," 434).

But many of Cleary's readers seem to find comfort in books, reading when they are bored or when they are "lonely, sad, or afraid"; one child wrote that "My father says the library is my best friend" ("Newbery," 435).

Leigh's Story

All these children's voices combined to form that of the protagonist of *Dear Mr. Henshaw:* Leigh Botts, only child of divorced parents, who turns to Mr. Henshaw and to books for comfort in his deep loneliness. Having received letters from readers suggesting "books featuring themselves as central characters," in 1982 Cleary heard, from "several boys unknown to one another: 'Please write a book about a boy whose parents are divorced.'" ("Newbery," 435). Cleary, looking for a change and "stereotyped as al-

ways writing a certain kind of book," found herself ready to write
a "different sort of book"—a book about a boy, for "girls, it appeared to me, had taken over children's literature" ("Newbery,
435). As happened during the creation of her other works, elements from Cleary's life began to come together to form the story:

> Those thoughts that are jumbled in an author's mind be-
> gan to separate themselves and cling to this nucleus. An
> overheard sentence spoken in grief by a strange woman:
> "It's so terrible when his father promises to call and
> doesn't." A remark by a teacher: "This kid in my class
> rigged up a burglar alarm for his lunch box. It made a
> terrible racket." These were joined by boys' pride in fa-
> thers who drive tractor-trailer rigs, grief at the loss of a
> pet, loneliness in a new school. My own idle thoughts
> about sending children lists of questions were no longer
> idle. Letters to an author who sends questions and de-
> mands answers followed by a diary seemed right; let the
> boy reveal his own feelings, for I believe children who
> want to write should look within themselves, not within
> the books of others. ("Newbery," 435–36)

The Young Writers program introduced during the 1970s formed
another element ("Dear," 23). Cleary created Boyd Henshaw as
both her antithesis and as the author of works she had thought
of writing but could not:

> a young foot-loose male whose books did not resemble
> mine. Creating Mr. Henshaw, from a name plucked from
> an obituary column (I read names anyplace I can find
> them!) was great fun, for he writes the books I have
> wanted to write but could not. His *Ways to Amuse a Dog*
> goes back to the 1940s, when I first heard that booksell-
> ers' legend of the woman who misunderstood the title of
> a book called *Forty Days of Musa Dagh* and asked for
> *Forty Ways to Amuse a Dog*. This struck me as a splendid
> idea for a book because most of the dogs I knew were

bored. *Moose on Toast* came out of a visit to Alaska, where a librarian asked, with a touch of desperation in her voice, whether I would like to take home some moose sausage. Her husband had shot the moose, and the family of three was faced with eating a thousand pounds of moose meat from their freezer. When I mentioned this to other librarians as having humorous possibilities for a story, no one was amused. All had a moose or part of a moose in their freezers. This discouraged me but would not discourage Mr. Henshaw, who would spend his time in Alaska climbing mountains instead of speaking at banquets and would be hungry enough to eat moose, even though I was told it is dry and stringy. Mr. Henshaw's third and more serious book *Beggar Bears,* about bear cubs in Yellowstone National Park, who are taught to beg instead of forage and whose mothers die from eating plastic bags, is another book I could not write because I lack a naturalist's knowledge. Foot-loose Mr. Henshaw was free to travel and research bears. ("Newbery," 436)

Cleary's knowledge of trucks and truckers came from her son's experiences working summers, and from a visit to a truck repair yard, "not an easy experience," according to Cleary, "for the dusty truckers found my asking questions amusing and I had to be wary of having my leg pulled" ("Newbery," 436–37). All these details combined in the deeply moving story of a lonely boy learning to pick up the pieces after his parents' divorce.

Leigh Botts is an ordinary young boy whose favorite book—as he writes its author, Boyd Henshaw, in second, third, fourth, and fifth grades—is *Ways to Amuse a Dog.* Reading—at Mr. Henshaw's request—another of his books, Leigh sends to Mr. Henshaw a list of questions, only to get questions from Mr. Henshaw in return. At first refusing to answer them, Leigh reluctantly does after his mother forces him to; his answers, written over the course of the next two weeks in November, make him realize that writing is not so bad when it is not for a book report.

Leigh is lonely and unhappy. His parents are divorced, and Leigh lives with his mother in a tiny cottage; his trucker father, who does not see the boy often, has taken Bandit, the Botts's dog, with him in his truck. New in the neighborhood and in school, Leigh has made no friends and feels that no one notices him, except to take the delicacies he sometimes has in his lunch, courtesy of the caterer for whom his mother works. Finally, someone does notice him: Leigh helps the school custodian with the flag one morning and gets a job helping him every morning.

At Mr. Henshaw's suggestion, Leigh begins to keep a diary, which he addresses as Mr. Henshaw. He chronicles his troubles with his lunch, which he cannot speak to his teacher about because the new boy should not be a "snitch." Christmas brings no visit from Leigh's father, but another trucker does drop off the wonderful quilted down jacket Leigh has longed for. Putting a fictitious name on his lunch bag works for a while; after Leigh's lunch is rifled again, Mr. Fridley, the custodian, suggests a burglar alarm. A story contest sponsored by the school proves more difficult than Leigh had anticipated, for he finds he keeps imitating the authors he reads.

Though Leigh's father had promised to call him, he does not; but when Leigh calls in order to hear the telephone ringing, he is surprised to hear his father answer. Leigh believes his father's explanation that he was going to call that night but is horrified to hear that his father has lost Bandit, who had jumped from the truck during a stop. Then, in the background, Leigh hears another boy's voice calling Leigh's father: the boy's mother is ready to go out. Leigh realizes that his father is not alone.

By the next day, Leigh has realized that he really does not hate his father and also that his father would not have called as he said he was going to, since he was going out. Talking to his mother in his despair, Leigh learns that he is not—as he had thought—responsible for the divorce. After the talk and a cozy supper in the car, watching the ocean, Leigh feels better about his mother, though he still is not sure how he feels about his father.

Life seems to have reached a nadir, however. Leigh begins his story for the contest, but it is too much like one of Mr. Henshaw's; enraged by someone stealing the cheesecake out of his lunch, Leigh almost drop-kicks someone else's lunch. Mr. Fridley stops him though; he does not want to see Leigh get into trouble. Everyone, he tells Leigh, has problems; Leigh must learn to think positively.

Though the next day begins badly, Leigh's life begins to look brighter. While taking a walk after a rotten day, Leigh follows signs to a grove of butterfly trees, where monarch butterflies spend the winter. When the sun comes out, clouds of butterflies take wing all around Leigh, and his spirits rise with them. The next days are busy ones: Leigh's father sends him $20 in an awkward attempt to say how sorry he is about Bandit; Leigh begins another story for the contest. But the story, about a wax trucker who melts each time he crosses the desert, somehow does not seem right; Mr. Henshaw answers Leigh's letter about the story by explaining that perhaps Leigh is not ready to write a whole story.

Since he has learned about alarms, Leigh gets a metal lunch box and begins to read about electricity; on the advice from the owner of a hardware store, he makes an alarm for his lunch box. At noon the next day, he realizes he has a problem: the alarm is still armed; and when he opens the box, the alarm goes off. Suddenly everyone notices Leigh, with admiration. One admirer is Barry, who would like an alarm, too, and now Leigh has a friend with whom to "goof around." Leigh's lunch is now safe, for the lunch thief does not strike again.

A telephone call from Leigh's father is awkward, though, with Leigh unable to say what he wants. The call does start Leigh thinking about his father; since his story for the contest is due, Leigh dashes off a description of a good day he had had with his father, hauling a load of grapes. The story wins Leigh only Honorable Mention, but when the winning poem turns out to have been plagiarized, Leigh gets to accompany the other winners to lunch with a famous author of books about girls. Leigh's lunch becomes even more special when the author praises his work and calls him an author.

Finally, Leigh's father visits, hauling a load of broccoli from a nearby farm. It is a short but important visit: Bandit has been found, and Leigh tells his father of his accomplishments. Despite his father's interest in getting back together with Leigh's mother, it becomes clear that this will not happen. At the end of the visit, Leigh sends Bandit with his father, for company; his father needs Bandit's company more than Leigh does. Pensive after the visit, Leigh realizes that broccoli may have been the reason his father came to the area, but it was love that brought him further, to visit his family.

Epistolary *Dear Mr. Henshaw* was, reviewers pointed out, a change of pace for Cleary: "Cleary tries something different this time around," said the reviewer for *Booklist,* calling it "a more serious story";[2] noting that Cleary was "forsaking her well-trodden path," *Horn Book* called the work "a poignant story with an unmistakable ring of truth."[3] All applauded Cleary's use of the form, especially the way it helped Leigh's characterization, giving "a clear sense of his life, his thinking process and his coming to grips with his father's absence"; it also helped show "his hurt and his hopes as well as his childlike confusion mixed with flashes of understanding of his clear-eyed, hard-working mother and his essentially irresponsible father" (*Horn Book,* "Henshaw").[4] Though the reviewer in *Booklist* felt that the work "lacks the wit and ingenuity for which Cleary's stories are known," the writer admitted that "the book stacks up well against any in the middle-grade problem genre." Other reviewers agreed with the latter statement, though they admired her use of humor: "as usual, Cleary's sense of humor leavens and lightens what might otherwise be a heavy work of social realism," wrote the reviewer for *School Library Journal,* while *Horn Book* felt that "the story is by no means one of unrelieved gloom, for there are deft touches of humor in the sentient, subtly wrought account of the small triumphs and tragedies in the life of an ordinary boy."

Leigh and Mr. Henshaw

Dear Mr. Henshaw is not, perhaps, as widely popular as the Ramona books and the Henry Huggins series, but that, Cleary has noted, is as it should be, for "in a world in which children's lives vary so widely, there is no reason why every child should like every book" ("Newbery," 438). Or perhaps, every adult, for the first letters Cleary received about the book were from adults, some of whom, according to Cleary,

> said it was the best book I had ever written; others expressed disappointment, even indignation, that I had not written a book as funny as the *Ramona* books. This surprised me. Writers of humor for children often hear that they "just write funny stories" and are made aware, even though they know it is wrong, that serious books are considered superior. A couple of people said they liked the book themselves but expressed doubts about giving it to children because it wasn't funny and because Leigh's parents were not reconciled at the end—a conclusion that I felt would be sentimental, dishonest, and a source of false hope to many children. Teachers wrote that the book would be valuable for classroom discussion because so many pupils came from single-parent homes. Mothers struggling to rear sons without help from fathers wrote moving letters of appreciation. ("Newbery," 437)

Letters from the work's intended audience—though some stated that their writers "liked Leigh, but they liked Ramona better"— showed that other young readers cared intensely about Leigh and the book:

> The first came from a boy with two parents, whose father owns a gas station in Leigh's town. He said he read *Dear Mr. Henshaw* straight through the day he bought it and five times the next week. Others said it was my best

book. Children found more of the humor in the story than
adults and expressed interest in Leigh's lunchbox alarm,
although one girl wrote a wistful letter saying she never
had anything good in *her* lunch. Another girl said she
was *so* glad Leigh's parents didn't get together at the
end. Many told me how hard life is in a new school, that
their lives were very much like Leigh's, or that there
were "lots of kids like Leigh" in their school. Several letters ended "Please don't send *me* a list of questions." One
boy wrote, "I was really moved by the book. I felt as
though I was gona [going to] wake up from a dream state
and find myself in Leigh's body." ("Newbery" 437–38;
brackets in original)

In 1984 Cleary, whose *Ramona and Her Father* and *Ramona
Quimby, Age 8* were Newbery Honor books, was awarded the
Newbery Medal for Leigh's story.

It is not, of course, unbelievable that Leigh's story should hit so
close to home for its intended audience, written as it was at the
behest of and from the letters of young readers. Leigh Botts is, as
Cleary points out, more than just a fictional character; like most
of her protagonists, he is an Everychild: "all the brave and lonely
children I have ever known who have found books and libraries
to their best friends" ("Newbery," 438). In an odd way, Leigh mirrors Cleary's first character, Henry Huggins: both ordinary boys
are only children who care about their parents and their dogs, and
their stories are made of the stuff of everyday life; just as Leigh
is a product of the letters Cleary had received from her fans,
Henry is the product of earlier readers' interests and concerns.
But each also reflects his time, and so their lives are very different: Henry, secure in his two-parent, 1950s home life, worries
mostly about the everyday concerns of growing up, such as getting a bicycle or handling a paper route; Leigh, insecure in his
1980s, one-parent life, is lonely and angry about the new situation, and growing up for him involves learning to deal with his
parents' divorce. Just as Henry was the ordinary child for his
time, so Leigh is the ordinary child for his; and so Leigh is time-

less in the way Henry is, concerned as he is with the kind of emotions that do not change. *Dear Mr. Henshaw* explores Cleary's theme of the ordinary child with ordinary problems helping himself, but it also shows that some problems are too big for the child to solve by himself.

There is little to set Leigh apart from other children: his main concerns are school and his family, friends, and his dog. Like many children, he reads the same book over and over, getting a lot of academic mileage out of it: having *Ways to Amuse a Dog* read to him in second grade, Leigh reads it for himself in third, makes a diorama of the book in fourth, and does a book report on it in fifth; it is to this book that Leigh later turns for comfort in the way many children do. Though Leigh hopes to become a writer, he wants little else out of the ordinary, only to live in a happy family with his parents and his dog, with friends and a secure place in school.

At the beginning of the sixth grade, this ordinariness begins to seem a curse: the new kid in a new neighborhood and a new school, Leigh feels himself blend in with the others, sensing that no one notices him much. Calling himself "just a plain boy" (14), Leigh emphasizes that he is "sort of medium," standing in the middle of the row when the class lines up according to height (15). As one reader points out, Leigh describes himself in terms of what he is not rather than what he is[5]: not "Gifted and Talented," Leigh is "not stupid either" and does not like soccer "the way everybody at this school is supposed to." In his physical description, he emphasizes that he does not "have red hair or anything like that," nor is he "real big like my Dad" (15). Leigh is, he feels, "the mediumest boy in the class" (15), and the only time he would not "seem so medium" is sitting in the truck with his father (30).

Leigh's problems are only too familiar to most of his readers. Having made no friends so far, at school Leigh walks the careful line of the new kid in town, avoiding doing the wrong things (such as going to the teacher about the lunch bag thief) yet never seeming to do the things that would win him attention and friends; though he does not like soccer, Leigh stays after school to play with the others, "so they won't think I am stuck up or anything," but nothing seems to work. "Maybe I'm just a boy nobody pays much attention to," decides Leigh. "The kids here pay more attention to my lunch than they do to me" (25). It is with real surprise that Leigh realizes that Mr. Fridley, the custodian, and the school librarian have noticed him (35, 55). Leigh also has the odder, but not unusual, problem of having the delicacies from his lunch stolen. His triumph lies partly in his solving of the two problems with one blow, as he emphatically calls attention to himself by accidentally setting off his lunch box alarm, thus gaining the attention of Barry, who becomes Leigh's friend, and warning off the lunch thief. "I began to feel like some sort of hero," Leigh writes. "Maybe I'm not so medium after all" (101–2).

But not all problems in a child's life are ones he can solve, and Leigh's is his parents' divorce, a problem familiar to many of Cleary's readers. Finding life "humorous, sorrowful, and filled with problems that have no solutions," Cleary deals with the divorce honestly, neither giving it the emphasis it would have received in the usual problem novel nor making light of it by hinting at the manufactured happy ending of a reconciliation ("Newbery," 437). The picture of divorce in *Dear Mr. Henshaw* is a divorce seen from a child's-eye view, with Leigh's emotional response that of any child caught in a divorce, running the gamut from confusion to anger. Confused about what has happened, Leigh resents his new situation, living with a hardworking mother in a tiny house while his dog is with his father on the road. Though he realizes that she is busy working part-time while taking classes at the community college, he misses the home-cooked meals she used to prepare. Leigh is confused, too, about his father's treatment of him: the way his father does not call when he promises he would and then calls him "kid" as if unable to remember Leigh's name (28). Like many children in divorced families, Leigh tries to find someone to blame for the divorce, first becoming angry with his mother, then feeling that he may somehow have been the cause. But Leigh's mother points out, divorce is a problem between adults, and "it takes two people to get a divorce" (49). Faced with a problem that he cannot solve and that will not go away, Leigh must find a way to deal with it; slowly he learns to accept the situation and acknowledges that his parents will not get back together.

In learning to deal with the situation, Leigh also must learn to deal with his irresponsible father and to accept this much-less-than-perfect parent. Having put Henry Huggins's parents firmly in the background of his story, Cleary had put Ramona Quimby's parents somewhere in the middle distance of hers; Leigh's parents are firmly in the foreground, and part of Leigh's growing up involves learning that they are not perfect, while he discovers how to deal with this knowledge. Themselves struggling to adjust after the divorce, Leigh's parents are shown in all their vulnerability, making mistakes, sometimes unhappy, and sometimes unsure.

Leigh's handsome, rowdy father appears in person only at the end of the novel, but, as expected, he dominates his son's life. He is the antithesis of the perfect parent: in love with the open road and with the idea of being his own boss, he makes promises he does not keep, forgets to send support checks and forgets, too, to call his son. As Leigh puts it, though "the judge in the divorce said he has a right to see me" (31), Leigh's father makes little effort to do so; he cannot even manage to deliver Leigh's gift for Christmas, sending it with another trucker. Leigh finds his father figures elsewhere: in Mr. Fridley, who gives him advice and keeps an eye on him; in the hardware store owner, who helps Leigh with the alarm and calls Leigh "son" when his father calls him "kid" (96); and, especially, in Mr. Henshaw, the long-distance recipient of Leigh's problems and fears. Leigh's father and Bandit seem linked, for both love trucks and the open road, and neither is ready to settle in one place; both are important in Leigh's idea of a unified family. At the novel's low point, Leigh learns that not only has his father lost Bandit, but he is dating someone and has lied about intending to call his son. But Leigh's mother reminds him that his father is not a bad man; it is just that he "will never grow up" (112).

In an unconscious and intensely revealing gesture, Leigh begins a story in which his father is symbolized as a trucker made of wax, melting a little more each time he crosses the desert (89).

He abandons it because, as Mr. Henshaw reminds him, a "character in a story should solve a problem or change in some way," and Leigh realizes that "a wax man who melts until he's a puddle wouldn't be there to solve anything and melting isn't the sort of change you mean" (91). Leigh's father does not change the way Mr. Henshaw means, and he is not "there to solve anything," either. By the end of the novel, battered by the emotions his father brings out and bolstered by his mother's love and explanations, Leigh has learned to deal with his father in a new way, finding that he can love his father even while he has learned not to count on anything his father says (132). Sending Bandit with his father is an affirmation of his love—for Leigh cannot bear to think of his father being alone—and an acknowledgment that things never will be as they were before the divorce.

Leigh's steadier mother, who works part-time while trying to earn her degree as Licensed Vocational Nurse, is no superwoman: Leigh grudgingly records every meal out of the freezer or a can, unconsciously contrasted with the delicacies she prepares as a caterer. Though she has answers for many of Leigh's concerns, she herself is still dealing with the divorce, and she has moments of great vulnerability; she does not pretend that blame for the divorce lies only on Leigh's father. Unhappy at home and too young to think things through, she had thought she had found a shining knight when she met Leigh's father, and, probably, she grew up and he did not (74–76). As she sits pensive after her ex-husband's visit, having denied any possibility of reconciliation, it seems clear that she too has come to terms with her new life.

Serious as the novel is and weighty as Leigh's problems are, it is finally a story of triumph. The Leigh at the end of the work is a more confident child who has triumphed over what he can change and come to terms with what he cannot. Defining himself in terms of what he is not at the novel's beginning, Leigh has realized at the end that while he may not be a soccer player or Gifted and Talented, he *is* a burglar-alarm maker and an author.

In a way, Cleary does in *Dear Mr. Henshaw* what she had set out to do in her first book: write about a child growing up to become a writer ("Regina," 23). Answering Mr. Henshaw's questions, Leigh realizes that writing can be enjoyable (31), and he begins to take his favorite author's advice, keeping a journal as Mr. Henshaw suggests; by allowing a protagonist to speak for himself, Cleary shows how a writer thinks. Just as the book is the story of Leigh and his triumphs, so it is a sort of letter from Cleary to her readers, as she discusses writing and the relationship between author and reader, and author and work.

The epistolary form of the novel is appropriate, as Cleary uses material with which she is very familiar. In a sense the book documents the relationship between author and reader, as many of Leigh's letters show the things Cleary has commented that her own readers do: Leigh sends Mr. Henshaw a picture of himself as Cleary receives pictures from her own readers (4; "Talking," 11); he writes a business letter because that is what the students are learning to do, just as many of Cleary's readers write to her as part of schoolwork (4; "Newbery," 432); spelling in the letters Cleary receives is as erratic it is in Leigh's early letters, where a boy who has learned that "the *i* goes before *e* so that at the end it will spell *end*" in "friend" asks Mr. Henshaw to "keep in tutch" (2). Especially, Leigh makes demands on his favorite author, asking for "a list of your books that you wrote, an autographed picture and a bookmark . . . by next Friday" as he sends a list of ten questions for Mr. Henshaw to answer (7–8).

The form also allows Cleary to make points she has wanted to make, about the lists she gets from readers, about doing library research, and about demands on an author's resources (especially time). Showered with questionnaires, Cleary found herself wondering "what would happen if I sent children lists of questions to answer" ("Dear," 22); faced with answering yet again such requests as "What are your books about?" and "Give me some tips on writing," Cleary finds that "the ghost of my mother whispers over my shoulder, Stand on your own two feet. Go to the library. Read" ("Newbery," 433). So Leigh finds the answers to most of the questions he has sent Mr. Henshaw on the back flap of the dust cover of one of his books (9), while Mr. Henshaw comments that his "favorite animal was a purple monster who ate children who sent authors long lists of questions for reports instead of learning to use the library (9); and Mr. Henshaw sends to Leigh the list of questions Cleary wanted to send her own readers. Cleary is faced with demands that have ranged from petitions for a personal memento ("Dear," 22) or something from her wastebasket—"along with an explanation as to how the discarded item relates to my life" ("Newbery," 433)—to demands for "free stuff" to plaintive requests for handwritten answers ("Dear," 25); she has wondered if "the 'me' generation . . . [has] produced a 'gimmee' generation" ("Newbery," 433) and if all the activity might be interfering with her work ("Why," 42). So Leigh constantly reminds Mr. Henshaw that he understands "how busy you are with your own books" (10) and promises not to send him his letters and compositions.

The form allows Cleary to give those tips on writing for which she has been asked again and again, as the reader watches the formation of a young writer. Faced with Mr. Henshaw's own questions to him, Leigh begins to enjoy writing unconnected with schoolwork. In contrast to those Leigh has sent Mr. Henshaw (superficial questions that can be answered with a trip to the library), the ones Leigh receives deal with deeper issues, allowing Leigh to explore who he really is as he answers such questions as "Who are you?," "What bothers you?," and "What do you wish?." Mr. Henshaw also sends Leigh some valuable "tips on writing," encouraging him to "read, look, listen, think and write" (14). Involved with the young authors program at school, Leigh struggles through the writing process, with Cleary emphasizing originality of idea and voice, writing about something one knows and has strong feelings about (119), and giving precise details (108–9). Watching Leigh attempt and fail again and again to write a story, the reader realizes that Mr. Henshaw is correct when he tells the boy that he probably is not ready to write one and agrees with famous author Angela Badger that perhaps "the ability to write stories comes later, when you have lived longer and have more understanding" (119). In a sense, the entire book stands as an example of how to write, for it is deeply felt, wonderfully detailed, and written in Leigh's fresh voice. Ironically, Leigh succeeds in exploring in the book the things he fails to write about for the young writer's contest: from his "Great Lunchbox Mystery," to the melting wax man, to the butterfly grove, reinforcing the idea that good literature is constructed from what the author knows and understands.

Just as important, the epistolary form allows Cleary to present an ordinary boy's life in a way that helps the reader understand him inside and out, making Leigh a three-dimensional character whose life and problems seem very real and allowing the reader to watch Leigh come to terms with his new situation and become more mature. Many readers have noted that the book is not as funny on the surface as her other works, though children have found more humor in the work than have adults ("Newbery," 437). Cleary reminds us, through Leigh, "a book doesn't have to be funny to be good, although it often helps" (56). One reason the book is not as superficially humorous as the kind of books usually associated with Cleary is that Leigh expresses his pain, confusion, and loneliness. This strengthens the book, but it also allows Cleary to write what is essentially a problem novel without being melodramatic or preachy. Less articulate than an adult writer, Leigh can chronicle painful scenes with deep impact without being overdramatic; his inarticulate simplicity gives the book real power.

More serious than many of Cleary's other novels, written in a different style and voice than her other novels, *Dear Mr. Henshaw* nevertheless contains many elements her readers have come to expect. The ordinariness of Leigh's life and the understated humor of the book are familiar to Cleary's readers. Cleary also here indulges in the type of humor that adults appreciate more than do children: noticing that "authors like Mr. Henshaw usually wear old plaid shirts in the pictures on the back of their books," Leigh does not worry that he is underdressed for his expected lunch with Angela Badger, for Leigh's shirt "is just as old as [Mr. Henshaw's], so I knew it was OK" (114). Leigh's mother notes, of a suitor, that "Charlie is divorced and has three children to support. What he really wants is someone to help support Charlie" (52).

This book about the breakup of a family struck home to many young readers of the 1980s, many of whom had gone through the

same thing: "Children said the book made them feel better because it told them they were not alone," Cleary has noted, while
many teachers "told how valuable the book had been in bringing
the children's problems into the open." Though uncomprehending
teachers were given the "idea of writing to authors and have their
classes copy out the questions Leigh asked Mr. Henshaw, con-
cluding with, 'Please give me some tips on writing,'" others have
used the list Mr. Henshaw sent Leigh to spark writing in their
students, resulting in "fascinating vignettes of childhood in the
United States today" ("Dear," 25). As has been detailed, many
young readers respond intensely to the work. Appearing thirty-
three years after Henry Huggins, Leigh has, of course, a more
contemporary feel; he also stands at one end of a logical progression, from the straight humor of Henry Huggins's books, to the
humorous worries of Ramona Quimby, to Leigh's own deeper worries. The "Our Gang" of Cleary's earlier books has evolved to a
lonelier, more isolated child no less typical of his time and no less
triumphant in his growing up.

7

Young Romance

So popular are Henry Huggins, Ramona Quimby, and Cleary's other works for elementary school-age children that many of Cleary's readers do not realize that she also has produced works for young teens. From 1956 to 1963, Cleary wrote *Fifteen, The Luckiest Girl, Jean and Johnny,* and *Sister of the Bride*—four works detailing the agonies and joys of first crushes and teenage love.[1] Though older than Cleary's other protagonists, Jane Purdy, Shelley Latham, Jean Jarrett, and Barbara MacLane are no less ordinary; and their typically uneven romances are chronicled with Cleary's characteristic down-to-earth humor. Emphasizing the power, joy, and pain of first love, Cleary also focuses on its fleeting quality and the fact that neither life nor love is really perfect.

The Course of Love

Fifteen
Like *Henry Huggins,* Cleary's first work for adolescents seems to have been written at the behest of young readers. Speaking at a junior high school, Cleary was asked by students "why she didn't write similar stories for youngsters in their age group" (Burns

and Hines, 745). The result was *Fifteen,* published in 1956, a book different from her works for younger children not only in theme but in style. Writing for a new audience proved refreshing for Cleary: "Trying my hand at something different—a book for teenagers, a fantasy, or an animal story—recaptures the 'first fine careless rapture' of writing a first book. I find change refreshing" (quoted in Fitzgibbons, 167). Accustomed, however, to writing swiftly moving works in a fairly simple style for younger children, Cleary soon realized that she would need to change her style for older ones: "When I read the first draft of the first chapter of *Fifteen,* I was surprised to find it almost as terse as a telegram. I had to start over and slow down" (Fitzgibbons, 167). Some things did not change, however, for the emphasis still is on the triumphs and trivialities in the life of an ordinary person.

Jane Purdy is painfully aware of her ordinariness, especially when she compares herself to wonderful Marcy; but then Jane meets a wonderful boy. One fact lies in the way of their relationship: Jane does not know his name. But he has learned hers and calls; he is Stan Crandall, and he asks Jane for a date. At first the date is wonderful, but after a movie about which Jane remembers little, they see Marcy and her date at the local hangout. Shy Jane begins to doubt how successful her date has been. But watching from the darkened house as Stan pulls a bicycle out of the bushes and rides off, Jane realizes that he is not all that confident, and she remembers the little, unconfident things he had done during the evening. Her first date with Stan has been truly wonderful.

Then Stan asks Jane to go to the city with two other couples (including Marcy and her boyfriend) to have dinner at a Chinese restaurant. The date begins on an offbeat note when they all ride in his delivery truck, since his father has taken the family car. Miserable because of the strange food and because Stan seems to talk more to Marcy than to her, Jane is heartsick that she has spoiled their date. But Stan assures her that he finds her "different" and appreciates the fact that she did not make fun of riding in the delivery truck.

As "Stan's girl," Jane feels special and dreams of things to come, especially the first school dance. But he takes another girl (an old family friend much like Marcy), and Jane is exasperated with herself for taking their relationship seriously; she no longer feels special. It is Jane, however, who gets a ride in Stan's new Model A. His explanation that he had promised to take the old friend before he knew Jane—and that he had not enjoyed the date—makes Jane jubilant. She finds herself acting like Marcy and actually allows June's boyfriend to kiss her for 50¢. Seeing that Stan is hurt, she also realizes that that was why she had kissed the boy. But Stan does not call when he should, and Jane knows he is disgusted with her. Since acting like Marcy caused the trouble, Jane decides to act like herself; if Stan does not like it, it simply will have to do. This decision relieves Jane: she also learns that Stan was rushed to the hospital for an emergency appendectomy before he had a chance to call.

When she decides to send flowers and selects them before learning that the shop will not deliver, Jane finds herself walking behind a gaudy arrangement first to the hospital and then to Stan's house, when she learns he has been discharged. But audacity sees her through; her triumph is complete when Stan invites her to the class steak bake and movie. The date is a revelation of Stan's feelings and of her own new confidence, and she is thrilled when he gives her his ID bracelet. But they never get to be alone; even their first kiss is accompanied by the family cat with a dead gopher and Jane's father praising the cat. The evening did not go quite as planned, but Jane knows that she is his girl, and that is all that matters.

Reviewers were charmed by Jane's love story, praising its humor and Cleary's understanding of teenagers. "The story has some of the same humor, and an understanding of teen-agers comparable to the author's understanding of eight-year-olds as shown in the stories of Henry Huggins and his friends," wrote the reviewer for the *Bulletin of the Center for Children's Books.*[2] The reviewer for *Saturday Review* agreed: "The author of the inimitable 'Henry Huggins' proves her versatility and her understanding of adolescence. . . . The same humor that has endeared Mrs. Cleary to younger boys and girls marks this story of Jane and her friends."³ While the *Bulletin* contented itself with calling the book "pleasant, light reading," the *Review* prophesied that "Fifteen-year-old girls, girls not yet fifteen, and anyone who has ever been fifteen will love this story." In 1958 the work was awarded the Dorothy Canfield Fisher Children's Book Award.

Fifteen is the most formulaic of the four works for adolescents, with some elements of traditional romance. Its plot follows a simple formula: Jane meets Stan and sets her heart on him; after a series of dates and misunderstandings, he gives her his ID bracelet and her first kiss. The work also has many elements of traditional romance. There is the glamorous, confident Other Woman, in the shape of Marcy and of Bitsy, the old friend Stan takes to the first school dance instead of Jane. There is the sense of the heroine's simple virtue winning out over the sophistication of her rival: Stan's interest in Marcy seems to be mostly in Jane's mind, and he himself says that he is disenchanted with Bitsy after what she says about his job; the fact that Jane makes no comments about it is part of her charm for him. There is the lack of communication that keeps Jane apprehensive about whether or not Stan actually enjoys being with her, as she frets over why he has not asked her to the school dance and why he does not call her after she has allowed another boy to kiss her. Finally, there is the promise at the end of the work of everlasting love, as Jane cherishes Stan's first kiss and the knowledge that "she was Stan's girl. That was all that really mattered" (254). The emphasis, however, is not on love as such—though she finds Stan exciting, Jane does not delude herself into thinking she really loves him—rather, it is on their gradually developing relationship. From the first date to going steady, Cleary presents a relationship that unfolds slowly as Jane and Stan learn about each other.

The first of Cleary's works for adolescents, *Fifteen* has the simplest love story. As Cleary produced work after work detailing the love stories of ordinary girls, the formulae, the girls, and the romance became more and more complex.

The Luckiest Girl

Cleary wrote a Henry Huggins book before publishing *The Luck-iest Girl* in 1958. Sixteen-year-old Shelley Latham is more expe-rienced than Jane but is no more expert about her romantic tangles, which are complicated by her difficult relationship with her mother. Change is what she needs, Shelley decides, and change is what she gets when she spends a school year in Cali-fornia with her mother's friend, Mavis Michie. Now she can break up with an old boyfriend, escape her demanding mother, and meet the boy she has always wanted to meet.

California is very different from what Oregonian Shelley is used to, and so is the casual Michie family. The students at the new school are friendly, and Philip Blanton, the boy of her dreams, is in her biology class. But it is Hartley Lathrop, from Shelley's homeroom, who is her first California date. The end of their comfortable evening is awkward, for as Hartley tries to get closer, Shelley realizes that Katie Michie is spying on them, and she is clumsily brusque. The next week Hartley is restrained, and Shelley cannot explain about Katie. But Philip asks her out, and, though it is an awkward evening, with many silences, now begins a golden time for Shelley. She even wears a raincoat her mother had bought her to the school dance; when a girl has made a name for herself at a new school and dates a wonderful boy, it does not seem to matter what kind of raincoat she wears.

Semester grades—and a D in biology—burst Shelley's bubble; she must work to bring up the biology grade. Philip cannot play on the basketball team or date Shelley for the rest of the year because he has flunked biology. Suddenly all is changed, espe-cially biology. Her views about her mother change, too, after she witnesses an appallingly familiar scene between Katie and Mavis. Mothers and daughters are, Shelley realizes, in a sort of tug of war that neither wins. Suddenly, she does not feel so bad about being rebellious. Hoping to mask her difficulties with Philip, Shelley sets out to recapture Hartley's interest: she will write to her mother about him, and she misses his companion-ship. Comfortably arguing with Hartley over an article for journalism class, Shelley finds that she is having more fun with him than she had with Philip, especially after she explains about the brusque end of their first date. She has little in common with Philip; having enjoyed the admiration of the other girls more than Philip himself, she had mentally turned him into the boy she wanted him to be. Now she feels good because Hartley likes her and she likes him; but there is the problem of Philip's liking her.

Her tension ends at the school carnival, where Philip has a date of his own; suddenly Shelley is relieved to know that their relationship is over. As the days slide by, Shelley is happy. Listening to Katie and Mavis bicker over Katie's preparations for a dance, Shelley realizes that the tensions between her and her mother are a natural part of life, with Shelley wanting to be an adult and her loving mother wanting Shelley to remain her child. Then come the last day of school and Shelley's last date with Hartley, a quiet evening during which Shelley suddenly realizes that she is in love. Sad at saying goodbye, as Shelley swings in the Michies's back yard, she realizes that this sadness is part of growing up.

The reviewer for the *Bulletin of the Center for Children's Books* was as charmed by *The Luckiest Girl* as by *Fifteen*, again praising the work's humor and the realism with which Cleary presented the relationships between her characters: "A moving and honest story of adolescence, well-rounded and frequently humorous. The relationships between children and adults, and among the children and young people, are portrayed with perception and told with restraint."[4]

Shelley herself is a more interesting personality than Jane Purdy, probably because she is older and more experienced. She is more confident than Jane, who is self-conscious to the point of obsessiveness, and her excitement about her new life in California seems to fuel her self-confidence. Cleary allows the already-complicated romance of this energetic character to be complicated further by her sometimes-combative relationship with her mother, which she deals with from afar by watching the Michie family. In this work, Cleary deals with mother–daughter relationships, the difficulties of a teenager learning to understand herself, and the difficulty not knowing oneself can bring to relationships, with the emphasis on romance.

The Luckiest Girl begins as a formula romance, with Shelley meeting and resolving to go steady with the boy of her dreams, but the romance is complicated by the fact that she does not really know what she wants and pursues the wrong relationship as a result. Shy and handsome, Philip seems exactly the kind of boy Shelley longs for after what seems a lifetime with boring, predictable Jack. But dates with him do not go well, as Shelley desperately casts about for things to do or to talk about; it is only when she is forced to date Hartley that she realizes how little she and Philip have in common. It is less-handsome Hartley who plunges into the Michies's nontraditional life-style in a way Philip never would, and whose dates with Shelley are full of comfortable conversations and arguments over their common interests. Having not gotten to know Philip, Shelley has no inkling of his real interests and has made him in her mind into the kind of boy she wants; eventually, she realizes, "because [Philip] was not really the boy she had wanted him to be, she would have come to feel about him the way she felt about Jack," for there would be something he did "that she would wish he would not do, and then she would know that she was tired of him" (251). But with Hartley she feels comfortable and close. A real relationship must be based on really knowing the other person, not simply on physical attraction.

Jean and Johnny

The Luckiest Girl was followed a year later by *Jean and Johnny*. Having explored the idea of an inexperienced girl in the wrong relationship, Cleary turned to it again in the story of Jean Jarrett, published in 1959, as Jean pursues an infatuation with a handsome charmer.

Their relationship begins at a dance Jean watches with Elaine Mundy, her best friend; enchanted by the beauty of the scene, she accepts as if in a dream when a boy asks her to dance. Reality quickly intrudes and she breaks off, but she is surprisingly happy, for at last she has been singled out. Now Jean finds herself dreaming and spending time in front of the bathroom mirror. Elaine, though, efficiently organizes Jean for that next, inevitable meeting, and the two girls gather information on the boy, whose name is Johnny Chessler. When Elaine actually goes up and talks to Johnny, what he says makes it clear that he knows they have been watching him. Humiliated, Jean is dazzled when she literally runs into Johnny in the hall and he calls her a "cute girl": she has been noticed.

Now he speaks whenever they meet in the hall and even learns her name. If she stays after her last class, she can walk out of school with Johnny and his friend, Homer. Learning that Johnny is trying out for the variety show, Jean even joins the Costume Club. When Jean finds Johnny walking with a beautiful girl one day, his wink shows her that the girl means nothing to him; but walking home alone, Jean uncomfortably realizes that she and Elaine never seem to see each other and are growing apart.

When Johnny asks to come over one night, Jean prepares happily. But an hour after he is due, Johnny cancels; Jean's disappointment is mollified when he informs her that she has a cute nose. It is the next Saturday that Johnny comes by and takes Jean to the local drive-in for cokes and to listen to Johnny on the school's radio program. Jean makes the next date, to the upcoming girls' choice dance. The thrill of finding the perfect dress is marred by an overheard conversation between a woman whose son is in a situation much like Jean and Johnny's. Shattered, Jean realizes that his bits of attention have not been worth the pain she has suffered and caused her friends, and a photo Elaine had taken of them shows the truth about their relationship: Johnny cool and handsome and Jean strained and unhappy. She no longer wants to take Johnny to the dance.

But Johnny breaks the date, citing a sick grandmother. Taking Elaine's advice, Jean asks unglamorous Homer. She even finds herself enjoying their evening, despite painful shoes and the pain of seeing Johnny attending with another girl. Homer also tells her some disquieting things about Johnny. It has not been a dream date, but she was more comfortable with him than she had been with Johnny. The Johnny she liked does not exist, but she will not forget him, for he was the first boy to single her out.

Reviewers enjoyed Jean's story, noting its humor and realism. "Mrs. Cleary has drawn another fifteen-year-old heroine with as sure a touch as that which pictured Jane in *Fifteen*," wrote the reviewer in *Horn Book*, noting that "younger teen-age readers will discover just as complete an empathy for the new Jean. Blithe humor freshens the ordinary enough incidents while a perceptive inclusion of details important to Jean's contemporaries makes everything as real as next door."[5] The reviewer for the *Bulletin of the Center for Children's Books* agreed, pointing out that the book's "not-unusual plot" is "handled with freshness and restraint" and that "[e]xcellent characterizations and natural touches of everyday incidents enhance the warmth and humor of the style."[6] *Jean and Johnny* was also proclaimed a notable book by the American Library Association.

Having explored the basic boy-meets-girl formula in *Fifteen* and discussed what constitutes a real relationship in *The Luckiest Girl,* in *Jean and Johnny,* Cleary takes it one step further by exploring the nuances of the impossible crush on the wrong boy. Like Shelley, Jean gets herself into the wrong relationship, not because she knows what she really wants in a relationship but because she knows what she does not want. Working to appear more attractive, casually managing to be where Johnny is, learning where he lives for giggling walkbys, milking every word and action for its deeper significance, calling him simply to hear his voice, Jean indulges in the kind of behavior typical of any shy girl with a crush. In Jean's case, she has the pleasure of going out with him, but eventually she realizes that that pleasure has not been worth the tension and pain she has experienced. For just as Shelley realizes that handsome Philip is not the boy she thought he was, Jean discovers that exciting Johnny may seem interesting but is shallow, flattered by her attention but not caring enough to be honest. Having had his license taken away for speeding, Johnny is unwilling to walk to Jean's house in the rain, so he calls her—an hour late—and lies about why he has not come. Finding that he and Jean will have to be driven to the dance by her parents, he cancels their date with the story of a sick grandmother, preferring to attend the dance with a girl who has her own car—a girl whom he had slighted one day when Jean saw them walking together by implying, with a wink, that she meant nothing to him. It is uninteresting, unhandsome Homer who not only is interesting in his own right, but who cares enough about Jean to treat her with respect.

As in *The Luckiest Girl,* Cleary emphasizes the comfortable relationship over the glamorous one, the average boy over the exciting one; Homer, awkward dancer and just as awkward at engineering their first kiss, is not the kind of boy whose dates will be thrilling, but he is nice, and Jean will not have to wonder whether or not he really likes her. But in *Jean and Johnny,* Cleary also points out that the boy who does not seem right at the time probably will seem very right later. Susan, Jean's sister, meets Ken Cory—"Old Repulsive"—after several years and finds that he has grown from an awkward, blotchy-skinned, bucktoothed adolescent to a poised adult who is not handsome but who possesses an attractive gentleness and strength and regard for her (104, 158). Jean realizes that, perhaps, "that was what a lot of girls should do—all they could do, really—wait for the boys to grow up" (282).

Sister of the Bride

The last of Cleary's works for adolescents was published four years later, in 1963, after *Emily's Runaway Imagination, Henry and the Clubhouse* and the works based on "Leave It to Beaver." In *Fifteen,* Cleary had explored a girl's first relationship; *The Luckiest Girl* and *Jean and Johnny* involved knowing when a relationship is real; in *Sister of the Bride,* Cleary emphasizes that young love is not always the real thing.

Walked home by klutzy Tootie Bodger, who is more interested in her than she is in him, Barbara MacLane envies her older sister, Rosemary, with whom Barbara simply wants to catch up. Then Rosemary calls: she is engaged to marry Greg Aldredge. Barbara now despairs of ever catching up with Rosemary, but she begins to dream of what is to be sure to be a romantic wedding, if it occurs. (Their parents are less than thrilled with the thought, and Rosemary and Greg must combine to convince them.) Barbara begins to think about her own wedding, only two years away if she works it right. Tootie will not do, but handsome Bill Cunningham might.

Rosemary's wedding plans are exasperating: she wants a practical wedding without a "middle-class" engagement ring, to which she will wear a suit and invite only family and friends (maybe). But not even Rosemary can disappoint her grandmother when she brings the lovely lace veil she had worn over fifty years ago; and Barbara realizes joyfully that now Rosemary *must* have a lovely wedding to go with it. Her own wedding plans seem to be going well, as her relationship with Bill grows on the strength of her baking cookies and his remembering the anniversary of their meeting.

Rosemary's hectic wedding plans make it seem "do it yourself," mostly by the rest of the family. The veil is fancier than the dresses they can afford, but the family cat demolishes it and the remainder is perfect as a fingertip-length veil and short jacket. The bride who wants her life free of "things" enjoys a shower by her mother's friends and sports an engagement ring, and Barbara feels she is losing her sister. The next days hold disappointments for Barbara: there will be no exciting shopping for her dress, and she is not invited to help buy the wedding dress, though she too will wear it some day. Just as bad, though Bill enjoys the cookies she gives him, he does not ask her out. The dingy little apartment Greg and Rosemary will share is far from Barbara's dream of a shiny newlywed household. But she realizes that Rosemary does not care how bad it is, for marriage is more than the glitter and newness pictured in magazines: it is love and trust, and Greg is lucky to be marrying Rosemary, who understands and is prepared for this.

The wedding nears and Barbara perhaps has a broken heart, for Bill graduates without inviting her to the seniors' party. His visit the next day with a shirt for Barbara to mend is the last straw, and she makes her feelings clear. When he calls for a date and she refuses, Barbara realizes that she likes Bill but does not love him; she should have gone out with him. But Tootie turns out to be just as interesting at the rehearsal dinner.

It is a lovely wedding, though Barbara is not so sure she will be the next bride. Bill calls for a date just as they leave for the wedding, and Tootie asks her out, so she has dates with two boys that weekend and is living a life of her own. Suddenly her dreams of being a bride seem childish, and she is eager to discover whether she likes Bill or Tootie most.

Reviewers seem to have appreciated the humor and timeliness of the work. Calling the book a "pleasantly realistic" and "lightly humorous" family story with "warmth, honest sentiment, and affectionate humor," the *Bulletin of the Center for Children's Books* emphasized its "good writing style" and "good values."[7] *Horn Book* pointed out that *Sister of the Bride* was "a lighthearted novel on a serious theme," praising Cleary's "understanding of today's young people and her remarkable ability to express it in their terms, with warmth and humor" in a "fast-moving story rooted in the serious contemporary problem of early marriages."[8]

With its carefully–detailed difficulties planning and executing the wedding and with Barbara's frustrations with her "suitors," *Sister of the Bride* is one of the most humorous of the works. Cleary not only explores the difficulties of bringing together two families, but the dynamics of the family unit as Barbara and Gordy battle and make up in the age-old way of siblings. By the end of the work, Barbara has learned something about her relationship with her brother and, more important, realized that love and marriage are more complex than she had imagined.

While Cleary explores the nuances of young love in her first three works for adolescents, in the last she emphasizes that it is not really permanent, for it is not really love. Entranced by visions of Rosemary's wedding, Barbara talks herself into working toward the same thing, without realizing the realities involved. As in *Jean and Johnny* and *The Luckiest Girl*, Cleary focuses on the idea that the boy who seems boring may be the right boy after all, as Tootie Bodger turns out to be more interesting than Barbara had imagined. But the emphasis is not only on finding the right boy, but finding him at the right time: sixteen-year-old Barbara attempts to seem domestic but cannot bring it off and realizes that she is too young to be interested in settling down, as Rosemary is doing. What she has at the end of the work is a weekend with two dates, not one boyfriend. Still in love with the orange blossom idea of romance and marriage, Barbara finds both her romantic version of what the wedding will be like and her romantic notions of marriage itself dissolved. Her focus is on the idea of beautiful new silver and china and of beautiful, shiny new things in a beautiful, shiny new life, at odds with the handthrown pottery, burlap placemats, dingy little apartment, and unglamorous apartment-managing of Rosemary's new life. Rosemary, in real love, knows how unglamorous her life will be, how terrible the apartment is, and is prepared for this; Barbara, unsure at the beginning of the book what real love is, is prepared for none of it, which is as it should be. Early marriage is not the answer, Barbara realizes, and her grandmother agrees, for Barbara is at the age in which she should have fun; there is lots of time for real love.

Adolescent Love

Published in the late 1950s and early 1960s, Cleary's four works for adolescents possibly have not been as popular as her works for younger children. But all have remained in print, and *Fifteen,* especially, has demonstrated great longevity. There have been British, Dutch, and Japanese editions. In the late 1970s, it was "the most popular book with girls" in South Africa (Fitzgibbons, 170); Aidan Chambers, listing works for British reluctant readers, calls the work "the standby, the natural, the first title we think of suggesting"—to boys as well as to girls.[9] In the United States, the work has generated letters from fans aged eight to eighteen, many from the Midwest; after a few years in which Cleary received few letters, around 1975 the volume increased (Fitzgibbons, 167). All four works were republished in 1980, without illustrations, in Dell Laurel Leaf's "Young Love" series, consisting of works from the Laurel Leaf line "which contain a strong element of romance."[10]

As in Cleary's works for younger children, in her works for adolescents her readers have found stories of ordinary life. With their emphasis on love, these books nevertheless have as their protagonists ordinary girls experiencing ordinary struggles with family and friends as they learn about relationships and about growing up.

As in Cleary's other works, the protagonists of these books are not extraordinary; nonglamorous and insecure, these are characters with whom most adolescent girls can identify. The lives of the four are not filled with adventure: they go to school and dream of the future. Jane Purdy babysits and dreams of being married. Jean Jarrett, whose family has little money, sews her own clothes; uninterested in the spotlight, she does not mind being "the salt-of-the-earth type" (50–51) who melts into the background at school; and she looks forward to a life of middle-class domesticity. Barbara MacLane fights with her younger brother and dreams of romance. Shelley Latham's life is exciting only by contrast with the one she has left behind in Oregon, a place which a friend in California finds as exotic and romantic as Shelley finds California. Even she, however, must concentrate on passing biology.

Shelley is perhaps the most confident of the four, taking part in school activities with aplomb and seeming to worry little about the impression she is making in the strange school, though she does worry about her relationship with Philip. Free of the expectations of family and old friends, in California she seizes the chance to rethink and explore what she can be. The others, however, evince the insecurities and tendencies to focus on the trivial aspects that many adolescents do. Jane, especially, is such a mass of insecurities that one critic has called *Fifteen* "a teenage version of *The Diary of a Nobody*" because of her "obsessional tendency to endow small matters with great significance."[11] Constantly comparing herself with glamorous, popular Marcy, Jane worries about every nuance of her dates with Stan Crandall and longs for Marcy's confidence; during the triple date, Jane convinces herself that she has worn the wrong clothes and ruined the date because of her unfamiliarity with Chinese restaurants. Overshadowed by a sense of Marcy's perfection, Jane must realize what Stan already knows, that what she herself has to offer is enough—a fact she proves to herself when she airily carries off carrying a monstrous flower arrangement through town. Barbara and Jean bring their insecurities upon themselves. Though Barbara seems secure in her actions, she yearns to "catch up" with her two-years-older sister and feels her insecurities only when comparing herself with Rosemary; seeing her sister, Barbara feels her youth and longs for all her sister has. Jean's insecurities result from her pursuit of more glamorous Johnny: like Jane, she finds herself attempting to interpret every action and word and nuance of her conversations with Johnny and also compares herself with a more glamorous rival.

Their love stories are not extraordinary, either. In all four works, Cleary emphasizes that love can be powerful and painful, and that it may not always last. Also, in typical Cleary style, its course does not run smoothly, even after girl and boy have realized that they are right for each other. The experience Cleary seems interested in chronicling is the experience of an ordinary girl learning about love: emotional love rather than physical relationships are emphasized, as the protagonists work their way through the tangles of miscommunication and cross-purposes. Focusing on the does he/doesn't he insecurities of the early part of a relationship, each of the four works emphasizes the exciting opening of a new relationship rather than what could happen next; the Kiss seems, in these works, the ultimate sign of the bond that has been formed. There is no sense that the girls' relationships could lead to anything more. Only Shelley and Jane are kissed, and then only once, at the end of their respective works: Jane on page 253 of a 254-page work; Shelley, two pages before the end of the work. A startled Jean finds herself being *asked* by Homer if she "would be interested" in kissing him at the end of their first date, and she refuses him; Barbara does not even go on a date in her book.

What Cleary does explore are the first flutterings, the hopeless

crushes, the wrong relationships that any teenager could experience—all the while pointing the way to relationships more satisfying and more lasting. Taken in chronological order, the
romantic relationships in these works grow ever more complex as
Cleary moves from chronicling the simple, formula romance to
showing that young love is no panacea. From the basic boy-meets-
girl formula of *Fifteen,* Cleary moved to *The Luckiest Girl,* in
which what begins as a formula romance is complicated by the
fact that the protagonist is too young to know what she really
wants. Jean, too, while more ready for the cares and realities of
marriage, is too young and inexperienced to keep herself from
being swept away by glamorous, inappropriate Johnny. In *Sister
of the Bride,* Cleary contradicts the earnestness of young romance
by pointing out that young love is not really love; it is mostly
infatuation, not prepared for the unglamorous aspects of marriage. None of the works negates the deep emotions felt by their
young protagonists, but Cleary makes it clear that real, permanent love is something different.

Romance is no panacea: just because one is in love, life does not
suddenly become perfect. Ordinary life has a way of intruding
unromantically, and humorously, even into real love in Cleary's
works. Blissfully in love, Rosemary MacLane must think about
"Plato: Teacher and Theorist" when she really wants to think
about Greg and the upcoming wedding (*Sister,* 121); Shelley finds
a romantic moment with Hartley being eagerly observed by thir-
teen-year-old Katie, curled up on top of the refrigerator (*Luckiest,*
88). Jane, especially, finds ordinary life intruding on her romance:
longing to sneak away with Stan when they learn that the movie
the junior class is about to see at their picnic is an educational
film about American history, she nevertheless is ushered with
Stan to their seats, to find themselves sitting beside the class
faculty adviser; their first kiss is accompanied by the low, triumphant wails of the family cat, who has dropped a dead gopher at
Jane's feet (*Fifteen,* 254). Romance, in Cleary's works, is not for
the humorless.

As they learn about love, Jane, Shelley, Jean, and Barbara also
learn about life and themselves. Jane, shy and insecure in her

first relationship, makes the biggest leap: the climax of *Fifteen* may be when Stan pronounces Jane his steady, but another major turning point already has occurred when Jane bluffs her way past her friends, carrying that enormous flower arrangement. Jane has longed to be like cool, confident Marcy or like intellectual Liz. Her attempt to become an intellectual does not last long, for she quickly realizes that this is not what she really wants; her attempt to act like Marcy leaves her and Stan miserable. Now resolving to be herself—whether or not Stan will like her—Jane finds that what she has to offer is enough as she discovers within herself the confidence to laugh at her predicament and to answer both Marcy's catty remarks and Liz's intellectual superiority. Realizing that she does not really know Philip, Shelley also comes to realize that she has been almost as unknowing about herself, planning to go to college without really knowing why and not knowing what she really wants out of a relationship. Her stay in California, where there are no expectations about who she is or what she will do, gives Shelley the freedom to develop her interest in journalism and to come closer to finding what she really wants in life. Always able to accept herself as a girl who stays in the background, Jean is content with this role and with her future as a housewife and mother, but she finds satisfaction in joining the Costume Club and taking part in school activities, activities that seem to bolster her self-confidence just as Johnny is draining it. Lost in her attempts to be like her sister and floating in clouds of orange blossoms, Barbara comes to realize that being herself and living on her own schedule is much more satisfying. The girls' self-knowledge seems designed to anchor them more firmly in their relationships. Jane is rewarded for her struggle with the flowers by learning from Stan's family the extent of his affections for her; both Shelley and Jean realize exactly what they are looking for in relationships; sticking to her own schedule, Barbara finds that she has two dates that weekend with two very different boys.

Just as the view of love in these works grows more complex, so do the families and family relationships in them, for family life is as important in these works as in the works for younger readers.

Jane is an only child whose parents are protective but malleable. Shelley too is an only child, but her relationship with her mother is difficult: Cleary shows the reader two strong wills battling, as Shelley tries to become independent of a mother who is loathe to release her only child. The emphasis of her story is as much on her understanding this and realizing that it is normal as it is on love: troubled by her new stubbornness and rebellious feelings, Shelley learns how normal they are by watching Katie and Mavis and Mavis and her mother. The last two works present larger families: Jean is the younger sister, which sometimes is difficult, as Susan tries to give her advice; their father also can be difficult, banning babysitting and being stern about approving of the boys they date. Younger sister Barbara is the middle child who is long- ing to "catch up" with her older, more glamorous sister, quarrel- ling with her younger brother. She too works out her relationships in the course of the book, realizing that she also has a life as important as her sister's and learning to get along better with their brother.

Possibly because these are works for older readers, Cleary em- phasizes the parents as individuals even if, to their children, they are dull. Parents may not seem perfect, Cleary points out in these works, but they are people, too. Mr. Purdy's pride in the family cat gives Jane some uneasy moments; Mrs. Latham seems an un- sympathetic figure at the beginning of the book but is touching as she reaches into her memories of being a teenager during the depression to deal with Shelley and Mavis reveals that she once was desperate to be "Soph Doll" (*Luckiest*, 80). Individualistic Tom and Mavis Michie leave the laundry hamper open for the cat, hang out laundry to dry by moonlight, and organize ironing par- ties; Mavis's arguments with her mother give Shelley insight into her relationship with her own mother. The Jarretts seem dull to their children because their jobs exhaust them, not because they themselves are dull; Mrs. Jarrett's contests are both the trial and the delight of the family. Mrs. MacLane tries to make it clear to Rosemary that she is not the only member of the family busy dur- ing semester finals; Mr. MacLane prides himself on his punctua- tion and his print shop.

Again, it is the ordinary qualities of ordinary life that become extraordinary in the works. The struggle to become independent from suddenly unsuitable parents, the difficulties of having little money just as one is desperate for pretty clothes, and the awkward relationships with siblings: all are familiar to Cleary's readers. The ordinary become extraordinary is most evident in *The Luckiest Girl,* as Shelley's new friends watch in amusement and envy her enjoyment of the elements of California life they have taken for granted, and she listens in surprise as a friend marvels at the ever-running drinking Oregon fountains Shelley takes for granted.

It is just this picture of ordinary life that helps make these four books the most dated of Cleary's works. The emphasis on clothes, so important to teenage readers, especially helps put the books into their time frame. The dresses the girls wear while not in school may seem unnaturally formal to today's reader, who might find Jane's fuss over white gloves puzzling; the contrasts between the clothes of Cleary's less-sophisticated protagonists and more-sophisticated girls has been lost in time. That Jean could buy a fashionable party dress for $17.95, shoes dyed to match for $6.99, and a Coke for 10¢ is startling by today's standards. The girls' naivete also seems surprising: Jane's lack of experience with Chinese food and Shelley's surprise at how different California looks may seem strange to readers who are used to finding Chinese restaurants in almost every town and seeing the landscape of California on the television screen. That the girls have little interest in driving or in having access to a car—Shelley and Barbara, both sixteen, each drive the family car once, on business—seems odd in a time when fourteen-year-olds look forward to learning to drive.

In the works' presentation of the future each girl has to look forward to, they also may seem dated. Shelley is the only protagonist who is thinking of having a career; that Jean, at age fifteen, actually looks forward to a life of "dishpans, mops . . . [d]iapers, [and] budgets" seems unrealistic and dull. Adult readers may disapprove of the emphasis on "securing an eligible male" (Thompson, 43) in these works, though this is the preoccupation of most

teenage girls; *Fifteen* is the most insistent in this regard, for in
the other three works the protagonists do not find that special
boy by the end of the work. In fact, *Fifteen*'s "insistent adulation
of the male" struck one critic as "irritating" (Thompson, 44).
Jane's fixation on Stan's ID bracelet as symbol of their relationship—it is mentioned eight times in the book—seems more amusing than anything else, especially her ecstasy when—eyes on the
movie screen in front of them—he reaches over and clicks it pro-
prietarily onto her wrist; their later kiss is almost anticlimactic.

These works have a stronger autobiographical element than
any other of Cleary's work, as she drew on her own experiences
as a teenager. Jane's trying afternoons babysitting lively young
children may have been drawn in part from Cleary's experiences
babysitting in high school (*Yamhill*, 238–39). Only-child Shelley's
difficulties with her mother, unwilling to grant her child's independence, probably were modelled on Cleary's difficulties with
her own mother, just as unwilling. Beverly's relationship with
Gerhart inspired Shelley's relationship with Jack, so boring because the two have nothing in common. Like Shelley, young Beverly was invited by a relative whose husband taught physical
education to stay with them in California and go to school for the
winter. Cleary, though, attended junior college instead of high
school, an invitation that her father, like Shelley's, decided she
would accept (*Yamhill*, 265; 269). For Cleary as well as for Shelley, California seemed a Never-neverland in which she could escape from the expectations of her family (especially her mother)
and of the boy she was dating (*Yamhill*, 251). *Jean and Johnny*
also is close to Cleary's own experiences at about the same age:
like Mr. and Mrs. Jarrett, Mr. and Mrs. Bunn seemed to their
daughter to sleep through the evening, uninterested in going out;
Mr. Cleary, like Mr. Jarrett, retired to the breakfast nook when
Beverly had friends over (*Yamhill*, 206); like Jean, young Beverly
wrote to pen pals (*Yamhill*, 260). Also like Jean, Cleary, unsuitably dressed and taking decorations to the Masonic Lodge, was
asked to dance (*Yamhill*, 215), though, unlike Jean, she never saw
her partner again; Beverly served the same kind of cookies with
whipped cream between them to Gerhart that Jean makes for her

date with Johnny, and, like Jean and Johnny's, they remained uneaten (*Yamhill*, 220). The Bunns's lack of ready money during the depression, with Beverly's mother entering contests to win money for the family, added authenticity to the Jarretts's similar economic difficulties, with Mrs. Jarrett entering contests to give her family small luxuries (*Yamhill*, 180). The deemphasis on popularity in Cleary's works for adolescence seem inspired at least partly by Cleary's experiences with the cliques in her own high school (*Yamhill*, 183).

What keeps these books alive for their readers is what allowed Cleary to put so much of her own experience, in the 1930s, into these works written in the 1950s and 1960s: the timeless qualities of young romance. The first flutter, the exciting insecurity, the hopeless and inappropriate crushes—all are the same today as they ever were. The details of clothing and daily life may have changed since the works were first published, but the essential details—of being a teenaged girl—and their emphasis on the quirkiness and humor of daily life makes them as fresh and readable for young readers as they were when first published.

Afterword

What Cleary has accomplished in her thirty-odd books is the championing of the ordinary child: the child as she is, with faults and doubts, rather than the child as adults would have her, repenting her mistakes and resolving to be good; the child involved in his own problems, which seem unimportant only to adults. In her presentation of real life, Cleary stands as a repudiation not just of the didactic realism of the early twentieth century, but of the problem-laden new realism of the later twentieth century.

By the time Beverly Bunn was reading, there had been a shift from the little paragons of virtue and education prevalent in the early nineteenth century to the more natural, slightly mischievous child of the later part of the century; but the emphasis into the twentieth century still was on the bad child made good and the good child made better by adversity. Beverly Bunn disliked the "goody-goody" five little Peppers and longed for humorous stories about real children playing together such as the girls in Carroll Watson Rankin's *Dandelion Cottage* or natural children realistically portrayed such as Dencey, in Caroline Dale Snedeker's *Downright Dencey*. In the movies, she found what she wanted in the Our Gang comedies and wondered where the books were that humorously explored such relationships.

Cleary's protagonists, while not really bad, are not paragons of virtue; Otis Spofford was kept from the shelves in some libraries because of his lack of repentance, and even in college classes there are a few students who worry that Ramona Quimby is not a good influence. In her humorous depiction of the ordinary trials of everyday childhood, Cleary also stands in contrast to the problem novels of new realism, with their conjugated problems and their protagonists beset by alcoholism, divorce, and abuse. Grimly realistic books about drug addiction, sexual abuse, divorce, and other "problems children are powerless to solve" are to Cleary as unrealistic as the novels she read when a child: "I feel it is presumptuous of adults to feel they can offer solutions in fiction to troubled children. Writers, I feel, should write of childhood as they know it and leave children free to discover what they need" ("Regina," 24).

This humorous version of life is what Cleary's readers may remember best about her works—this and her well-meaning, sometimes-befuddled characters. *Dear Mr. Henshaw,* Cleary's most complex novel to date, is as satisfying in its careful balance of the serious and humorous aspects of life as it is thematically. But Cleary's most memorable accomplishment so far is probably that energetic bundle of complexities, Ramona Quimby, whom we watch grow through eleven books, from Henry Huggins's nemesis to a girl with a nemesis of her own. Henry himself, determined and persistent, gamely coping in a humorously chaotic life, is just as memorable, popular forty years after his first appearance in print. The novels' rich picture of ordinary life in the United States satisfies contemporary readers, who see their own lives reflected, and may prove as satisfying to future readers seeking a window into twentieth-century life.

Cleary has given to children's literature a sense that ordinary life itself is enough to hold a reader's interest and carry a work of fiction; the difficulties inherent in going to school and dealing with peers are enough. Any reader who has watched Henry Huggins fall into his difficulties or Ramona Quimby imagine her way into hers would agree; life is complex enough as it is. Cleary has never wanted to write books like *"Ramona Solves the Mystery of the Haunted House and Finds a Baby Brother"* or *"Henry and Beezus Play Doctor"* ("Newbery," 438), nor has she found it necessary, for her popularity seems to have been assured from the beginning.

What Cleary has chosen to dwell on are the smaller problems of everyday life—the problems that children can solve themselves—and the result is a chronicle of everyday life in the twentieth century. An emphasis on humor has not kept her from exploring worries about teachers and school and struggles with peers, fears of abandonment and of the dark, and of not fitting in. These are carefully detailed and given their proper weight in works rich in details of family relationships and family life. As real life has changed, so has the ordinary life in Cleary's novels. The norm of Henry Huggins's close-knit suburban family has given way to the norm of Leigh Botts's splintered family in Cleary's works, as in life. "Mrs. Cleary," Margaret Novinger notes, "may be called the Boswell of the average child" (Novinger, 81).

Part of this emphasis on the complexity of everyday life is the complexity of relationships: all Cleary's works have relationships with family and friends as their focus. The triumph of the individual in Cleary's novels includes both a triumph over immediate problems and a renewal of relationships. Emily Bartlett is friends again with Fong Quock; Socks's place in his family is secure; Henry and Ribsy are together and safe in the Huggins family; Ramona is snug in her place in the Quimby household; Leigh Botts forgives his father and is assured of his mother's love; and Shelley Latham finds new understanding of her demanding mother. The end of most of the works—especially the last book of the various series—finds their protagonists comfortably centered in their families and their worlds.

The protagonists in Cleary's books are well on their way to maturity. "To grow up is the ambition of normal children," Cleary has reminded us, and her works help assure her readers that they have grown ("Laughter," 562). Ramona's popularity may lie in the fact that she is not as old as most of the members of her audience; looking at her, they can judge how far they have come. They also can absorb what it is to be grown up. Cleary presents her readers with characters struggling toward adulthood and allows them to discover what being grown up really means. Growing up, Ralph S. Mouse finds, is not just growing older chronologically; it is taking responsibility. Henry begins to empathize with others; Ramona starts to see herself from the outside and to realize that others, too, are probably nice on the inside, even if that niceness "curdles" on the outside. Leigh learns to accept things as they are. Showing her readers that they are, indeed, growing up, Cleary gives them examples of others doing the same.

Where Cleary's work will go from here is difficult to assess. Having produced thirty-seven books and two short stories since 1949, Cleary has earned the right to slow down, though she shows no signs of retiring; *Muggie Maggie* was published in spring, 1990. What kind of work Cleary will write next also is difficult to assess: those thirty-seven books represent every genre from picture book to realistic fiction to fantasy to historical fiction to adolescent fiction to autobiography. One thing is certain, however: Cleary will continue to offer her readers humorous insight into themselves and the world around them, entertaining them with tales of characters much like themselves who, like all of Cleary's characters, are "winning at growing up."

Notes and References

Preface

1. Margaret Novinger, "Beverly Cleary: A Favorite Author of Children," in *Authors and Illustrators of Children's Books,* ed. Miriam Hoffman and Eva Samuels (New York: R. R. Bowker, 1972), 79; hereafter cited in the text.
2. James Zarrillo, "Beverly Cleary, Ramona Quimby, and the Teaching of Reading," *Children's Literature Association Quarterly* 12 (1988):131–35.
3. Suzanne Rahn, "Cat-Child: Rediscovering Socks and Island MacKenzie," *Lion and the Unicorn* 12 (1988):111–20.
4. David Rees, "Middle of the Way: Rodie Sudbery and Beverly Cleary," in *The Marble in the Water* (Boston: Horn Book, 1979, 1980), 90–103; hereafter cited in the text.
5. Susan Thompson, "Images of Adolescence," *Signal* January 1981, 37–59; hereafter cited in the text.

Chapter One

1. Beverly Cleary, "Writing Books about Henry Huggins," *Top of the News,* December 1957, 11; hereafter cited in the text as "Writing."
2. Beverly Cleary, *A Girl from Yamhill* (New York: Morrow, 1988), 11; hereafter cited in the text as *Yamhill.*
3. Beverly Cleary, "Laura Ingalls Wilder Award Presentation," *Horn Book* 51 (1975):362; hereafter cited in the text as "Wilder."
4. Beverly Cleary, "Books Remembered," *Calendar,* July 1982–February 1983, n.p.; hereafter cited in the text as "Books."
5. Deborah Churchman, "Children's Literature: A Source of Hope and Morality," *Christian Science Monitor,* 6 June 1983, 17; hereafter cited in the text.
6. Beverly Cleary, "Low Man in the Reading Circle, or, A Blackbird Takes Wing," *Horn Book* 45 (1969):287; hereafter cited in the text as "Low."

7. In David Reuther, "Beverly Cleary," *Horn Book* 60 (1984):443; hereafter cited in the text.

8. Beverly Cleary, "Newbery Medal Acceptance," *Horn Book* 60 (1984):431; hereafter cited in the text as "Newbery."

9. Shirley Fitzgibbons, "Focus on Beverly Cleary," *Top of the News,* Winter 1977, 168; hereafter cited in the text.

10. Paul C. Burns and Ruth Hines, "Beverly Cleary: Wonderful World of Humor," *Elementary English* 44 (1967):744; hereafter cited in the text.

11. "Beverly Cleary: A Practicing Perfectionist," *Early Years,* August–September 1982, 25; hereafter cited in the text as "Perfectionist."

12. Beverly Cleary, "Why Are Children Writing to Me Instead of Reading?" *New York Times,* 10 November 1985, 42; hereafter cited in the text as "Why."

13. Mary June Roggenbuck, "Beverly Cleary—the Children's Force at Work," *Language Arts,* January 1979, 59; hereafter cited in the text.

14. Beverly Cleary, *Ramona the Pest,* illus. Louis Darling (New York: Morrow, 1968), 75; hereafter cited in the text.

15. Beverly Cleary, Regina Medal Acceptance Speech, *Catholic Library World* (1980):23; hereafter cited in the text as "Regina."

16. Beverly Cleary, "On Talking Back to Authors," *Claremont Reading Conference Yearbook* (1970):4; hereafter cited in the text as "Talking."

17. Beverly Cleary, "The Laughter of Children," *Horn Book* 58 (1982):556; hereafter cited in the text as "Laughter."

Chapter Two

1. Beverly Cleary, *Henry Huggins,* illus. Louis Darling (New York: Morrow, 1950, 1978); *Henry and Beezus,* illus. Louis Darling (New York: Morrow, 1952); *Henry and Ribsy,* illus. Louis Darling (New York: Morrow, 1954); *Henry and the Paper Route,* illus. Louis Darling (New York: Morrow, 1957); *Henry and the Clubhouse,* illus. Louis Darling (New York: Morrow, 1962); *Ribsy,* illus. Louis Darling (New York: Morrow, 1964). These works are hereafter cited in the text.

2. May Hill Arbuthnot, et al., *Children and Books,* 3d ed. (Glenview, Ill.: Scott, Foresman, 1964), 441; hereafter cited in the text.

3. "Henry Huggins," *Saturday Review,* 11 November 1950, 48; hereafter cited in the text.

4. "Henry Huggins," *Booklist* 47 (1950):46–47; hereafter cited in the text.

5. Beverly Cleary, "Dear Author, Answer this letter now . . .," *In-*

structor, November–December 1985, 22; hereafter cited in the text as "Dear."

6. *"Henry and Ribsy," Booklist* 51 (1954):21; hereafter cited in the text.

7. *"Henry and Ribsy," Publishers Weekly,* 10 July 1954, 131; hereafter cited in the text.

8. *"Henry and Ribsy," Bulletin of the Center for Children's Books,* 8 (1954): 28; hereafter cited in the text.

9. *"Ribsy," Bulletin of the Center for Children's Books* 18 (196), 35; hereafter cited in the text.

10. *"Ribsy," Horn Book* 40 (1964):615; hereafter cited in the text.

11. "Beverly Cleary," *Publishers Weekly,* 23 February, 1976, 55; hereafter cited in the text.

12. Celia Herron, "Cleary Thinks Books Should Be Fun," *Christian Science Monitor* 14 May 1982, B6; hereafter cited in the text.

13. Claudia Lewis, "Beverly Cleary," in *Twentieth-Century Children's Writers,* ed. D. L. Kirkpatrick (New York: St. Martin's Press, 1983), 183; hereafter cited in the text.

Chapter Three

1. Beverly Cleary, *Beezus and Ramona,* illus. Louis Darling (New York: Morrow, 1955); *Ramona the Brave,* illus. Alan Tiegreen (New York: Morrow, 1975); *Ramona and her Father,* illus. Alan Tiegreen (New York: Morrow, 1977); *Ramona and Her Mother,* illus. Alan Tiegreen (New York: Morrow, 1979); *Ramona Quimby, Age 8,* illus. Alan Tiegreen (New York: Morrow, 1981); *Ramona Forever,* illus. Alan Tiegreen (New York: Morrow, 1984). These works are hereafter cited in the text.

2. *"Beezus and Ramona," Horn Book* 31 (1955):365; hereafter cited in the text.

3. *"Beezus and Ramona," Publishers Weekly,* 13 August 1955, 670; hereafter cited in the text.

4. *"Ramona the Pest," Saturday Review,* 11 May 1968, 38; hereafter cited in the text.

5. *"Ramona the Pest," Horn Book* 44 (1968):419–20; hereafter cited in the text.

6. *"Ramona the Brave," School Library Journal,* April 1975, 50; hereafter cited in the text.

7. *"Ramona the Brave," Horn Book* 51 (1975):266; hereafter cited in the text.

8. *"Ramona the Brave," Bulletin of the Center for Children's Books* 28 (1975):175; hereafter cited in the text.

9. *"Ramona the Brave," Booklist* (1975):1010; hereafter cited in the text.

10. *"Ramona and Her Father," Booklist* 74 (1977), 285; hereafter cited in the text.

11. *"Ramona and Her Father," Bulletin of the Center for Children's Books* 31 (1977):58; hereafter cited in the text.

12. *"Ramona and Her Father," Horn Book* 53 (1977):660; hereafter cited in the text.

13. *"Ramona and Her Mother," Booklist* 75 (1979):1361; hereafter cited in the text.

14. *"Ramona and her Mother," Bulletin of the Center for Children's Books* 32 (1979):172; hereafter cited in the text.

15. *"Ramona and Her Mother," Christian Science Monitor,* 15 October 19779, B11; hereafter cited in the text.

16. *"Ramona Quimby, Age 8," School Library Journal,* August 1981, 54; hereafter cited in the text.

17. *"Ramona Quimby, Age 8," Christian Science Monitor,* 14 May 1982, B12; hereafter cited in the text.

18. *"Ramona Quimby, Age 8," Booklist* 78(1981):42–3; hereafter cited in the text.

19. *"Ramona Quimby, Age 8," Horn Book* 57 (1981):533; hereafter cited in the text.

20. *"Ramona Forever," Booklist* 81 (1984):62; hereafter cited in the text.

21. *"Ramona Forever," Horn Book* 60 (1984):590; hereafter cited in the text.

22. *"Ramona Forever," Christian Science Monitor,* 1 March 1985, B5; "Ramona Forever," *School Library Journal,* September 1984, 115; hereafter cited in the text.

23. *"Ramona the Pest," Junior Bookshelf* 36 (1974):92; hereafter cited in the text.

24. *"Ramona the Brave," Junior Bookshelf* 40 (1976):20; hereafter cited in the text.

25. Elaine Scott, *Ramona: Behind the Scenes of a Television Show* (New York: Yearling, Dell, Bantam Doubleday Dell, 1988):4; hereafter cited in the text.

26. In a brief, undated, anonymous article entitled "Speaking of Ramona . . .," Cleary tells about an idea she got from a reader: "'a boy wrote and told me that his little sister was just like Ramona, and how she wrapped a worm around her finger and pretended it was a ring.' Mrs. Cleary thought that it did sound like something Ramona *would* do. In *Ramona the Pest,* Ramona's worm engagement ring was a big hit on the playground" (vertical file, Children's Room, Minneapolis Public Library).

Chapter Four

1. Beverly Cleary, *Ellen Tebbits,* illus. Louis Darling (New York: Morrow, 1951, 1979); *Otis Spofford,* illus. Louis Darling (New York: Morrow, 1953); *Leave It to Beaver* (New York: Berkley Publishing Corporation, 1960); *Here's Beaver* (New York: Berkley Publishing Corporation, 1961); *Beaver and Wally* (New York: Berkley Publishing Corporation, 1961); *Mitch and Amy,* illus. George Porter (New York: Morrow, 1967); *The Hullaballoo ABC,* illus. Earl Thollander (Berkeley, Calif.: Parnassus, 1960); *The Real Hole,* illus. Mary Stevens (New York: Morrow, 1960); *Two Dog Biscuits,* illus. Mary Stevens (New York: Morrow, 1961), illus. DyAnne DiSalvo-Ryan (New York: Morrow, 1986); *The Growing Up Feet,* illus. DyAnne DiSalvo-Ryan (New York: Morrow, 1987); *Janet's Thingamajigs,* illus. Dyanne DiSalvo-Ryan (New York: Morrow, 1987); *Lucky Chuck,* illus. J. Winslow Higginbottom (New York: Morrow, 1984); *Emily's Runaway Imagination,* illus. Beth and Joe Krush (New York: Morrow, 1961). These works are hereafter cited in the text.

2. "Ellen Tebbits," *Booklist* 47 (1951):405; hereafter cited in the text.

3. "Ellen Tebbits," *Horn Book* 27 (1951):408; hereafter cited in the text.

4. In *Good Books for Children,* rev. ed., comp. Mary K. Eakin (Chicago: University of Chicago Press, 1962), 259; hereafter cited in the text.

5. "Ellen Tebbits," *Publishers Weekly,* 4 August 1951, 484–85; hereafter cited in the text.

6. "Otis Spofford," *Booklist* 50 (1953):18; hereafter cited in the text.

7. "Otis Spofford," *Publishers Weekly,* 15 August 1953, 647; hereafter cited in the text.

8. Margaret Ford Kieran, "New Books for Children," *Atlantic Monthly,* December 1953, 98; hereafter cited in the text.

9. "Mitch and Amy," *Saturday Review,* 18 March 1967, 36; hereafter cited in the text.

10. "Mitch and Amy," *Horn Book* 43 (1967):346; hereafter cited in the text.

11. "Mitch and Amy," *Bulletin of the Center for Children's Books* 20 (1967):136; hereafter cited in the text.

12. "Lucky Chuck," *School Library Journal,* September 1984, 100; "Lucky Chuck," *Bulletin of the Center for Children's Books* 37 (1984):162; hereafter cited in the text.

13. Charlotte Jackson, "Books for Children," *Atlantic Monthly,* December 1961, 119; Alice Dalgliesh, "Things That Go Bump in the Night," *Saturday Review,* 28 October 1961, 35; hereafter cited in the text.

14. "Emily's Runaway Imagination," *Bulletin of the Center for Children's Books* 15 (1961):40; hereafter cited in the text.
15. Irwyn Applebaum, *The World According to Beaver* (New York: Bantam Books, 1984), 8; hereafter cited in the text.

Chapter Five

1. Beverly Cleary, *The Mouse and the Motorcycle,* illus. Louis Darling (New York: Morrow, 1965); *Runaway Ralph,* illus. Louis Darling (New York: Morrow, 1970); *Ralph S. Mouse,* illus. Paul O. Zelinsky (New York: Morrow, 1982). These works are hereafter cited in the text.
2. Beverly Cleary, *Socks,* illus. Beatrice Darwin, (New York: Morrow, 1973); hereafter cited in the text.
3. "The Mouse and the Motorcycle," *Saturday Review,* 13 November 1965, 58; hereafter cited in the text.
4. "The Mouse and the Motorcycle," *Horn Book* 41 (1965):628; hereafter cited in the text.
5. "Runaway Ralph," *Horn Book* 46 (1970):386; hereafter cited in the text.
6. "Runaway Ralph," *Saturday Review,* 9 May 1970, 44; hereafter cited in the text.
7. Ellen Fader, "Ralph S. Mouse," *School Library Journal,* August 1982, 94; hereafter cited in the text.
8. "Ralph S. Mouse," *Bulletin of the Center for Children's Books* 36 (1982):6; hereafter cited in the text.
9. "Ralph S. Mouse," *Horn Book* 58 (1982):648; hereafter cited in the text.
10. "Socks," *Bulletin of the Center for Children's Books* 27 (1973):23; hereafter cited in the text.
11. "Socks," *Publishers Weekly,* 27 August 1973, 282; hereafter cited in the text.
12. Judy N. Staley, "Socks," *Children's Book Review Service,* September 1973, 3; hereafter cited in the text.
13. "The Mouse and the Motorcycle," *Junior Bookshelf* 39 (1975):33; hereafter cited in the text.
14. "Runaway Ralph," *Junior Bookshelf* 39 (1975):104; hereafter cited in the text.

Chapter Six

1. Beverly Cleary, *Dear Mr. Henshaw,* illus. Paul O. Zelinsky, (New York: Morrow, 1983); hereafter cited in the text.

2. "Dear Mr. Henshaw," *Booklist* 80 (1983):80; hereafter cited in the text.

3. "Dear Mr. Henshaw," *Horn Book* 59 (1983):570; hereafter cited in the text.

4. "Dear Mr. Henshaw," *School Library Journal,* September 1983, 120; hereafter cited in the text.

5. Charlene K. Coates, class discussion, West Chester University, West Chester, Pa., 22 April 1989.

Chapter Seven

1. Beverly Cleary, *Fifteen,* illus. Joe and Beth Krush (New York: Morrow, 1956); *The Luckiest Girl* (New York: Morrow 1958); *Jean and Johnny,* illus. Joe and Beth Krush (New York: Morrow, 1959); *Sister of the Bride,* illus. Beth and Joe Krush (New York: Morrow, 1963). These works are hereafter cited in the text.

2. "Fifteen," *Bulletin of the Center for Children's Books* 10 (1956): 48; hereafter cited in the text.

3. "Fifteen." *Saturday Review,* 17 November 1956, 60; hereafter cited in the text.

4. "The Luckiest Girl," *Bulletin of the Center for Children's Books* 12 (1958):44; hereafter cited in the text.

5. "Jean and Johnny," *Horn Book* 35 (1959):485; hereafter cited in the text.

6. "Jean and Johnny," *Bulletin of the Center for Children's Books* 13 (1959):5; hereafter cited in the text.

7. "Sister of the Bride," *Bulletin of the Center for Children's Books* 17 (1963):24; hereafter cited in the text.

8. "Sister of the Bride," *Horn Book* 39 (1963):506; hereafter cited in the text.

9. Aidan Chambers, *The Reluctant Reader* (Oxford: Pergamon Press, 1969), 46; hereafter cited in the text.

10. Berta Parrish and Karen Atwood, "Romantic Fiction Revisited," *ALAN Review* 13 (Spring 1986):53; hereafter cited in the text.

11. Susan Thompson, "Images of Adolescence," part 1, *Signal,* January 1981, 53; hereafter cited in the text.

Selected Bibliography

Primary Works

Fiction

Beaver and Wally. New York: Berkley Publishing Corporation, 1961.

Beezus and Ramona. Illustrated by Louis Darling. New York: Morrow, 1955.

Dear Mr. Henshaw. Illustrated by Paul O. Zelinsky. New York: Morrow, 1983.

Ellen Tebbits. Illustrated by Louis Darling. New York: Morrow, 1951, 1979.

Emily's Runaway Imagination. Illustrated by Beth and Joe Krush. New York: Morrow, 1961.

Fifteen. Illustrated by Joe and Beth Krush. New York: Morrow, 1956.

A Girl from Yamhill. New York: Morrow, 1988.

The Growing Up Feet. Illustrated by DyAnne DiSalvo-Ryan. New York: Morrow, 1987.

Henry and Beezus. Illustrated by Louis Darling. New York: Morrow, 1952.

Henry and Ribsy. Illustrated by Louis Darling. New York: Morrow, 1954.

Henry and the Clubhouse. Illustrated by Louis Darling. New York: Morrow, 1962.

Henry and the Paper Route. Illustrated by Louis Darling. New York: Morrow, 1957.

Henry Huggins. Illustrated by Louis Darling. New York: Morrow, 1950, 1978.

Here's Beaver. New York: Berkley Publishing Corporation, 1961.

The Hullabaloo ABC. Illustrated by Earl Thollander. Berkley, California: Parnassus, 1960.

Janet's Thingamajigs. Illustrated by DyAnne DiSalvo-Ryan. New York: Morrow, 1987.

Jean and Johnny. Illustrated by Joe and Beth Krush. New York: Morrow, 1959.

"Josie Lays Her Down to Sleep." *Woman's Day,* 5 February 1985, 36ff.

Leave It to Beaver. New York: Berkley Publishing Corporation, 1960.
The Luckiest Girl. New York: Morrow, 1958.
Lucky Chuck. Illustrated by J. Winslow Higginbottom. New York: Morrow, 1984.
Mitch and Amy. Illustrated by George Porter. New York: Morrow, 1967.
The Mouse and the Motorcycle. Illustrated by Louis Darling. New York: Morrow, 1965.
Muggie Maggie. Illustrated by Kay Life. New York: Morrow, 1990.
Otis Spofford. Illustrated by Louis Darling. New York: Morrow, 1953.
Ralph S. Mouse. Illustrated by Paul O. Zelinsky. New York: Morrow, 1982.
Ramona and Her Father. Illustrated by Alan Tiegreen. New York: Morrow, 1975, 1977.
Ramona and Her Mother. Illustrated by Alan Tiegreen. New York: Morrow, 1979.
Ramona Forever. Illustrated by Alan Tiegreen. New York: Morrow, 1984.
Ramona Quimby, Age 8. Illustrated by Alan Tiegreen. New York: Morrow, 1981.
Ramona the Brave. Illustrated by Alan Tiegreen. New York: Morrow, 1975.
Ramona the Pest. Illustrated by Louis Darling. New York: Morrow, 1968.
The Real Hole. Illustrated by Mary Stevens. New York: Morrow, 1960.
Ribsy. Illustrated by Louis Darling. New York: Morrow, 1964.
Runaway Ralph. Illustrated by Louis Darling. New York: Morrow, 1970.
Sister of the Bride. Illustrated by Beth and Joe Krush. New York: Morrow, 1963.
Socks. Illustrated by Beatrice Darwin. New York: Morrow, 1973.
Two Dog Biscuits. Illustrated by Mary Stevens. New York: Morrow, 1961.
Illustrated by DyAnne DiSalvo-Ryan. New York: Morrow, 1986.

Nonfiction

"Acceptance Speech." *Claremont Reading Conference Yearbook* (1983), 89–90. Speech on acceptance of George G. Stone Award.
"Books Remembered." *The Calendar,* July 1982–February 1983, n.p. Discussion of the books of Cleary's childhood.
"Dear Author, Answer This Letter Now . . ." *Instructor,* November–December 1985, 22–5. Discussion of Cleary's fan mail.
A Girl from Yamhill: A Memoir. New York: Morrow, 1988.
"The Laughter of Children." *Horn Book* 58 (1982):555–64. Discussion of humor in Cleary's works.

"Laura Ingalls Wilder Award Presentation." *Horn Book* 51 (1975):359–64.

"Low Man in the Reading Circle, or, A Blackbird Takes Wing." *Horn Book* 45 (1969):287–93. Discussion of Cleary's reading problem and the books she read as a child.

"Newbery Medal Acceptance." *Horn Book* 60 (1984):429–38.

"On Talking Back to Authors." *Claremont Reading Conference Yearbook* (1970), 1–11. Discussion of Cleary's popularity.

Regina Medal Acceptance Speech. *Catholic Library World* 51 (1980:22–6.

"Why Are Children Writing to Me Instead of Reading?" *New York Times*, 10 November 1985, Book Review sec.:42. Discussion of Cleary's fan mail.

"Writing Books about Henry Huggins." *Top of the News*, December 1957, 7–11.

Secondary Works

"Beverly Cleary." *Publishers Weekly*, 23 February 1976, 54–5. Discussion of Cleary's popularity.

"Beverly Cleary: A Practicing Perfectionist." *Early Years*, August–September 1982, 24–5ff. Cleary and her working method.

Burns, Paul C., and Ruth Hines. "Beverly Cleary: Wonderful World of Humor." *Elementary English* 44 (1967):743–7ff. Description of Cleary's works up to 1967.

Churchman, Deborah. "Children's Literature: A Source of Hope and Morality." *Christian Science Monitor*, 6 June 1983, 17. Cleary's view of life, with Lloyd Alexander and Lois Lowry.

Epstein, Connie E. "Beverly Cleary: An Outstanding Children's Books Author for Our Time." *Catholic Library World* 51 (1980):274–5. Discussion of Cleary and her works.

Fitzgibbons, Shirley. "Focus on Beverly Cleary." *Top of the News*, Winter 1977, 167–70. Discussion of Cleary and her works.

Geller, Evelyn. "WLB Biography: Beverly Cleary." *Wilson Library Bulletin* 36 (1961):179. Biography of Cleary.

Herron, Celia. "Cleary Thinks Books Should Be Fun." *Christian Science Monitor*, 14 May 1982, B6. Interview with Cleary.

Lewis, Claudia. "Beverly Cleary." In *Twentieth-Century Children's Writers*, 2d ed., edited by D. L. Kirkpatrick, 182–84. St. Martin's, 1983. Bibliography, biography, and short analysis.

Novinger, Margaret. "Beverly Cleary: A Favorite Author of Children." *Southeastern Librarian*, Fall 1968, 194–202. Reprinted in *Authors* and *Illustrators of Children's Books,* edited by Miriam Hoffman and Eva Samuels, 70–83. New York: R. R. Bowker Company, 1972. Discussion of Cleary's work up to 1972.

Rahn, Suzanne. "Cat-Child: Rediscovering Socks and Island MacKenzie." *The Lion and the Unicorn* 12 (1988):111–20. Discussion of *Socks* and Ursula Williams's *Island Mackenzie.*

Rees, David. "Middle of the Way: Rodie Sudbery and Beverly Cleary." In *The Marble in the Water,* 90–103. Boston: Horn Book, 1979, 1980. Discussion of the Ramona books and Rodie Sudbery's works.

Reuther, David. "Beverly Cleary." *Horn Book* 60 (1984):439–43. Cleary and her works, from the point of view of her editor.

Roggenbuck, Mary June. "Beverly Cleary—the Children's Force at Work." *Language Arts,* January 1979, 55–60. Discussion of Cleary's works up to 1979.

Roozen, Nancy. "Presentation of the Recognition of Merit Award to Beverly Cleary." *Claremont Reading Conference Yearbook* (1983), 87–8.

Zarrillo, James. "Beverly Cleary, Ramona Quimby, and the Teaching of Reading." *Children's Literature Association Quarterly* 16 (1988): 131–5. The Ramona books as instructional material for reading teachers.

Index

Reuther, David, 10
Ribsy, 17, **19–49**, 51, 59, 76, 95, 134; illustrated, 10; relationship with Henry Huggins, 185
Risely, Mrs., 133, 137
Rogers, Mrs., 77

St. Nicholas League, 6
Saylor, Joe, 39
Sheriff Bud, 37–38, 76
Socks, **132–36**, 137; as substitute child, 119; as substitute older sibling, 135–36; relationship with Bricker family, 185
Spofford, Mrs., 114, 115, 116
Spofford, Otis, **96–100**; as "bad boy", 98–100; as bully, 114; as bully in *Ellen Tebbits*, 95, 98; as nonparagon of virtue, 183; Cleary's life reflected in, 117; contrasted with "fiction" characters, 99–100; develops as character, 98–99; illustrated, 10; in *Ellen Tebbits*, 93, 94
Stewy, 96, 97, 112
Story of Dr. Dolittle, The (Lofting), 5
Stumpf, Bernadette, 102, 104
Stumpf, Mrs., 115–16
Susan, 56–57, 59, 63

Tailor of Gloucester, The (Potter), 3
teacher, Beatrice Quimby's. *See* Mr. Cardoza. Beverly Bunn's, calls her a "nuisance", 5; influence on writing, 16–17; inspires her to write for children, 6–7. *See also* Falb, Miss. Otis Spofford's, 96. Ramona Quimby's. *See* Binney, Miss; Griggs, Mrs.; Rogers, Mrs.; Whaley, Mrs. Ryan Bramble's. *See* Kuckenbacker, Miss
Tebbits, Ellen, 17, **92–96**, 97; Cleary's life reflected in, 117–18; compared with Emily Bartlett, 110; illustrated, 10

Tebbits, Mrs., 114, 116; compared with Austine Allen's mother, 115
themes in Cleary's works:
childhood, in *Ramona and Her Father*, 68
divorce, in *Dear Mr. Henshaw*, 154–55
family dynamics, in *Socks*, 135–36, 138, 141
family life, in *Dear Mr. Henshaw* contrasted with Henry Huggins's, 185; in Henry Huggins books, 48–49; in Henry Huggins books contrasted with Leigh Botts's, 185; in *Ramona and Her Father*, 66–69; in *Ramona and Her Mother*, 71; in *Ramona Forever*, 81; in Ramona Quimby books, 84, 87–89; in *Ramona Quimby, Age 8*, 77–78; in *Socks* and Ralph S. Mouse books, 140–41; progression of from Henry Huggins to Leigh Botts, 18, 185; progression of in Ralph S. Mouse books, 142
family relationships, in Ramona Quimby books, 116; in works for adolescents, 177–78
fears, childhood, reflected in Ramona Quimby books, 86; Beverly Bunn's, 4–5; in *Ramona the Brave*, 60, 61–62
growing up, deemphasized in nonseries books, 111–12; importance of in books, 185–86; in *Beezus and Ramona*, 55; in *The Growing-Up Feet*, 105–106, 112; in Henry Huggins books, 85; in *Janet's Thingamajigs*, 105–106; in *Lucky Chuck*, 112; in *The Mouse and the Motorcycle*, 124; in Ralph S. Mouse books, 138–39; in *Ralph S. Mouse*, 131; in *Ramona and Her Mother*, 71–72; in *Ramona Forever*, 82; in Ramona Quimby books, 85–86; in *Ramona Quimby, Age 8*, 78; in

The Author

Pat Pflieger received her M.A. in children's literature from Eastern Michigan University and her Ph.D. in American studies from the University of Minnesota–Twin Cities. Now she teaches courses in children's literature. She is the author of *A Reference Guide to Modern Fantasy for Children* (1984).

The Editor

Ruth K. MacDonald is a professor of English and head of the Department of English and Philosophy at Purdue University. She received her B.A. and M.A. in English from the University of Connecticut, her Ph.D. in English from Rutgers University, and her M.B.A. from the University of Texas at El Paso. To Twayne's United States and English Authors series she has contributed the volumes on Louisa May Alcott, Beatrix Potter, and Dr. Seuss. She is the author of *Literature for Children in England and America, 1646–1774* (1982).